PAVEL SCHEUFLER

Josef **Binko**

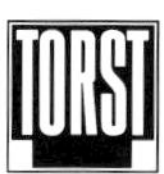

TORST

Kniha byla vydána za laskavé pomoci Viktora Novotného
a ve spolupráci s Ministerstvem kultury České republiky.

Za pomoc při vydání knihy děkujeme
Národnímu technickému muzeu v Praze.

ISBN 80-7215-281-5

FOTO**TORST**

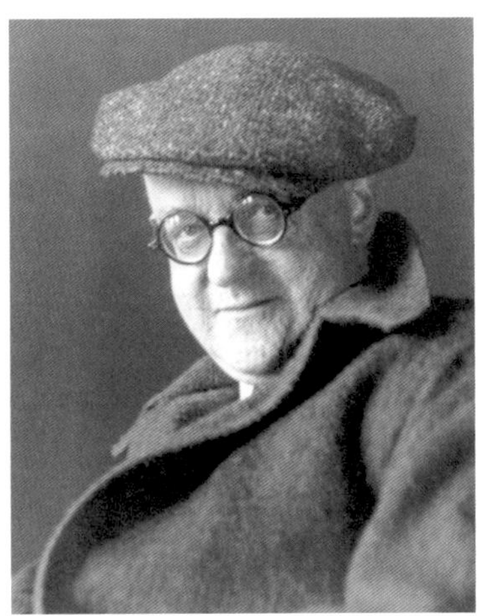

Josef Binko: His Life and Photography

The life of Josef Binko (1879–1960) is closely tied to the little town of Krucemburk in the Bohemian-Moravian Uplands and the tannery there. Until it was nationalized by the Communist government in 1948, the tannery had been owned by members of the family for three centuries.[1] Binko's deep sense of being part of that family and the region is clearly expressed in his photographs.

Binko succinctly characterizes Krucemburk in his unpublished memoirs. "The little town of Krucemburk," he writes, "is located in the Bohemian-Moravian Uplands, as if pasted onto the slope of the hill that protects it from the north winds, with little houses built almost one on top of the other. There is a church and real mountain cemetery at the top, from where, all around, there is a lovely view of nothing but hills and woods [...] which are now mostly thinned out, but in my youth were dense, and from there one of the two streams of the river Doubravka stem, and flow through the whole system of man-made lakes above the village and below it [...]. This is why it was here, with its abundance of spruce bark and flowing water, that a tannery was built."[2]

Binko's great uncle, Gustav Skřivan (1831–1866), a teacher of mathematics at the Prague polytechnic, may have had an indirect influence on Binko's first getting into photography. While a student at Vienna, Skřivan got to know Josef Maximilian Petzval (1807–1891), physicist, professor of mathematics, and father of the modern photographic lens. In his memoirs Binko writes that Skřivan took Petzval to Krucemburk, and adds that several glass negatives, which they had prepared themselves (that is, coated with wet gelatin), survived from that period.[3] Skřivan seems to have been truly familiar with photography, and may have influenced Binko's father Ladislav, who lived with Gustav in Prague while a student at the business school founded and run by Antonín Skřivan (1818–1857), Gustav's uncle.[4] The Binko and Skřivan families were united in 1851, when the tanner Eduard Binko (of Žďár nad Sázavou), Josef's grandfather, married Julie Skřivanová, Gustav's sister. Their father, Augustin Skřivan, was Mayor of Krucemburk from 1850 to 1867 and owner of the local tannery.[5]

Josef was born in 1879, the second son of Ladislav and Emma Binko. He attended school in Prague, where courses were taught in Czech; his favorite subjects were mathematics, descriptive geometry, and anything else related to technology. Later, obeying his father's wishes and with some regret that he couldn't study engineering as his elder brother Ladislav was doing, he attended the Czechoslav Business School, and graduated from it in 1897. His father's pragmatic thinking meant that Josef "was destined for the commercial side," whereas Ladislav, who studied chemistry at the Czech Technical University, "was destined for production." "I often regretted that Dad hadn't decided otherwise, but at the time he probably couldn't have acted as I would have wished."[6] The youngest son, Dušan, was born in 1884, and studied at the tanning school in Halberstadt, Saxony. His expertise was mainly in the demanding production of chrome-tanning. This method, which employs chrome salts, constitutes a link between tanning and photography, particularly pigment processes of printing, which are also based on chrome salts. Moreover, gelatin is still used today in the production of photographic material that has a similar chemical composition as the lower layer of rawhide.

All three sons, Ladislav, Josef, and Dušan, grew up in an educated family environment. Their father spoke fluent German as well as some French, English, and Russian, and had in his youth even studied Sanskrit. As in many families at that time he actively went in for music, and, as Binko recalled, his father was a good pianist, organist, and later a cellist as well. "Even in his later years he enjoyed playing piano trios, quartets, and quintets with us, and we all kept up to date with modern music, the arts, and sciences, and he thus remained abreast of the times."[7] He was also a member of the Umělecká beseda arts society.

Binko inherited a love for music from his father. Together with photography it was the chief topic of the correspondence with Ludvík Boháček, a close friend from his school days. Later, as the owner of a textile company in Prague, Boháček regularly provided Binko with sheet music; the descriptions of what he sent to Binko provide a good idea of the two friends' taste in music.[8] It seems that Binko was a great admirer of the music of Fibich and Bruckner and also loved the music of Dvořák.[9] He liked to play Chopin, Grieg, and piano-duet arrangements of Dvořák's *Slavonic Dances*, Beethoven's symphonies, and Smetana's *My Country*. With his father, Dušan, and some friends, Binko formed a quintet, and they

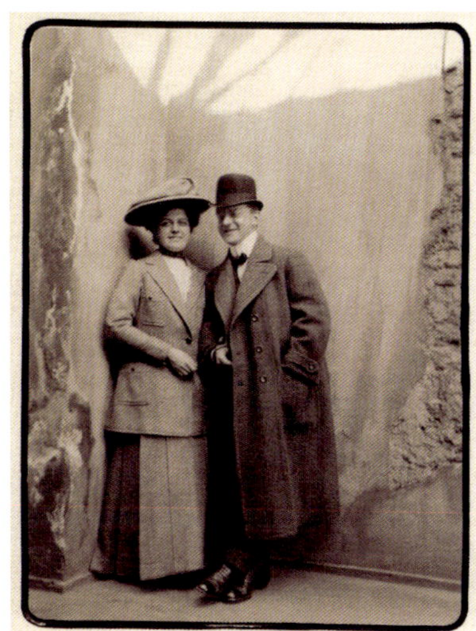

Josef Binko with his wife, 1910

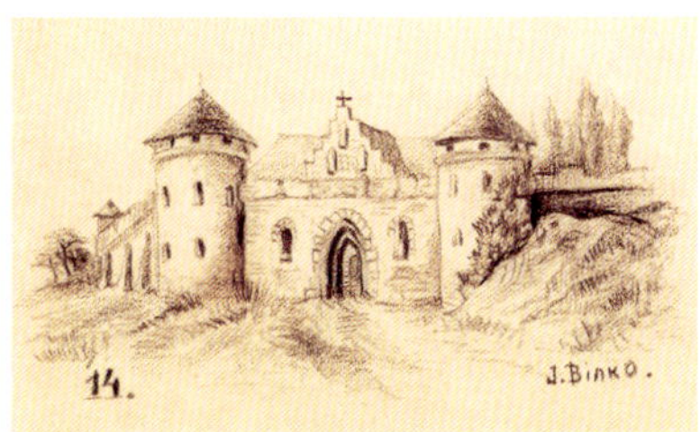

From Binko's sketchbook

often played pieces by Russian composers. Binko's interest in music should be borne in mind when considering his photography. His pencil, chalk, and charcoal studies that have been preserved also testify to his sensitivity and skill as a draftsman.

After graduating from the Czechoslav Business School, Binko returned to Krucemburk and began working in the accounts office of the tannery, while having to learn a variety of manual tasks and work with machines, all under the supervision of an experienced journeyman. "Three years later I qualified for my apprenticeship certificate. In the finishing room, I came to like working with my hands, and after some time I worked half days doing piece-work in a group, thus earning enough extra money for my personal needs, mainly for sheet music and books. I was not yet receiving any wage, and my pocket money was too modest."[10]

In his memoirs, which focus on the development of the family business, Binko does not mention his interest in photography even though it was something he did throughout his active life. He may have neglected to mention it because he considered it something both obvious and personal. He probably began to take photographs as a student at the business school in Prague, during summer vacation in Krucemburk in 1894 or 1895. His earliest photos were in 9 × 12 cm and 13 × 18 cm formats. One of them bears a note about a certain Mr. Křesťan, "who used to help me carry the wooden camera with my cassettes and plates."[11]

In the late 1950s, Karel M. E. Paspa (1899–1979), a photographer and member of the National Technical Museum Society, proposed to Binko near the end of his life that he donate his photographs and equipment to the National Technical Museum in Prague. In a letter Binko wrote to his son Ivan, in response to the proposal, he described the difficulties he had faced when starting out in photography. "I'll be glad that someone takes care of it, because – although I make no claim to any recognition – it would be a pity if all that work were lost, particularly when I recall the difficult circumstances in which I began to devote myself to photography. At first it was only on Sundays, providing there was at least a bit of sunshine. Only after the introduction of silver-bromide paper did it become possible to photograph in the evening too. But back then I wasn't permitted even to imagine running out with a camera or sitting down in the darkroom during working hours. And, anyway, for years I had no darkroom, and was dependent on the summer to work in the gazebo, and to get everything I needed with the extra money I made from doing manual labor in the factory."[12]

Binko clearly considered photography something for special moments and concentration, not something to record activities with. In the "Old Villa," where the whole family lived at the time, there was no darkroom. Perhaps his father did not even know he was taking photographs. It is clear, however, that Binko was taking photographs long before settling down to run the family business and before he had money to spend on his hobby.

The start of his career was relatively hard. Towards the end of his life he mentioned this in a letter to his son Ivan: "You must bear in mind that when we were young we really had to be frugal, and our father, an intelligent man, expected us to have the same self-discipline as he had when he worked his way up, at least to send us to school in Prague."[13]

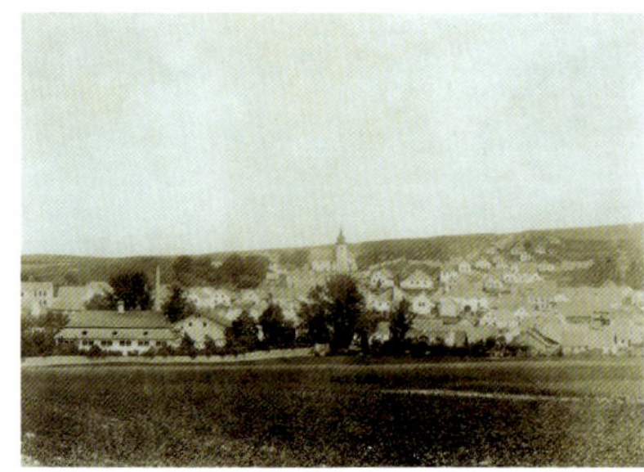

Krucemburk

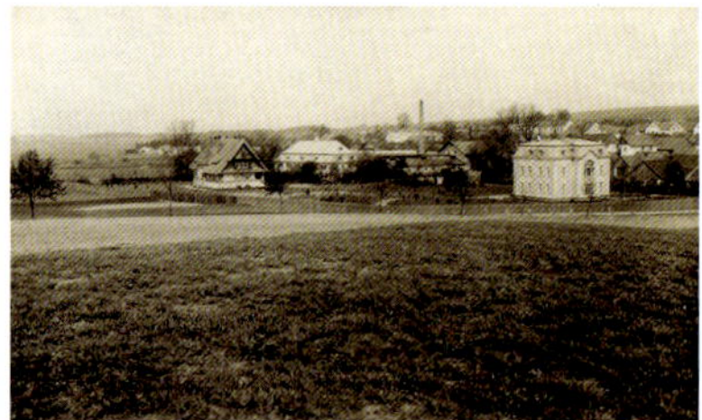

Krucemburk with the Red Villa and White Villa

In the early years of the twentieth century production in the family factory was fundamentally modernized, including electrification and the building of the machine room and boiler room, which Binko also took part in and photographed. "After this, and after getting practical experience, I could finally go out into the world and see how things work there, which I had long wanted to do because I knew I was quite unfamiliar with the local market for rawhide," he wrote in his memoirs.[14] In 1904, Binko was hired in various tanneries of a leather company with head offices in Vienna and Pest and 27 bulk-buying centers in Hungary and Galicia, in areas that are mainly in what is now Slovakia. The company also supplied leather to large companies in Germany and, Binko recalls in his memoirs, "It was there that I learnt to sort, receive, purchase, and ship, and also sometimes consign a freight-car [...] of goods home to Dad." It seems that even when busy at his job abroad he occasionally found time to take photographs.

In his various curricula vitae, Binko mentions having worked abroad in the years 1904–06. In 1906, his mother, grandmother, and grandfather died, each shortly after the other. It was thus necessary "to abandon other plans and begin again where I had left off before traveling to gain experience." One can only imagine what those plans were. But they were most likely linked with his return to Krucemburk. It was probably a time of difficult decisions, but, ultimately, responsibility for family tradition, respect for his father, and love for the place of his childhood predominated. The young man had got to know Prague, Vienna, and Pest, and could now compare them to each other. Krucemburk had back then a population of about 1,600. It was the site of six annual trade fairs, and it had a post and telegraph office, its own doctor with a pharmacy in his home, and a new school house; several clubs were active there; and apart from the tannery it was home to other industries as well.[15] Although it was a small provincial town, it was buzzing with activity, and it was where his brothers and roots were. His decision may have also been influenced by a pianist and singer he was in love with but who died prematurely.

The year 1907 is, according to his curricula vitae, when Binko began to work in his own factory.[16] It was also when Boháček sent him sheet music and books from Prague and the beginning of his friendship with a leading Czech modern architect Josef Gočár (1880–1945), who had been introduced to the Binko family by the important Czech sculptor Josef Štursa (1880–1925).[17] Gočár later designed the "Red Villa" for Binko, which historians of architecture consider his first independent work. The house, built near the villa of Binko's elder brother in 1908–09, is fascinatingly beautiful, though from a purely functional point of view it is somewhat impractical. With elements of the Moravian cottage and the English country house, the Binko villa was meant for a single family.

Binko designed his own darkroom. It was originally intended for the first floor, where it may have even existed for a short while, but was ultimately built in a ground-floor room designed for a maid. "I am just amazed!" Boháček wrote to him on 23 May 1911. "Once again you have a new darkroom and you're now bombarding me with beautiful new pictures, each one better than the last and each different." It thus appears that in 1909 Binko had a darkroom in the planned space and that it was here he developed his first "Cupidos," that is, flat 9 × 12 cm negatives taken with a Cupido camera, the earliest of which are dated 13 September 1909. It was also here that he made a series of oil prints of photographs from his honeymoon in May 1910. Possibly, it was already here, too, that he kept the enlarger he and Dušan had built (perhaps the first vertical enlarger in the Bohemian Lands).[18]

The new darkroom on the ground floor was systematically arranged. It was obviously designed by a person who knew much about what was required. A rare description of it is provided in a diagram preserved by the photographer's grandson Jan Binko. (The numbers refer to the diagram): "The whole room, which is still intact today, is 4 × 3.4 meters in area. Everything was arranged systematically, and was kept absolutely tidy. In the middle there was a table with a glass top (2), around which were chairs. To the right of the entrance there was a washbasin (10). On the left there was a long table (4) with drawers. One of the drawers held a Leica camera, which he used at the time; another contained film, and another held some equipment. On the very bottom, under the drawers, there were shelves with wooden boxes containing prints and negatives. At the front end of that table stood a slide projector (7), a large black box, and in front of it was a small projection screen on a stand (6), which, when not in use, was attached to the projector. I remember how Granddad used to show me a few pictures right in the lab, which could be projected the length of the table. At the end of the table was a lamp with two bulbs, a red and a white one (5). Its contacts were exposed – I remember that well because I got a shock from it.

The right-hand side of the darkroom (1) was particularly interesting. It was the most important for how the whole room worked. It was completely built up and divided into three booths. The booth on the left was for enlarging. I remember the Leitz Focomat, which I still have, but in Granddad's time the vertical enlarger stood there, which is now in the National Technical Museum (P1). Above the enlarger was a little cabinet with glass doors, which contained old cameras that were no longer used. In the middle there was a thick, slightly tilted glass tabletop (P3), with a lead trough at the wall to drain off water. The water mains were in the wall above it. Above the glass tabletop there were shelves. Two lamps with a liquid filter hung on the lower shelf (P4). Between them was a typical lamp for glass filters (P2), which I remember was an intense green. Above, there were two more colored bulbs. On the shelves there were glass jars and flasks and other similar things. In the first part of the main wall there was also a glass table, and on it stood pharmacist's scales (P5). That was the area for preparing solutions. Above it were shelves, on which every possible chemical was lined up. And that's where the directions for the developers hung. In the little cabinet at the top there was other photography equipment, an arc lamp, and resistance for the arc lamp. Under the table were little shelves with bowls and other similar trays and tanks. There was a double window in the room (3). The room could be made dark within two minutes. The inner shutters were opened, a frame with black cardboard was put into the space, four sliders were slid in, and the shutters were closed. The same thing was done with the second half of the window. And a black curtain was also drawn." The appearance of the main wall of the darkroom and also with the unique vertical enlarger is made from the original equipment at the permanent "Interkamera" exhibition at the National Technical Museum in Prague. This is a uniquely preserved exhibit.

On 10 May 1910, Binko married Terezie Chladová, the daughter of a brewer and mayor of Pardubice. Her younger sister, Antonie, later married Dušan Binko, and another sister, Marie, married Gočár.

Josef and Terezie Binko set out on their honeymoon to Dalmatia by way of Vienna, Trieste, Miramare, Pula, Dubrovnik, and Spalato. From the trip he made an original wedding gift and a lasting souvenir: a series of 103 tinted bromoil prints.[19] This is the largest extant series of pigment prints on a single theme made by a Czech. Nine months later a son, Ivan, was born to Josef and Terezie, and was soon followed by a brother, Jan, and a sister, Věra.

For Binko the years before the Great War were undoubtedly happy ones and, from the point of view of work, intensive. He became a recognized expert, sitting, for example, on the Board of the Chamber of Trade and Commerce in Vienna and in the Austrian War Ministry department for leather production. In addition to business trips he undertook several big journeys abroad at this time, during which he could take photographs. Interestingly, apart from his contacts with the Foto-Fon photography and publishing company, no evidence has been found of his membership in Czech amateur photography societies or contacts with Czech photography magazines; we have evidence only of his contacts with German periodicals to which he subscribed and some of which remain in his library to this day.[20] It may have been because of the quality of printing in Czech photography magazines at the time or even a certain disparaging attitude among élite Czech amateur photographers toward what most interested Binko about photography – namely, prints made with the pigment processes. Boháček, also an amateur photographer – who, if we are to judge from his letters, kept a close eye on the arts scene in Prague – makes no mention of the photography exhibitions of 1911 that we now consider to have been of prime importance. Czech amateur photography was in a complicated situation back then and even though the 1911 exhibitions signaled a change in the opinions of Prague amateur photography clubs, they continued to stagnate for a long time and the disparaging attitude toward pigment prints, at least among some amateur photographers, continued, whereas documentary-like photographs tended traditionally to enjoy

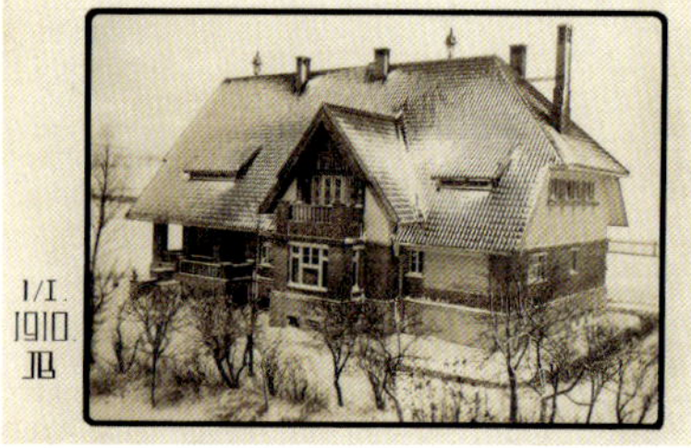

The Red Villa

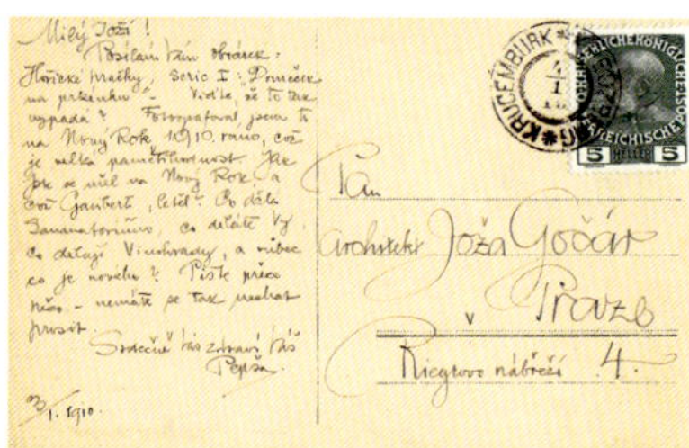

The reverse of the postcard from Josef Binko to Josef Gočár

12

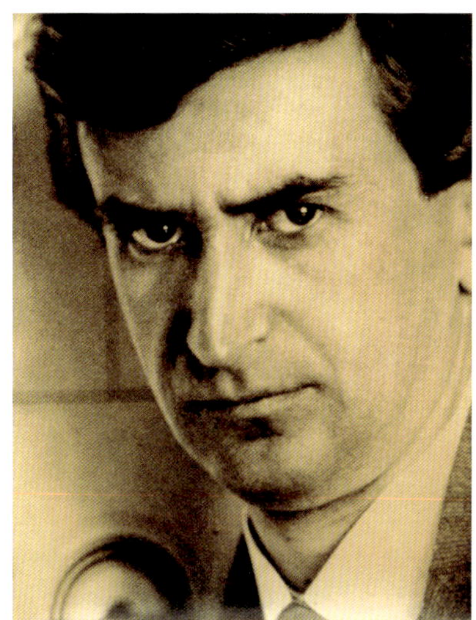

A portrait of the architect Josef Gočár

their support. One has only to recall the expulsion of Jaroslav Petrák (1887–1917), the first important photography theorist and author of several publications, from the Prague Club of Amateur Photographers in March 1913. The quality of printing in the Bohemian photography magazines was probably the chief reason Binko, in 1911, chose the German *Photographische Rundschau und Mitteilungen* as the first journal in which to publish his photographs. One issue of the journal contains twelve photos by him.[21] The annual *Die Photographische Kunst im Jahre 1911* published four Binko landscapes and a portrait. No Czech photography magazine at the time could have provided him with so much space and such high-quality printing. His choice of periodical and interest in being published are evidence both of Binko's perfectionism and of his desire to "make himself known as a photographer," in other words to go beyond the bounds of "taking photographs as a purely personal matter for myself, family, and friends." He thus made it clear that he considered his photos more important than merely emotional evidence of his life and of the life of his family.

The new home and darkroom provided Binko with a powerful impulse to take photographs. This period of his photography can be reconstructed quite well. From 1909–14 we have a coherent series of film negatives, which are deposited in the Museum of Decorative Arts in Prague. This was the key period of Binko's photography and also the main source of pictures for the present publication. September 1909, when the first dated 9 × 12 cm sheet-film negatives were made, marked the end of what is more or less Binko's first photographic period; at present we know only the positives, because the negatives have unfortunately not been found.[22] In this period he was taking photographs only occasionally, with long breaks, having converted the gazebo into his darkroom. He photographed mainly on glass plates. His turning to a more systematic approach to photography is connected not only to economic stabilization and his new standing in the family business, but also to the purchase of a camera for the preferred sheet film and the building of the darkroom in his new house.

The landscape was the chief object of Binko's photographic interest both before 1909 and afterwards. It was not, however, a symbolic landscape or a landscape of dramatic suggestion with an existential subtext, such as appears in the early work of František Drtikol (1883–1961), nor was it the landscape of dusky moods, as in the work of Vladimír Jindřich Bufka (1887–1916). It was rather a graceful landscape whose charm consisted in harmony. Binko's landscapes contain order and harmony, and if a number of the photos also have a certain charming dreaminess, it is chiefly because of the landscape itself, not the photographer. Krucemburk and its environs are, from the point of view of the landscape artist, a truly exceptional place. "Nowhere else will you find the kinds of sky you get in the Bohemian-Moravian Uplands," Binko apparently used to say. A tendency to treat the Uplands poetically appears in the works of a number of Czech painters, for example Antonín Chittussi (1847–1891), Antonín Slavíček (1870–1910), and Jan Zrzavý (1890–1977). Zrzavý, in fact, expressly stated that he wished to be buried in Krucemburk. Another painter, František Kaván (1866–1941), during his stays in the village of Vitanov near Hlinsko in 1909–22, also used to be inspired by the beauty of the Uplands. It was typical of Binko's interest in art that he approached Kaván in Vitanov, photographed him, and acquired a few of his paintings.[23]

Another special interest of Binko's was the vernacular architecture all around Krucemburk. In addition to the purely aesthetic point of view, he gave this side of his photography a certain documentary accent. By contrast, the photos from his garden have a powerful emotional charge, often becoming almost purely emotional. The garden and the man-made lake called Řeka, in Krucemberk, remained his favorite topics throughout his life and they appear also in his 35mm photos from the 1940s.

Binko often printed his landscape photographs using pigment processes. They comprised various techniques based on colloids, mostly of organic origin (gelatin or gum arabic as binders) soaked in a solution of bichromates (as sensitizers). With exposure to UV light the layers of a chromed binder harden in proportion to the length of time exposed. The image thus has the form of a subtle relief according to the degree of hardened binder. The relief can be used as a plate for printing the image or the image can be made more visible by coloring the layers of binder. Oily pigments can be used, which are repelled by the water soaked into the raised areas or, by contrast, water-soluble pigments can be used, which are absorbed by the raised places.

Pigment prints, which enable one to make substantial changes to the original image in the negative, occupy an important place in Binko's photography. The resulting picture in most of the pigment prints greatly depends on the skill and experience of the photographer, who can sometimes (depending on the kind of process) change the tonal values and coloring of the print. The print was thus an expression of the personality of its maker, and was original in the sense of traditional artistic values. Binko was initially fascinated with gum bichromate print and pigment printing. After 1907 he devoted himself also to oil-pigment prints, and, beginning in 1911, to bromoil prints too. Binko's gum bichromate prints were usually 30 × 40 cm, whereas his bromoil prints were always 18 × 24 cm. His oil-pigment prints had the same format as the bromoil, but he tended to make the oil-pigment prints in smaller formats, even as small as 9 × 12 cm. A set of enlarged paper negatives for gum prints has also been preserved. He made some of his portraits (for example, those of Boháček) in variations, using several techniques. In terms of the quantity and quality of his prints, Binko was among the most important Czech photographers of Art Nouveau pictorialism. Some of his works, particularly those of the garden, made in 1912–20 with soft-focus lenses and backlighting or with the contrast of light and dark areas are among the first manifestations of purist pictorialism, which was later developed, for example, by Josef Sudek (1896–1976).

In addition to pigment prints, Binko devoted himself to work with slides. In those days slide projection was very popular in Bohemia. As in other families, an evening of relaxation at the Binkos' would often consist not only in making music and reading aloud, but also in showing slides. Binko had high-quality slide-projection equipment for showing those "light pictures," which were projected in the great hall, a large room in the middle of the house with a cathedral ceiling. The slide projector, of which, unfortunately, only part has survived, was adapted for 12 × 12 cm plates, and was factory made.

In some of his letters Binko recalls beautiful moments "when on winter evenings I projected many slides in the hall."[24] His grandson Jan also mentions this in recollections of his early childhood. For Binko, this way of spending his free time undoubtedly meant both spiritual enrichment and an expression of a natural family closeness. Binko's hobbies were merely recreation, "rest" in today's sense of the word; his main concerns were for the prosperity of the tannery and the well-being of its employees. (One recalls here another Czech amateur photographer, the physician Jaroslav Feyfar [1871–1935] from the little north Bohemian town of Jilemnice, who also spent many hours making music for pleasure, had, similarly to Binko, a library of 2,000 volumes, and regularly went to the theatre in Prague like Binko went to concerts.)

In letters from the last ten years of his life Binko often recalled moments of music-making. In his memoirs it is the richness of his intellectual life, which stands out. He also spent his leisure time going on excursions to the countryside and other towns. This is reflected in Binko's photographs as well. It is fair to call some of the photos from his trips "urban landscapes." Some are emotional commentary on architectural detail. Only rarely do they contain scenes of the hustle and bustle of life in the street. When photographing architecture in towns, Binko tried to ensure that people would not appear in his photographs. Where they do show up in the streets, they are not intended as examples of any particular kind of person or situation, but merely as part of the unstaged state of affairs at that moment.

A special place in Binko's work is held by photographs of urban architecture. Binko visited many towns and cities in his own country and abroad. He often took photographs in Prague and Kutná Hora. Of the photos with urban subject matter, he seems to have most valued the photos taken in Rothenburg, Germany, on 5 September 1912, which he later turned into a series of 43 oil-pigment prints.[25] It is hard to know why he chose Rothenburg over the other cities he passed through on that trip (Nuremberg, Ulm, Munich, Salzburg, and Königsee), when the Nuremberg photos, for example, are equally interesting. The photos are not a description of the sites of the town; rather, they are a record of feelings evoked by scenery and details characteristic of the place. Almost all the negatives made during a single day he turned into oil-pigment prints. His "5 September 1912" series, he said, were the result of the fortunate constellation of place, weather, atmosphere, and personal biorhythm, so that

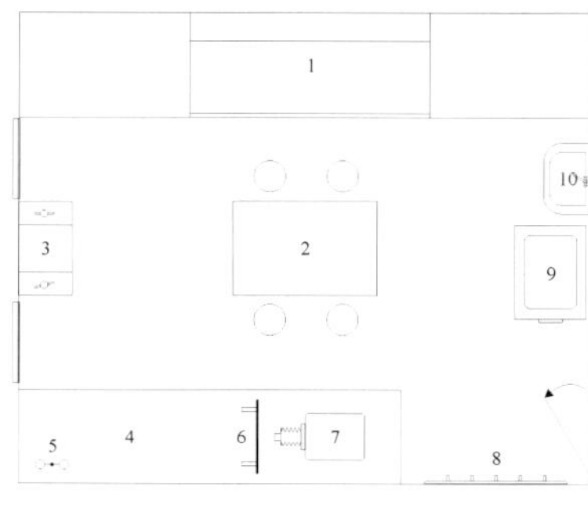

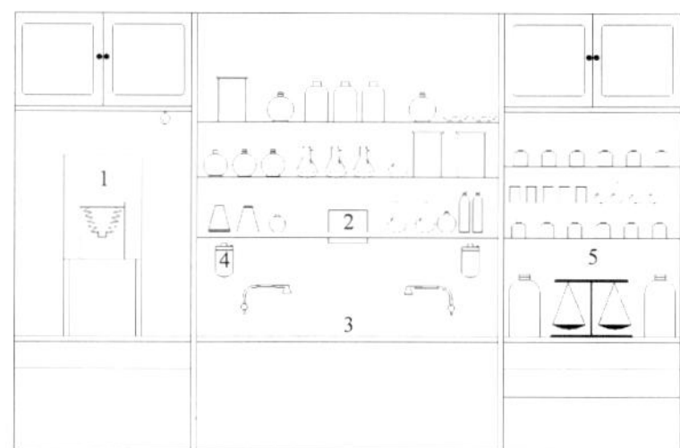

The arrangement of the wall of Binko's darkroom

in one city on a single day he took about five dozen photographs on large-format negatives, most of which he considered so interesting that he turned them into oil-pigment prints. The name of the set, "Rothenburg, 5 September 1912," also emphasizes that single day. The large number of high-quality photos is, in addition, evidence of the interplay between the photographer and his camera. We know of no other similar works by the amateur photographers of those days.

What Binko took his photographs with can be deduced from the set of cameras donated to the National Technical Museum, Prague, and also from the cursory remarks in his correspondence with Boháček. The one he used most frequently was the Cupido folding camera for 9 × 12 cm negatives with a high-quality six-element Dagor (that is, "Doppel Anastigmat Goerz") lens with f 6.8 / 20 in the central pneumatic shutter and speeds from one second to 1 / 250 of a second. The camera was made by Hüttig AG, Dresden (later ICA AG), some time after 1907, and Binko probably acquired it in the summer of 1909. Another important camera from his estate is the high-quality English-type wooden field camera for 13 × 18 cm plates, which was made about 1895. Binko worked with it before buying the Cupido. With a Voigtländer Alpin camera he made 7.5 × 10 cm stereoscopic photographs. According to a sales receipt from August 1916, Binko bought an Icarette for 6 × 6 cm negatives, which had a Novar 6.8 / 75 mm lens.[26] The list of negatives from just after the First World War mentions tests with an Ernemann camera for 6 × 4.5 cm plates. Binko's photo equipment at the height of his hobby was clearly diverse.

A smaller, but high-quality set of subject matter in Binko's photography consists of portraits. These were mainly of people closest to him: his grandfather, father, two brothers, and friends, and, later, his wife and her sisters. Rarely did he portray people who weren't close to him. The portraits also reveal Binko's journey from description to artistic emotional creation. His first prints made with pigment processes, which are portraits of his grandfather and father, are among his masterpieces and the best such works in early twentieth-century Czech photography. The portrait of Gočár posing in front of a tile oven is well known (it exists in several, differently cropped variations) and the portrait of Boháček is also exceptional. In addition to the transformation of the photo into a pigment print, Binko altered the negatives with pencil strokes, and some photographs (all of the great outdoors) carry the note "work with a needle."

Rarely did Binko make photographs that documented a certain event. Among the few exceptions is the procession of the nationalist Sokol physical education movement at their Sixth All-Sokol Rally on 29 June 1912. And because he took a camera on excursions with friends, Binko occasionally also took snapshots. Rarely, however, are they lively, spontaneous pictures; he has almost always arranged the people being photographed into a careful composition.

Clearly, Binko was a photographer who needed peace and quiet to compose. He needed to think the shot through, only rarely taking photographs spontaneously or quickly, even though his equipment could have handled that. This was more a matter of his attitude toward photography than of his mentality. For Binko, developing film and then making pigment prints was something fundamental, because it was somehow also a way to experience the shot again. What was important for him seems to be the experience and re-experience of the subject matter rather than some need to make a record or a snapshot that would immortalize a moment. This view is supported by a quotation from a letter of Binko's dated 18 December 1950 (a carbon copy of which survives): "Recently, while looking through old photographs, I suddenly found myself holding shots of our trip to the seaside, and I recalled how we picked up the seaweed on the dunes in Helgoland and swam in the sea [...]. For each of these pictures I'd be able to tell you exactly when it was made and what the mood was. That's a nice thing about photography: it somehow freezes our experiences and memories, which would otherwise surely loose vividness or would completely fall into oblivion. I must have hundreds of such photos from my journeys, and now I sometimes sit down with them and read them like a book."[27] The desire for order, peace and quiet, and harmony, which radiate from Binko's photographs, was also one of his basic attitudes toward life. In a letter of 6 May 1952, he wrote, "[It is] not only love for people, but also for everything beautiful, because that guarantees a calm, comfortable life."

Unfortunately, there is no extant writing that would have revealed Binko's views on photography or taking photographs in the years before the Great War. We can glean snippets of his views only from typewritten letters he wrote to various people in the last decade of his life, the carbon copies of which have survived, or deduct them from the reactions of Boháček, whose letters from 1910–14 have survived. Binko's attitude toward photography, however, can be deduced mainly from his extant works, and for this key period we have a rare opportunity to compare the negatives with the prints made from them. We can therefore compare what the photographer selected from the collection and how, using crops or other techniques, he adjusted the print. This can be seen well in the photographs from his honeymoon, from which he made 103 bromoil prints out of a total of 207 negatives. This set, the largest of its kind in Czech photography, is an emotional evocation of places the newlyweds visited together, and is also a magnificent, monumental gift to his wife. Some of the views or captured situations may therefore have suggested to them something intimate. The set clearly shows, however, how Binko dealt with the color tone of the oil-pigment print and how he made the crops, which were probably the result of much experimentation. Binko was one of the first photographers in the Bohemian Lands regularly to crop using the enlarger.

Undoubtedly, Binko diligently kept up to date with regard not only to the aesthetics of photography, but also to various technical tricks, which the photography manuals of the day were full of. In landscape photography Binko put great emphasis of course on the grouping of clouds and their expressiveness. Typically, Boháček asked him: "Please give me the recipe for making those clouds! I haven't managed anything like that yet. Does one need special plates or something else? I now use exclusively the Perutz [sic], and still haven't managed to get the clouds to come out. Or is there some other trick, which I haven't yet stumbled on? And please tell me about how the camera operates, which does the job so fantastically! Write me about it in detail!"[28] Binko's reply, unfortunately, has not been found, and we therefore don't know whether he used filters or special photographic material or a combination of both to conjure up the clouds. Although the technical aspects, no matter how important, cannot overshadow the emotional content of Binko's photographs, it is still useful to know how they were applied in his work. They are, among other things, evidence of the responsibility with which he approached his hobby.

During the First World War, the tannery met its wartime orders, and a wartime manager was assigned to it. Required as experts in tanning, the brothers Ladislav and Josef, similarly to other badly needed experts and many workers, were exempted from the draft. The youngest brother Dušan, however, spent the war on the battlefield. Between the two younger brothers there was a particularly close tie: they shared many of the same views, and their wives were sisters. Dušan was said to be remarkably handy and technically gifted. In the Old House where he lived he had a superb workshop, and the enlarger in his brother's darkroom was mainly his doing. He made a slide projector for himself (see below), which has survived to this day. Dušan also liked to photograph, and was more interested than Josef in taking photographs as documents.[29]

According to his memoirs Binko was in Prague during the exciting days of October 1918, which led to the declaration of Czechoslovak independence on the 28th. And he was very active at this time.[30] The hopes invested in the new republic of Czechoslovakia led him to carry out many organizational tasks, which demanded almost all his time. He took part, for example, in building a tanning school in Hradec Králové based on plans by Gočár. He held all the major organizational positions in the local tanning industry. And the tannery, in several stages, underwent fundamental remodeling, modernization, and expanded its operations. In 1923

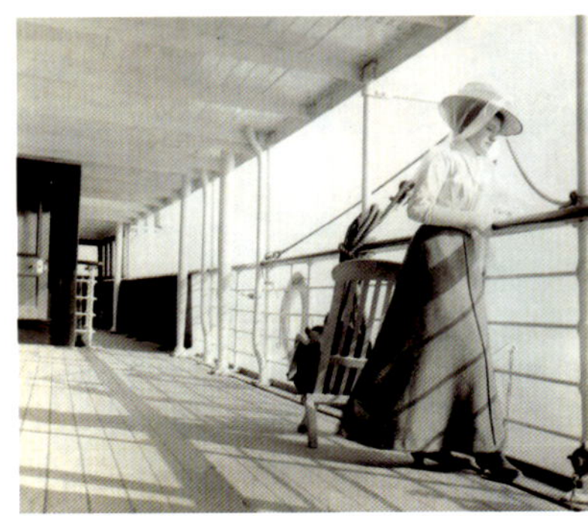

Binko's wife aboard the **Baron Gautsch**

Binko's father Ladislav died. It seems that in the early years of Czechoslovakia, Binko devoted himself to photography much less than he had before. A similar trend appeared among a number of other amateur photographers, for example, Feyfar, with whom Binko can to some extent be compared in terms not only of how remote the place he lived and worked was from the big towns, and the breadth and importance of his interests in the arts, but also in his way of life in the years before the First World War. Whereas Feyfar stopped taking photographs in the 1920s because he was occupied with another hobby (radio), Binko was extremely busy with organizational tasks. In 1920 he cancelled his last two subscriptions to photography magazines, one of which, the *Wiener Mitteilungen*, he had been receiving regularly since 1899. Perhaps, his interest in his hobby intensified when in 1925 he got a Leica, the first version of which, according to recollections of family members, he got immediately, since its advantages were obvious to him. His new Leica IIIa, a camera that went into production in 1935, remains in the family to this day, together with his large archive of 35mm negatives. They demonstrate that Binko was taking photographs till the early 1950s.[31]

In the late 1930s, the tannery business was so prosperous, that it required special warehouses in ten countries for its own goods. By contrast, during the Second World War production came almost to a standstill and the factory was in essence saved by piecework for the Baťa shoe factory in Zlín, Moravia. It was probably a time of recapitulation, recollection, and designing. Perhaps for that reason he used both new and old photographs to make albums as gifts for his children as well as individual photographs of the garden, the family with their dog, and places around Krucemburk. It seems that he became interested again in pigment prints too.[32]

The new political situation after the Communist takeover in February 1948 radically changed things in almost every area of life, particularly for people who had property. The tannery was nationalized on 28 April 1948. The difficult period is described with sadness – but without a trace of bitterness – in many passages of Binko's letters to his son Ivan, friends in the leather industry, and friends and acquaintances who had stayed with them in Krucemburk during the summer.

In the winter of 1953 the darkroom probably for the first time ceased to serve solely its original purpose, because it was the only room in the big house, which could be properly heated. Until the end of his life Binko was plagued by the new régime, which found him "in arrears in property taxes," and eventually even expropriated the Binko villa and garden.[33] Binko was particularly disheartened to know that the government had ordered the villa to be remodeled, and he was overcome with grief: "Everything I spent my whole life making and maintaining with such love is now gradually going to ruin."[34] In that general decline one can nevertheless find in Binko's letters to his children and friends words of consolation and hope. To Jan Novák, a former Czechoslovak consul in France and "summer friend," Binko sent Christmas greetings on 20 December 1953, writing: "But please don't think I'm complaining. On the contrary, I'm full of hope that better times will come, that I'll be healthy again, that we'll see you here again in spring, and that we will once again make up for all the sadness that has closed down on us, and that all mankind will again be rid of this horror of uncertainty, when a human being will again be a human being, when a lie will be a lie, and truth and honor will again be a something one simply takes for granted [...]. Today such thoughts, unfortunately, sound almost absurd, but what would be the point of life without hope?"[35]

In a letter to the painter and restorer František Petr (1884–1964), dated 3 April 1957, Binko writes: "we now live completely secluded from the rest of the world, and I have gradually become unaccustomed to people. True, I read assiduously, study the history of music and art in general, and look forward to this being perhaps a more pleasant summer, so that we can again toughen up and prepare for the future. I hope, no, I firmly believe, that we shall live to see better days and that makes us stronger – even though we definitely no longer make any plans at our age and live more in memories. I especially like to recall the nation in its prime, and thank the Lord I was allowed to experience those days at the height of my powers. When I think only of all the concerts I enjoyed in Prague and Vienna, the personal acquaintances with so many artists, writers, painters, and sculptors, people who are now famous, and all the galleries I'd visited almost everywhere in Europe [...]."[36]

While his father was still alive, Ivan Binko tried to make sure his father's photographic legacy would be preserved. When he met Paspa by chance in 1958, Paspa asked him if his father would consider making a gift of his equipment and work to the National Technical Museum in Prague. Paspa later visited Krucemburk in August 1959. The letter, which Ivan wrote to him after the visit, dated 31 August 1959, is an important source of information about the state of the darkroom and the photo archive toward the end of Josef Binko's life: "After you left I tidied up the whole laboratory. Today all the cameras are in one cabinet and the slides and slide projection equipment are in another. All the negatives are together and all the positives are together. I looked cursorily through the slides. They have hardly been attacked by mildew, but are rather damp and are coming unglued. [...] The negatives are mostly in good shape, and have for the most part not been damaged by any mildew either. Probably only the condensation on the glass of the negatives needs to be cleaned off. The negatives from his travels are on film from the Cupido and are in perfect shape. I've cleaned off the leather parts of the cameras. I've put together all the work done with collodion positive techniques [like ambrotypes and tintypes or ferrotypes] and, together with Grandfather or according to his negatives, catalogued them. They are all now deposited in a cupboard in Grandfather's room, so that they don't fall prey to mildew. I have saved the copies of the lists. The originals are inserted in the corresponding files, which I made for the individual series. That is all I managed to do during the holidays. It is still necessary to carry out a thorough cataloguing of the negatives. The negatives from the journeys have been catalogued precisely by Grandfather himself. The negatives from the Bohemian-Moravian Uplands and the family, however, have been catalogued according to what is sometimes only vague information, or have sometimes not been cataloged."

Thanks to the preserved correspondence of Ivan Binko and Paspa we can reconstruct the course of the subsequent, somewhat depressing talks concerning the donation of the photo archive and darkroom including the camera equipment.[37] While these talks were going on, Binko died on 11 February 1960. Ivan, at his own expense, took the donation to the National Technical Museum in Prague in September.[38]

Many other people in this country had fates similar to Binko's. No other person, however, left such a large number of precisely made pigment prints. Binko found beauty in music, in the woods, and in novels, in simple scenery, in the interplay of trees, clouds, haystacks, contours of the terrain and the hills of the Bohemian-Moravian Uplands. As with architecture, it would be fair to call these photographs "frozen music." They reflect, and evoke, old feelings and moods, since they fix memories. Music and photography engage – and also relax – two of the most essential senses – hearing and vision –, and perceptions overlap in the mind in a special unity and harmony. Binko didn't feel a need to give titles to his photographs that would show off how well read or educated or familiar with music he was or would imbue the photographs with other, deeper meanings. The titles are simple, designed solely for orientation, and lack symbolism. This was surely also because he really did take photographs chiefly for himself and for those closest to him. He was unconcerned with the opinions of the anonymous public, and didn't seek recognition as an artist. "All I wanted was to provide for your future," he wrote to his children in the 1930s about the factory and his efforts. "A bit of music-making, reading, and taking photographs are therefore bright moments in this universal misery," Boháček wrote in 1912.[39] Boháček's words, I believe, apply well also to feelings of the man to whom he wrote them. In Binko we can see the best, classic qualities of pure photographic work, and we may ask why one actually even takes photographs. Generally, it is not in order to make a work of art or to win the recognition of society, nor to make money. Binko's work, essentially unsophisticated, straightforward, simple, is a fine example of that. Binko took photographs for the private pleasure he got from the beautiful things of this world. His photography was above all about beauty: the beauty of nature in the Bohemian-Moravian Uplands, the beauty of urban architecture, the beauty within the people he knew, the experience of his honeymoon. It may strike today's ears as banal and non-academic to say simply that with his camera Binko sought out, captured, and, thanks to the special quality of photography, preserved beauty, yet I am convinced that this search was the true purpose of his photography.

Notes

1   See J. Janáček, "700 let Krucemburku – Křížové," MS, Krucemburk, 1966. Martin Skřivan first appears in the records as a master tanner in 1690. See also Josef Kynčl, *Průvodce Krucemburkem s rodinnými kronikami*, Krucemburk, 1918.

2   Josef Binko, "Paměti koželužny v Krucemburku," fifteen-page typescript, Krucemburk, 1956. Copies in the family archives.

3   Binko, "Paměti," p. 3.

4   Antonín Skřivan (1818 Krucemburk – 1887 Prague), Director of the Skřivan Business School, Prague; coined Czech business terminology. Gustav Skřivan (1831 Krucemburk – 1866 Prague), first Czech Professor of Mathematics at the Prague Polytechnic, associate member of the Royal Bohemian Learned Society. Responsible for establishing mathematics as a subject at Czech institutions of higher learning. See *Ottův slovník naučný*, 1903, vol. 23, pp. 313–14.

5   Augustin Skřivan (1805–1869) was prominent in Krucemburk public life, for example, as mayor, 1850–67. He was the brother of Antonín and father of Gustav.

6   Binko, "Paměti," p. 9.

7   Ibid., p. 6.

8   The letters of Ludvík Boháček are in the possession of Eva Kolářová. The whole correspondence from 1909–14 is imbued with Boháček's love for his friend and contains much interesting information about Binko's passion for photography. A letter of Boháček's dated 14 January 1913 included a list of 104 items of sheet music that he had sent to Binko since 1907. Some of the sheet music has been preserved in the family of Jan Binko.

9   Josef Binko was a life-long member of the Antonín Dvořák Society, Prague.

10   Binko, "Paměti," p. 10.

11   This is the negative marked "No. 3, group of friends at the sources of the river Doubravka." See the twelve-page list "Z pozůstalosti J. Binko předaný negativní materiál na skleněných deskách" (Negatives on glass plates, from the estate of J. Binko), which is owned by Jan Binko. The list was probably made by Ivan Binko with Josef Binko in 1958–59. Although not organized chronologically, it contains the numbers of the negatives according to individual formats and descriptions of each shot. Sometimes the precise date of the photograph is given. The earliest of the negatives (a garden with a granary, Krucemburk) dates from 16 July 1895. Nos. 1–2, with the year 1895 and marked as "original numbering," were photographs of the burnt-out flour mill in Krucemburk. Unfortunately these negatives, mainly glass, have been lost. (They were in the following formats: 9 × 12 cm, 13 × 18 cm, 18 × 23.5 cm, a panoramic 10 × 15 cm, stereoscopic 7.5 × 9 cm, 9 × 9 cm and 6 × 4.5 cm; all were in wooden boxes and crates). See also Note 24.

12   Letter to Ivan Binko, dated 10 October 1958. Archive of Eva Kolářová.

13   Ibid.

14   Binko, "Paměti," p. 8. (Ibid. for the two subsequent quotations.)

15   In 1910 Krucemburk had 216 houses and 1,616 residents. See Ivan Binko, "Data obce Krucemburk od založení podnes," MS, undated.

16   It is difficult to ascertain the dates more precisely, because the original written records concerning the Krucemburk tannery were destroyed after it was nationalized following the Communist takeover of 1948.

17   Štursa designed the Binko family grave in Krucemburk in 1904. Gočár first designed the exterior and interior of the new home of Ladislav, the eldest of the brothers. The house, called the "White Villa," was built in 1907–08.

18   As is clear from Ivan Binko's letter to Karel M. Paspa of 31 August 1959, the unique upright enlarger was probably given to Jan Pěnička shortly after 1950, and was found by Ivan Binko in the attic of Pěnička's Krucemburk house, no. 196. It was undamaged; only the Tessar lens had been "damaged by humidity and needed to be stuck back together." In a letter Binko requested Paspa to ask the National Technical Museum (NTM), Prague, to inquire whether Pěnička would donate the enlarger to it.

19   The series of 103 tinted bromoil prints, deposited in the NTM, were made from 207 film negatives, 9 × 12 cm, of photos taken during a journey on 13–29(?) May 1910. The negatives are deposited in the Museum of Decorative Arts in Prague. Individual bromoil prints from this series are also owned by members of the family.

20   The library (which today belongs to Jan Binko) contains, apart from about thirty other photographic periodicals, *Photographische Rundschau und Mitteilungen* (1912–20), Vogel's *Photographische Mitteilungen* (1900–11), Lechner's *Wiener Mitteilungen* (1899–1920), *Photographische Rundschau* (1908–11), Wachtl's *Der Amateur* (1905–08), *Kamera Kunst* (1909–12), and *The Studio* (1905–06), as well as five volumes of *Fotografický věstník* (1894–99). The collection of books constitutes a respectable cross-section of photographic literature published about 1900 (the latest titles – *Bromöldruckverfahren* and *Oeldruck und Bromöldruck* – were published in 1913 and 1915). All the books are in German and are further evidence that Josef Binko obtained his theoretical grounding in photography mainly in the 1890s.

21   See *Photographische Rundschau und Mitteilungen*, vol. 48 (1911), no. 17. These were mainly photographs of the outdoors in the Krucemburk area.

22   Binko's 9 × 12 cm and 13 × 18 cm glass negatives of the continuous series from 1895–1909, as well as his later glass negatives (of various formats) and slides, have not been found. They were to be transferred together with the list to the NTM, but, according to records in the NTM, the transfer was never made. Considering that the film negatives from 1909–14 were given to the Museum of Decorative Arts in Prague by Rudolf Skopec, a teacher, collector, and historian of photography, it is possible that Skopec, since he was interested in writing a book about Binko, also had the glass negatives and slides at his disposal, which were, regrettably, destroyed after Skopec's death. See also Note 38 below.

23   The letters of František Kaván are in the personal archive of Eva Kolářová. Josef Binko's negatives depicting Kaván's house, which were made on 21 May 1914, are deposited in the Museum of Decorative Arts in Prague.

24   Josef Binko to his son Ivan, in a letter dated 10 October 1958. Shortly before that, on 4 October, Ivan had written to his father about the wealth shown "on the slides of the German towns, which had vanished from the face of the earth during the war." The letters are in the personal archive of Eva Kolářová. Jan Binko has a list of 729 slides, which is organized according to how they are stored in nine boxes. It is clear from the list that the slides were a selection from trips abroad, beginning with the honeymoon in May 1910 and ending with a trip to Germany in August 1913. Of these photographs, 177 are from the Vysočina (the Bohemian-Moravian Uplands), Prague, and other towns in Bohemia and Moravia.

25   Josef Binko went on a "German journey" through Nuremberg, Rothenburg, Ulm, Munich, Salzburg, and Königsee on 3–12 (?) September 1912. Of the photographs taken on the trip, 241 negatives (9 × 12 cm) have been preserved in the Museum of Decorative Arts in Prague, of which Binko made a series of 43 bromoil prints entitled "Rothenburg 5. IX. 1912," which is deposited in the NTM, Prague. The individual prints also remained in the family. Eight photos from this series were published in *Photographische Rundschau und Mitteilungen*, vol. 50 (1913) nos. 20, 21, 23.

26   The sales receipt is in the personal archive of Jan Binko. In addition to a Novar lens, Josef Binko used a Tessar, which, he remarked, "made photographs that were too harsh; it didn't pass muster." (See the list of items donated to the NTM.) All the items donated by Binko to the Museum have the accession number 14 / 18.01.1963. The inventory numbers of the cameras are as follows: the 6 × 6 cm Icarette, no. 26 869; the 9 × 12 cm Cupido, no. 26 870; the 9 × 12 cm Kunstler Camera, no. 26 871; the no-name 13 × 18 cm English-style field camera, no. 26 872; the 6 × 9 cm Kodak Cartridge, no. 26 873; and the 3 × 4 cm Kodak III box camera, no. 26 874. The high-quality traveling camera for 13 × 18 cm

plates, from about 1895, is illustrated in Jiří Janda, *Kamery obskury: Fotografické přístroje z let 1840–1940*, Prague: National Technical Museum, 1982, p. 58, no. 36.

27   From a letter to Ivan Růžička, 18 December 1950. Archive of Eva Kolářová.

28   Letter from Boháček to Josef Binko, 19 February 1912. The two friends exchanged technical information about photography quite often. For example, the letters from Boháček of 28 March, 26 May, and 31 May 1913, include relatively detailed discussions of his own experience of making oil-pigment prints and suitable accessories. On 28 March 1913, Boháček asked his friend how to make a "Höchheimer Gummidruck," which required an enlarger, which Boháček also had.

29   As is clear from the 1911–12 correspondence of Dušan Binko and his future wife, photographic paper was the best present he could have received. Apart from photos of the Vysočina, a complete set of photographs has been preserved, for example, from the years of the First World War, of which no. 1 is dated 15 July 1914 and no. 383 is dated 1 February 1917. It includes photos of Italy, Sub-Carpathian Ruthenia, and Galicia. Most of the items from the estate of Dušan Binko, including the projector he made himself for 9 × 9 cm slides, belong to Simona Binková.

30   "Paměti," p. 11.

31   The spools with 35mm negatives, carefully catalogued, belong to Jan Binko, as do prints of some selected negatives.

32   The album "Vánoce 1942," (Christmas, 1942), which is a souvenir of the events of the year, belongs to Eva Kolářová. It includes one oil-pigment print; the rest are enlargements. This is the last example of Binko's impressive enlargements and pigment prints. From the later period there are only contact and small-format prints.

33   The court rulings, decisions, overturned decisions, new decisions, correspondence, and evidence of allegedly unpaid bills from the "People's Court," as well as appeals and protests, are a painful reminder of his persecution by the State, which lasted from 10 August 1950 to the end of Josef Binko's life. It is almost unbelievable that the Prosecutor General, on the basis of the appeals made by Ivan Binko to the Office of the Czechoslovak President and the Minister of Finance on 5 January 1956, ultimately protested against the rulings and proposed that they be quashed, which eventually did happen on 20 September 1956. Typically, this was immediately followed by reprisals: the National Committee in the town of Křížová decided on 18 February 1957 to evict Dušan Binko's widow from the Old Villa, where the family had lived for generations, and ultimately ordered the distrainment of the "Red Villa," the home of Josef Binko. On 11 January 1960 the tax authorities in Chotěboř put a lien on the property of Josef Binko for 23,000 Czechoslovak crowns; exactly one month later he died. During the probate of the Binko estate the tax authorities proposed that all property, chattels and real estate, should go to the State.

34   From a letter to his son Ivan, 14 January 1957. Archive of Eva Kolářová.

35   From a letter to Jan Novák, 20 December 1953. Archive of Eva Kolářová.

36   Archive of Eva Kolářová.

37   On 9 August 1960, Paspa wrote to Ivan Binko: "I am ashamed of the Museum, although I cannot do anything about these delays, and as a part-time employee I really do not have much influence. I have often urged them to act but without results. Frankly and confidentially: the Museum is somewhat in a state of chaos about both what it should think and how it should work." In the same letter Paspa asks Ivan Binko: "When you get around to organizing the written material, please save all

the documents and correspondence relating to photography, including sales receipts for material and so forth." In the same letter Paspa also mentions, as he had several times in the past, that he would like to write a book about Josef Binko and to get it published in the well-known "Umělecká fotografie" (Art photography) series of the Odeon publishing house. "If it works out, I'll need a lot of personal information from you and also the written material that would, in the present situation at the Museum, go missing." Archive of Eva Kolářová.

38   The three-page "List of objects donated by the late Mr. J. Binko of Křížová to the National Technical Museum in Prague" is owned by Jan Binko. Items 1–7 are camera equipment; Items 8–18 are "equipment and accessories for making prints," Items 19–29 relate to the darkroom. Section IV comprised 729 slides in a format of 9 × 12 cm; Section V is called "Photographic Pictures," at least 206, though not all, were described, and three items were marked "Various." The list says: "Glass and celluloid film negatives in formats from 9 × 12 cm to 13 × 18 cm and 6 × 6 cm, which were part of the donation, have not yet been described in detail and sorted. As soon as this work is finished, they will be handed over to the Museum with a special list. This includes several hundred items, from which all the family photos have to be excluded." The list also states that "The items and materials [...] were received on 22 April 1960 by Comrade M. Malík, an official of the National Technical Museum, and were, together with an expert report by Paspa, packed and made ready for transport by Czechoslovak Rail, to be shipped as soon as Czechoslovak Rail can manage it. The final confirmation of the receipt of the individual items by the administration of the NTM will be in writing after the items are included in the inventory of the NTM." It is signed by Ivan Binko and M. Malík. The items were transported at the expense of Ivan Binko on 21 September 1960. The negatives and probably also the slides, however, never made it to the NTM. The inventories of the NTM make no mention of them. The "Photographic Pictures" collection, which had been made ready for transportation, was probably reduced in size, and a small number of the photographs remained in the family. Eight of Binko's gum bichromate prints and oil-pigment prints were exhibited at the "History of Photography II" exhibition organized by Skopec at the Brno Art Centre in November 1961. It is quite clear that Skopec had Binko's key film negatives in his possession; it was he who donated them to the Museum of Decorative Arts in Prague, probably in 1975.

39   Boháček to Josef Binko, 19 February 1912. Archive of Eva Kolářová.

Fotografování a život Josefa Binka

Život Josefa Binka byl spjat s Krucemburkem a rodinným podnikem, továrnou na usně. Ta byla v dědictví příslušníků jednoho rodu po tři staletí.[1] Sounáležitost s předky a láska k rodnému kraji byly v životě Josefa Binka intenzivně přítomny a nacházely i svůj specifický výraz ve fotografické tvorbě.

Výstižnou charakteristiku Krucemburku (do roku 1851 Krucberku-Krucburku a v letech 1949–1990 Křížové) můžeme nalézt přímo v textu Josefa Binka, v jeho *Pamětech koželužny v Krucemburku: „Městečko Krucemburk leží na Českomoravské vysočině jako přilepeno na svahu kopce, chránícího ho před severáky, s domky postavenými skoro nad sebou, nahoře s kostelem a pravým horským hřbitovem, odkud je krásný rozhled kolkolem na samé kopce a lesy... dnes valně prořídlými, ale ještě v mládí stoletými, v nichž pramení jeden z obou potoků Doubravky, a protékal celou soustavou rybníků nad obcí i pod ní... Je tedy vysvětlitelno, že zde u zdroje smrkové kůry a na protékající vodě vzniklo koželužství“.*[2]

Na fotografické počátky Josefa Binka měl možná zprostředkovaně vliv jeho prastrýc Gustav Skřivan, který při studiu na polytechnice ve Vídni poznal Josefa Maxmiliána Petzvala, „otce fotografického objektivu“. Podle vzpomínky Josefa Binka přijel se strýcem Gustavem do Krucemburku o prázdninách i sám profesor Petzval: *„...a zůstalo z té doby několik fotografických snímků na deskách, jež si sami preparovali (tzv. mokrá želatina)...“*[3] Gustav Skřivan, který podle všeho byl s fotografováním skutečně obeznámen, mohl ovlivnit Binkova otce Ladislava, který u něho bydlel za svých pražských studií na obchodní akademii, kterou založil a vedl zase jiný příbuzný – Antonín Skřivan.[4] Spojení se jménem Binko přišlo roku 1851 sňatkem Julie, dcery krucemburského purkmistra a majitele koželužské manufaktury Augustina Skřivana[5], bratra Antonínova, s Eduardem Binkem, koželuhem ze Žďáru nad Sázavou.

Josef Binko se narodil roku 1879 jako druhorozený, a jak uvádí ve svých *Pamětech...*, jeho zálibou *„byla matematika, deskriptiva a vůbec technické předměty“*. Studoval na c. k. české reálce v Praze v Ječné ulici a poté – na přání otce a s jistou přiznávanou lítostí – nestudoval technické vědy (jako o dva roky starší bratr Ladislav), ale obchod na Českoslovanské obchodní akademii, kterou absolvoval roku 1897. Podle pragmatických pravidel rodinného podniku *„byl určen pro obchodní část"*, zatímco Ladislav, který studoval chemii na ČVUT, *„byl určen pro výrobní část". „Často jsem litoval, že tatínek nerozhodnul jinak, ale v té době asi nemohl jednat, jak bych si byl přál já".*[6] Nejmladší bratr Dušan, narozený roku 1884, studoval odbornou koželužskou školu v Halberstadtu. Svou odbornost soustřeďoval zejména do oblasti náročné výroby chromočinných usní.

Chromočinění, které je způsobem zpracování usní za působení chromových solí, zajímavě spojuje koželužství s fotografií, zejména s ušlechtilými fotografickými tisky, jejichž základem byly také chromové soli. Ostatně i želatina, až do dnešní doby při výrobě fotomateriálů stále používaná, má podobné chemické složení jako spodní vrstva surové kůže.

Všichni tři synové, Ladislav, Josef i Dušan, vyrůstali v kultivovaném rodinném prostředí. Jejich otec hovořil perfektně německy, částečně francouzsky, anglicky a rusky. V mládí se učil i sanskrt. Jako v mnoha rodinách té doby aktivně pěstoval hudbu, a jak vzpomíná Josef Binko, byl dobrý klavírista a varhaník a později i cellista . *„Rád si zahrál ještě v pozdních létech s námi klavírní tria, kvarteta i kvinteta, až do svého stáří, a sledoval stále s námi vývoj moderní hudby, umění i vědy, a tím zůstával stále na výši doby".*[7] Byl členem Umělecké besedy.

Lásku k hudbě podědil po svém otci i Josef Binko. Vzpomíná, jak na vandru, který strávil převážně ve službách vídeňsko-pešťské koželužské firmy, bylo v domě jejího majitele *„krásné Blüthnerovo křídlo"*, na němž mohl často *„ve společnosti svého šéfa přehrávat české skladby, hlavně Fibicha, ve Vídni skoro neznámého. Ba i s Mahlerem, ředitelem Vídeňské dvorní opery jsem se seznal, a s mnoha jinými".*[8] Hudba – a fotografování – byly také převažujícími tématy jeho dopisů s přítelem z doby studií Ludvíkem Boháčkem. Boháček, majitel obchodu s textilním zbožím v Praze, svého přítele průběžně zásoboval notovým materiálem, který dává dobrou představu o hudebním vkusu obou přátel.[9] Zdá se, že Josef Binko byl velkým přítelem zejména Fibichovy a Brucknerovy hudby, miloval také Antonína Dvořáka.[10] S oblibou hrál Chopina, Griega, čtyřručně úpravy pro klavír Dvořákových Slovanských tanců, Beethenovy symfonie i Smetanovu Mou vlast. S otcem a mladším bratrem Dušanem a některým z přátel vytvořili kvintet, který s oblibou hrával také ruské autory. Považuji za velmi důležité zvýraznit Binkovo hudební vnímání ve vztahu k jeho fotografování. Dochované náčrtníky se studiemi tužkou, křídou i uhlem svědčí o senzitivitě a talentu také v oblasti kresby.

Po absolvování Českoslovanské obchodní akademie v Praze, na níž se s Boháčkem seznámil, se Josef Binko vrátil do Krucemburku. Nastoupil do rodinné továrny *„v pisárně, a mezi tím se musel učit veškeré manuelní práce i práce na strojích, vždy pod dohledem staršího zkušeného tovaryše... Po třech létech jsem se tak dalece vyznal, že jsem mohl obdržet výuční list. Oblíbil jsem si některé ruční práce v úpravně tak, že jsem po dlouhý čas půldenně pracoval akordně v některé partě, a tak si přivydělával dosti peněz na svoje soukromé potřeby, hlavně ovšem na noty a knihy. Plat jsem tehdy nedostával žádný, a kapesné bylo příliš skromné"*.[11]

Ve svých *Pamětech...*, zaměřených na vývoj rodinného podniku, se Josef Binko vůbec nezmiňuje o své fotografické zálibě, i když fotografování jej provázelo celý aktivní život. Možná proto, že tuto činnost považoval jednak za samozřejmou, a také za velmi osobní. Fotografovat začal za doby pražských studií na obchodní akademii, zřejmě o letních prázdninách v Krucemburku v roce 1894 nebo 1895. Nejstarší záběry byly pořízeny na formáty 9 × 12 a 13 × 18 cm. Zajímavá je zmínka na popisce jednoho z nejstarších snímků o jakémsi panu Křesťanovi, *„který pomáhal nosit dřevěnou komoru s kasetami a deskami"*.[12]

O svých obtížných fotografických začátcích psal Josef Binko ke konci svého života synu Ivanovi jako odpověď na návrh ing. Karla Paspy předat fotografickou pozůstalost Národnímu technickému muzeu: *„Budu šťasten, že se toho někdo ujme, protože – ačkoliv si nedělám nárok na jakékoli ocenění nebo uznání – bylo by celé té práce škoda. Zvláště když si vzpomenu, za jak těžkých podmínek jsem se mohl fotografii věnovat. Byly to zpočátku jen neděle, kdy svítilo aspoň trochu sluníčko, a teprve po zavedení bromostříbrných papírů přibyly k tomu i večery. Ale tehdy mi nesmělo ani v duchu napadnout, vyběhnout si mezi pracovní dobou za plot s fotokomorou, anebo se usadit v temné komoře. Ostatně jsem po léta ani žádné temné komory neměl, a byl odkázán na léto pracovat v zahradním altánu a pořizovat si veškeré potřeby z peněz, jež jsem si přivydělal manuelní prací v továrně."*[13]

Je zřejmé, že Josef Binko považoval fotografování za věc svátečních chvil a soustředění, nikoli za věc podstatnou pro záznam nějakých aktivit. V takzvaném Starém domě, kde tehdy celá rodina žila, nebyla žádná fotokomora, nejistá je i povědomost otce o fotografování, stejně jako inspirace Gustavem Skřivanem. Jisté je jen to, že Josef Binko fotografoval dlouho předtím, než se usadil v řízení rodinného podniku a měl více finančních prostředků pro svou zálibu. O rozhodnutí věnovat se fotografické zálibě svědčí také předplácení fotografických časopisů, které započalo roku 1894 českým *Fotografickým věstníkem* a pokračovalo o pět let později *Wiener Mitteilungen*, které později doplňovaly ještě další časopisy.[14]

Jeho pracovní začátky byly poměrně tvrdé. V náznacích o tom na sklonku života psal synu Ivanovi: *„Nesmíš nikdy zapomínat, že jsme museli za mlada velmi, velmi šetřit, a že náš otec byl při své inteligenci zvyklý očekávat i od nás takovou sebekázeň, jakou on se těžce propracovával, aby nás mohl dát aspoň na studie do Prahy“.*[15]

V prvních letech 20. století došlo v rodinné továrně k zásadní modernizaci výroby díky elektrifikaci a stavbě strojovny a kotelny, na čemž se Josef Binko již podílel a fotograficky to zdokumentoval. *„Po této přestavbě a zaběhnutí v praksi, mohl jsem konečně nastoupit na zkušenou do světa, po čemž jsem již dávno toužil, protože jsem si byl vědom, že neznám dostatečně tuzemský trh surových koží,“* psal ve svých *Pamětech*…[16] Roku 1904 nastoupil Josef Binko praxi v cizích koželužnách ve službách vídeňsko-pešťské koželužské firmy, která měla *„27 sběren v Uhrách a Haliči, hlavně na nynějším Slovensku“.* Současně podnik dodával kůže velkým firmám v Německu a *„naučil jsem se tam třídit, přejímat, kupovat, expedovat, a poslat občas i vagon …zboží domů tatínkovi,“* vzpomínal v *Pamětech*… Zdá se, že i při svém pracovním vytížení si v cizině občas nalezl čas i na fotografování.

V úředním životopisu Josef Binko uváděl praxi v zahraničí v letech 1904–1906. V tomto roce zemřeli krátce po sobě dědeček, maminka a babička. Bylo nutno *„zanechat dalších plánů – a začít zase tam, kde jsem přestal před cestou na zkušenou“.* Jaké to byly plány, můžeme jen spekulovat. Ale nejspíše to nesouviselo s návratem do Krucemburku. Byla to asi doba obtížných osobních rozhodování, ale nakonec převážila zodpovědnost k rodinné tradici a respekt před otcem a jistě i láska k místu dětství. Mladý muž poznal Prahu, Vídeň i Pešť, mohl srovnávat. Krucemburk měl tehdy 1600 stálých obyvatel, konalo se tam šest výročních trhů, měl poštovní a telegrafní úřad, svého lékaře s domácí lékárnou, novou budovu školy, pracovalo tu několik spolků, vedle koželužny zde byly i další průmyslové podniky.[17] Bylo to maloměsto, ale kypělo ruchem a byly tam rodinné kořeny a bratři. Vliv na jeho rozhodnutí mohla mít také opětovaná láska k místní klavíristce a zpěvačce, která však předčasně zemřela.

Ve svých životopisech Josef Binko uváděl, že od roku 1907 započal *„činnost ve vlastní továrně“.*[18] Rok 1907 je ostatně i letopočtem, od něhož mu přítel Ludvík Boháček z Prahy do Krucemburku posílal noty a knihy. Od stejného roku se také může datovat počátek přátelství mezi Josefem Binkem a Josefem Gočárem, kterého rodina Binků poznala prostřednictvím sochaře Jana Štursy.[19] Gočár poté navrhl Josefu Binkovi takzvanou Červenou vilu, kterou historici architektury považují za první samostatné dílo mladého, leč tehdy již velmi nadějného architekta. Dům, stavěný poblíž vily staršího bratra v letech 1908–1909, je fascinující a krásnou stavbou, i když z ryze účelového pohledu poněkud nepraktickou. Dům s prvky moravské lidové chalupy a anglického venkovského sídla byl projektován pro život jedné rodiny.

V přízemí vily, v komoře navržené pro služebnou, vznikla podle návrhu Josefa Binka fotokomora, původně projektovaná do prvního patra. Možná, že v patře krátký čas dokonce byla. *„Žasnu, žasnu a zase žasnu! Ty už zas máš novou komoru a hned mne bombarduješ novými krásnými obrázky. Jeden lepší než druhý a každý jiný,"* psal přítel Ludvík 23. května 1911. Formulace *„zas máš novou"* naznačuje posun oproti dřívějšímu stavu. Můžeme se tedy odvážit hypotézy, že po dokončení stavby domu v roce 1909 měl Josef Binko komoru na projektovaném místě a v této komoře vyvolal první „Cupida", ploché filmy na formát 9 × 12 cm pořízené fotopřístrojem Cupido, z nichž nejstarší známé jsou datované 13. září 1909. V této komoře také vytvořil cyklus bromolejotisků ze své svatební cesty v květnu 1910. Je možné, že již zde měl zvětšovací přístroj vertikálního typu[20], jehož tehdy unikátní konstrukce byla zhotovena s pomocí mladšího bratra Dušana.[21]

Nová fotokomora v přízemí, zařízená v původně projektované místnosti pro služku, byla velmi systematicky a cílevědomě zařízená. Je jasné, že její koncepci vymýšlel člověk, který toho o organizaci práce v temné komoře již hodně věděl. Vzácné svědectví o jejím vzhledu zachoval ing. Jan Binko (čísla odkazují na nákres fotokomory): *„Celá dodnes stojící místnost má rozměry 4 metry × 3,40. Všechno bylo rozmístěno velmi systematicky a promyšleně, panoval tu úzkostlivý pořádek. Uprostřed byl stůl se skleněnou deskou (2), kolem něho židle. Vpravo od vchodu bylo umyvadlo (10). Po levé straně stál dlouhý stůl (4) se zásuvkami. V jedné z nich byl fotoaparát Leica, který se tehdy používal, v dalším filmy a v dalším nějaké příslušenství. Úplně dole pod zásuvkami byly na polici dřevěné krabice s fotografiemi a negativy. Na začátku tohoto stolu stál diaprojektor (7), velká černá bedna, a před ní stála na stojánku malá promítací stěna (6), v klidové poloze připevněná na projektoru. Pamatuji se, jak mně děda pouštěl přímo v laboratoři pár obrázků, které se mohly promítat na délku stolu. Na konci stolu byla lampa na dvě žárovky, červenou a bílou (5). Měla odkryté kontakty, pamatuji se na to dobře, protože jsem od nich dostal ránu.*

Zvlášť zajímavá byla pravá strana komory (1), která byla pro provoz fotokomory nejpodstatnější. Byla celá zastavěná a rozčleněná na tři boxy. Box vlevo sloužil ke zvětšování. Já zde pamatuji již Leitz Focomat, který pořád mám, ale za dědy tam stál vertikální zvětšovací přístroj, který je dnes v technickém muzeu (P1). Nad zvětšovákem byla skříňka se zasklenými dvířky, v níž byly uloženy staré fotografické přístroje, které se již nepoužívaly. Uprostřed byla silná skleněná deska s mírným sklonem ke stěně (P3), kde byl olověný žlábek pro odtok vody. Přívody vody byly ve zdi nad tím. Nad deskou byly police. Na dolní polici visely dvě lampy s kapalným filtrem(P4). Mezi nimi byla klasická lampa na skleněné filtry (P2), já zde pamatuji silný zelený. Nahoře byly ještě dvě barevné žárovky. Na policích stálo chemické sklo a další podobné věci. V pravé části hlavní stěny byl rovněž skleněný stůl, na němž stály lékárnické váhy (P5). Tam byl prostor pro přípravu roztoků. Nad tím byly police, kde byly vyrovnané všechny možné chemikálie. Také tam visely předpisy vývojek. Ve skřínce nahoře byla černá fotografická technika, oblouková lampa, odpor pro obloukovou lampu. Pod stolem byly poličky, kde byly misky a další podobné fotografické nádobíčko. V místnosti bylo dvojité okno (3). Zatemnit se mohlo během dvou minut. Vnitřní okenice se otevřela, do prostoru se vsadil rám s černým kartonem, zašoupla se čtyři šoupátka a okenice se zavřela. Totéž se učinilo s druhou půlkou oken. Navíc se ještě zatáhla černá záclona…" Vzhled hlavní stěny fotokomory i s unikátním vertikálním zvětšovacím přístrojem je vytvořen z původního vybavení ve stálé expozici Interkamera Národního technického muzea v Praze. Jedná se o ojediněle zachovanou památku.

10. května 1910 se Josef Binko oženil s Terezií Chladovou, dcerou sládka a primátora Pardubic. Připomeňme si, že její mladší sestra Antonie si později vzala Dušana Binka, další sestra Marie pak architekta Josefa Gočára. Vzájemné sympatie s Josefem Gočárem byly tak zpečetěny vskutku nevšedním způsobem: dva bratři Binkovi a Josef Gočár si vzali za manželky tři dcery někdejšího zámeckého sládka.

Novomanželé Binkovi se vydali na svatební cestu do Dalmácie na trase Vídeň, Terst, Miramare, Pola, Dubrovník, Spalato. Z cesty jako originální svatební dar a pro věčnou upomínku vznikl cyklus 103 tónovaných bromolejotisků.[22] Jde o největší dochovaný cyklus ušlechtilých tisků na jedno téma od českého autora. Za devět měsíců se Josefu a Terezii Binkovým narodil syn Ivan a poté druhý syn Jan. Jako třetí dítě se jim narodila dcera Věra.

Pro Josefa Binka byla léta před první světovou válkou nepochybně velmi šťastným a po pracovní stránce intenzívním obdobím. Jako uznávaný odborník získal i společenskou prestiž, zasedal například v prezidiu Vídeňského průmyslového svazu a v referátu pro koželužný průmysl Ministerstva války. Vedle cest pracovních podnikl v té době i několik velkých zahraničních cest poznávacích, na nichž mnoho fotografoval. Je zajímavé, že kromě kontaktů s fotografickou společností FOTO FON nebyly zjištěny doklady o jeho členství v českých klubech fotoamatérů a styky s českými fotografickými časopisy, ale naopak s časopisy německými, které odebíral a které zčásti zůstaly v jeho někdejší knihovně dodnes. Možná to bylo polygrafickou úrovní dvou tehdy vycházejících českých fotočasopisů, možná i určitým přezíravým postojem elity českých fotoamatérů vůči tomu, co Josefa Binka z fotografické tvorby nejvíce zajímalo – totiž vůči ušlechtilým fotografickým tiskům. Přítel Ludvík Boháček, sám fotoamatér, který podle dopisů pilně sledoval pražskou kulturní scénu, se o fotografických výstavách v roce 1911, které dnes z odstupu považujeme za klíčové, například vůbec nezmiňoval. Situace české amatérské fotografie byla tehdy složitá, a i když výstavy roku 1911 signalizovaly změnu v názorech pražských amatérských fotoklubů, setrvačnost ve stagnaci měla dlouhé trvání a vedla k přezíravému postoji vůči ušlechtilým fotografickým tiskům u části fotoamatérů. Tradičně se podpoře těšily spíše dokumentaristické fotografické projevy. Připomeňme si i vyloučení Jaroslava Petráka, prvního významného teoretika fotografie a autora několika publikací, z Klubu fotografů amatérů v Praze v březnu 1913. Patrně především polygrafická úroveň českých fotografických časopisů byla hlavním důvodem, proč Josef Binko volil v roce 1911 pro první publikování svých snímků *Photographische Rundschau und Mitteilungen*, kde bylo v jednom čísle otištěno celkem dvanáct Binkových snímků.[23] V ročence *Die Photographische Kunst im Jahre 1911* bylo pak otištěno ještě pět Binkových snímků (čtyři krajiny a jeden portrét). Žádný z českých fotografických časopisů mu tehdy nemohl dát takový prostor a takovou kvalitu reprodukce. Volba časopisu i zájem o publikování v ročence jsou dokladem jak Binkova perfekcionalismu, tak touhy „dát o sobě jako fotograf vědět", tudíž překročit mez „fotografování jako ryze osobní věci pro sebe, rodinu a přátele". Dal tak najevo, že svým snímkům dává větší váhu, že je nechápe pouze jako doklady svého života a života rodiny.

Skvělá fotokomora a nový domov, do něhož záhy přivedl manželku, poskytly Josefu Binkovi vskutku mocný impuls k fotografování. Zároveň jde o období, které můžeme po fotografické stránce dobře rekonstruovat. Z let 1909–1914 se totiž zachovala souvislá řada filmových negativů, které jsou dnes uloženy v pražském Uměleckoprůmyslovém museu. Pro Binkovo fotografování to byla klíčová doba a v ní je i obrazové těžiště naší knihy. Zářím 1909, z něhož pocházejí první datované planfilmové negativy formátu 9 × 12 cm, skončilo první Binkovo fotografické období, z něhož v současnosti známe bohužel jen pozitivy.[24] V tomto období fotografoval jen příležitostně, s delšími přestávkami, jako fotokomory využíval altánu v zahradě. Fotografoval především na skleněné desky. Obrat k soustavnějšímu zájmu o fotografii souvisel nejen s ekonomickou stabilizací a novým postavením v rodinném podniku, ale také s koupí fotopřístroje na výhodnější planfilmy a vybudováním fotokomory v novém domě.

Základním objektem Binkova fotografického zájmu – před rokem 1909 i po něm – byla krajina. Nebyla to však krajina symbolická, krajina dramatických nápovědí s existencionálním podtextem, jakou nalézáme v rané Drtikolově tvorbě, ani krajina podvečerních nálad a rozhraní dne a noci jako u V. J. Bufky, ale krajina spíše líbezná, krajina, jejíž podmanivost tkvěla v harmonii. V Binkových krajinách je řád, soulad a harmonie, a jestliže řada snímků má také jistou podmanivou snivost, je to díky krajině samé, nikoli kvůli prvnímu plánu autora. Dlužno podotknout, že Krucemburk a jeho okolí jsou z krajinářského hlediska vskutku mimořádným místem a nepřekvapuje ani, že si místo natolik zamiloval Jan Zrzavý, který si přál být v Krucemburku pohřben. „Taková obloha jako na Vysočině – není nikde," říkával prý Josef Binko. Obzvláštní náklonnost k poetickému zvýraznění Českomoravské vysočiny projevovali mj. také Antonín Chittussi a Antonín Slavíček. Také František Kaván, Binkův současník, těžil za svého pobytu ve Vitanově u Hlinska v letech 1909–1922 z krás Českomoravské vysočiny. Pro Binkův zájem o uměleckou tvorbu je příznačné, že Kavána ve Vitanově oslovil a získal od něho několik obrazů. Mezi oběma muži se rozvinula zajímavá korespondence, z níž například vysvítá, že Kaván, který Binkovi věnoval několik „svininek", jak svá díla charakterizoval, se na čas urazil, když mu Josef Binko za dar poslal protihodnotu. V jednom z dopisů Kaván Binka oceňuje *jako odborníka i vysoce umělecky nadaného na vše možné*.[25] Zvláštní oblastí Binkova fotografického zájmu byly také lidové stavby v širokém okolí Krucemburku, kde vedle ryze estetického hlediska uplatňoval i jistý dokumentaristický akcent. Naopak záběry ze zahrady, která při jeho domu vznikala, mají silný emotivní náboj, přecházející mnohdy až do ryze pocitové polohy. Zahrada a krucemburský rybník Řeka zůstaly nejoblíbenějšími Binkovými náměty po celý život a nalezneme je ještě na kinofilmových záběrech ze čtyřicátých let 20. století.

Krajinářské snímky Josef Binko mnohdy upravoval do formy ušlechtilých fotografických tisků. Ty představují soubor technik založených na koloidních látkách, většinou organického původu (želatina, arabská guma), napojených roztokem dvojchromanových solí. Působením světla dochází ve vrstvách chromovaných klihovin k utvrzování, které je úměrné osvitu. Obraz má tedy formu jemného reliéfu, tvarovaného podle stupně vytvrzení klihoviny. Reliéf se může využít jako matrice k tisku obrazu, nebo se obraz může zviditelnit vybarvením klihovinové vrstvy. U zbobtnalého reliéfu se například využije mastných barviv, která jsou odpuzována vodou nasáklou ve zbobtnalých místech, nebo naopak barviv ve vodě rozpustných, která zbobtnalá místa přijímají. V několika příkladech máme vzácnou příležitost srovnání různých výsledků Binkova uměleckého postupu.

Ušlechtilé fotografické tisky, které v principu umožňují podstatně změnit původní obraz z negativu, mají v chápání fotografické tvorby Josefa Binka velmi důležité místo. Výsledný obraz u většiny ušlechtilých tisků velmi závisel na zručnosti a zkušenosti autora, který mohl (nikoli u všech technik) pozitiv podstatně ovlivnit, včetně tonálních hodnot a barevnosti. Díla tak byla vskutku výrazem osobnosti svého tvůrce, byla originální ve smyslu tradičních hodnot umělcovy osobnosti. Binka nejprve zaujaly gumotisky a pigmenty, po roce 1907 se věnoval také olejotiskům a od roku 1911 bromolejotiskům. Binkovy gumotisky mívaly formát 30 × 40 cm, bromolejotisky vždy 18 × 24 cm. Stejný formát mívaly také olejotisky, u nichž se však častěji uplatňovala řešení v menším měřítku, většinou 9 × 12 cm. Zachoval se rovněž soubor zvětšených papírových negativů ke gumotiskům. Některé z portrétů (například Ludvíka Boháčka) uplatnil ve variacích více technik. Můžeme říci, že Josef Binko počtem a kvalitou svých ušlechtilých fotografických tisků patřil k vůbec nejvýznamnějším českým fotografům secesního piktorialismu. Některé práce, zejména ze zahrady, vytvořené mezi léty 1912–1920 měkce kreslicími objektivy s využitím protisvětla nebo kontrastu světlých a tmavých ploch, náležejí k prvním projevům puristického piktorialismu, rozvinutého pak například Josefem Sudkem.

Vedle ušlechtilých tisků se Josef Binko věnoval tvorbě diapozitivů, jejichž promítání bývalo tehdy v české společnosti velmi populární. Také u Binků patřívalo k rodinné večerní pohodě, kdy se střídalo s hudebními preludii a hlasitým předčítáním. Josef Binko měl kvalitní projekční vybavení pro projekce těchto „světelných obrazů“, které se promítaly ve velké hale, veliké prostoře uprostřed domu s výškou přes patro. Skioptikon, projekční přístroj pro diapozitivy, z něhož je dnes bohužel torzo, byl uzpůsoben pro formát desek 12 × 12 cm. Na rozdíl od zvětšovacího přístroje se jednalo o tovární výrobu. Na krásné chvíle, *„když jsem v zimních večerech promítal celou spoustu diapositivů v halle“*, vzpomínal Josef Binka v dopisech[26] a zmiňuje se o nich také vnuk Jan Binko ve svých vzpomínkách z raného dětství. Tento způsob naplňování chvil volna pro Josefa Binko nepochybně znamenal obohacování sebe sama ve smyslu duchovním a byl i výrazem přirozené rodinné semknutosti a pospolitosti. Binkovy záliby nebyly pouhou rekreací, odpočinkem v dnešním smyslu, byly jen jinou formou naplňování jeho života, kde na prvním místě bylo úsilí o rozkvět továrny a zabezpečení jejích zaměstnanců. Připomeňme si životní osudy jiného fotoamatéra, jilemnického lékaře Jaroslava Feyfara, který také trávil mnohé hodiny muzicírováním pro potěchu a podobně jako Josef Binko měl knihovnu s dvěma tisíci svazků a pravidelně jezdil do Prahy do divadla stejně jako Josef Binko na koncerty.

V dopisech z posledního desetiletí svého života Josef Binko často vzpomínal na chvíle muzicírování. Z těchto vzpomínek vyvstává bohatství jeho duševního života, spočívající i v aktivním prožívání chvil volna. *„Smetanovo klavírní trio, Dvořákovy dumky, Fibichův klavírní kvintet, a.t.d., a což teprve druhý Beethovenův klavírní koncert!! To jsme chvílemi ani nedýchali při hraní tohoto nesmrtelného díla. Ale i houslové sonaty nejen Beethovenovy, ale obě Griegovy, náš Laub, nebo Spohr… prostě tehdy jsme žili! … S přítelem Ludvíkem Boháčkem [jsme hráli] někdy od oběda do půlnoci, a s klavírní virtuoskou a učitelkou hudby slečnou Fingrovou, temperamentní a ušlechtilou, a neúnavnou; celou Mou vlast bez přestávky nebo čtyřruční klavírní výtahy Wagnerových oper. [Boháček] každý rok na sv. Václava dostal týden dovolenou od tatínka, a to poslal napřed pětikilový balík not. To byly jiné časy, aspoň pro mne, a když byl v Praze nějaký významný koncert, napsal mi, že už má pro mne lístek, a tatínek mi nikdy na ten den neodmítnul, naopak sám byl rád, když se mu poštěstilo někde se k nějakému koncertu dostat. A kolikrát jsem slyšel „slavnostní představení" Prodané nebo ke konci první války Libuši s Maturovou – jsou to sice jen vzpomínky, ale děkuji za ně osudu, byla to přímo životní vzpruha pro člověka zapřaženého do denního chomoutu."*[27]

K ativnímu prožívání volného času patřily vedle muzicírování také výlety do přírody a cestování, které se významně odrazily i v Binkově fotografické tvorbě. Část snímků z cest můžeme označit jako „městskou krajinu", část jako pocitové glosování detailů architektur. Jen vzácně se objevují motivy pouličního ruchu. K fotografovaným objektům Binko nestavěl stafáž, ale naopak se snažil, aby lidé na snímcích z měst nebyli. Pokud jsou lidé v ulicích zachyceni, nenesou žádnou významovotvornou roli (například ve formě zachycení určitého typu nebo situace), jde jen o nearanžovaný záznam daného stavu.

Osobité místo v Binkově tvorbě mají fotografie městské architektury. Binko navštívil mnoho tuzemských i zahraničních měst, mnohokrát fotografoval v Praze a Kutné Hoře. Z městských motivů si osobně patrně nejvíce cenil cyklu Rothenburg, vzniklého 5. září 1912 na jeho „Německé cestě", z něhož poté vytvořil cyklus 43 olejotisků.[28] Proč z trasy Norimberk, Rothenburg, Ulm, Mnichov, Salzburg, Königsee zvolil právě Rothenburg, když třeba norimberské snímky jsou rovněž velmi zajímavé, těžko soudit. Snímky nejsou popisem památek města, ale spíše jakýmsi záznamem pocitů ze scenerie a charakteristických detailů města. Téměř všechny negativy vytvořené během jediného dne uplatnil v bromolejotiscích. Jeho 5. září 1912 patřilo i podle Binka samotného k těm šťastným konstelacím místa, počasí, nálady i osobního biorytmu, že během jediného dne vytvořil ve městě na pět desítek velkoformátových negativů, z nichž většinu shledal tak zajímavou, že je přetvořil v bromolejotisky. Důraz na jeden jediný den je ostatně i v názvu souboru – „Rothenburg 5. 9. 1912". Množství kvalitních snímků zároveň dosvědčuje souhru fotografa s jeho fotopřístrojem. Neznáme jiný podobný dobový příklad ve fotoamatérské oblasti.

Čím Josef Binko tehdy fotografoval, lze rekonstruovat ze souboru přístrojů předaných do Národního technického muzea v Praze a také z letmých poznámek v korespondenci přítele Boháčka. Nejčastější používanou komorou byl tehdy sklopný přístroj pro formát negativu 9 × 12 cm Cupido s kvalitním Goerzovým šestičočkovým symetrickým tmeleným anastigmatem Dagor s parametry 6,8 / 20 v centrální pneumatické závěrce s expozicemi od jedné sekundy po 1/250 sekundy. Přístroj vyráběla firma ICA, respektive Hüttig AG v Drážďanech od roku 1907 a Josef Binko si jej pořídil zřejmě v létě 1909. Další významnou komorou z pozůstalosti byl kvalitní dřevěný cestovní přístroj anglického typu na formát desek 13 × 18 cm z doby kolem roku 1895, s nímž Binko pracoval před zakoupením Cupida. Aparátem Alpinka vytvářel stereoskopické snímky formátu 7,5 × 10 cm. Podle dochovaného účtu si v srpnu 1916 Josef Binko zakoupil Icarettu na formát 6 × 6 cm s objektivem Novar 6.8 / 75 mm.[29] Krátce po první světové válce zaznamenáváme v soupisu negativů zkoušky s aparátem Ernemann na desky 6 × 4,5 cm. Binkovo fotografické vybavení v době rozkvětu jeho záliby bylo tedy skutečně velkorysé.

Méně početnou, ale kvalitativně významnou námětovou skupinu tvoří u Josefa Binka portréty. Především se jednalo o portréty nejbližších: dědečka, otce, sourozenců a přátel, později také manželky a jejích sester. Jen vzácně zachytil lidi bez bližšího vztahu k nim. Na Binkových portrétech je dobře patrná jeho cesta od popisného zachycení k uměleckému pocitovému ztvárnění. Jeho první ušlechtilé tisky, portréty dědečka a otce, patří k mistrovským dílům, k těm nejlepším, jaké v české fotografii počátku 20. století vznikly. Slavný je Gočárův portrét před kachlovými kamny, existující v několika výřezových variacích, mimořádný je i portrét někdejšího spolužáka Ludvíka Boháčka. Vedle transformace snímku do podoby ušlechtilého tisku zasahoval Binko do negativů tahy tužkou, u některých snímků (vesměs z přírody) nacházíme poznámku „práce jehlou".

Jen málokdy pořizoval Josef Binko snímky, které můžeme označit za dokumentaci určité události nebo děje. Jistou výjimku tvoří průvod Sokolů při VI. všesokolském sletu 29. června 1912. A protože ho fotografický přístroj doprovázel na výletech s přáteli, zachytil občas i „momentku" z výletu. Málokdy se však jednalo o nějaký živý spontánní záběr, Binko téměř vždy snímek komponoval po dohodě se snímanými osobami.

Z naznačeného vyplývá, že Josef Binko byl typem fotografa, který měl potřebu v klidu komponovat, záběr promýšlet, že jen málokdy fotografoval spontánně, rychle, „od boku", i když to jeho fotografické vybavení dovolovalo. Nebyla to zřejmě věc mentality, ale spíše názoru na fotografii. Pro Binka bylo vyvolání filmů a následné upravování na ušlechtilých tiscích velmi podstatnou věcí, neboť se zároveň jednalo o formu jakéhosi druhého prožitku záběru. Podstatný byl pro něj prožitek motivu, nikoliv potřeba něco zaznamenat. Nikoli dokument okamžiku a jeho zvěčnění, ale jakési znovuprožití emoce bylo pro něj podstatné. Názor můžeme opřít o citaci z Binkova dopisu z 18. 12. 1950, jehož průklep se dochoval: *„Vzpomínal jsem nedávno, při prohlížení starých fotografií, když mi najednou přišly do rukou snímky z našeho společného zájezdu k moři. Jak jsme tahali chaluhy na duně u Helgolandu a koupali se v moři… U každého toho obrázku bych přesně mohl říci, kdy a za jaké nálady povstal. To je u fotografie pěkné, že jaksi ustáluje naše zážitky a vzpomínky, které by jinak jistě pozbyly životnosti a nebo úplně vypadnuly z paměti; a mám takových snímků ze svých cest jistě mnoho set, a nyní si tak někdy k nim sednu a čtu v nich jako v nějaké knize".*[30]

Touha po řádu, klid a harmonie, které čiší z Binkových fotografií, byly i součástí jeho životních postojů. V dopise ze 6. května 1952 píše: *„nejen láska k lidem, ale ke všemu krásnému, protože v tom je záruka klidné životní pohody".*

Bohužel se nedochoval žádný text osvětlující Binkův názor na fotografii a fotografování v letech před první světovou válkou. Střípky názorů můžeme posbírat až z dopisů z posledního desetiletí života, psaných na stroji v průklepech různým adresátům. A rovněž jen zprostředkovaně můžeme dedukovat Binkovy názory podle reakcí přítele Ludvíka Boháčka, jehož dopisy z let 1910–1914 se zachovaly. Binkův postoj k fotografické tvorbě tak rekonstruujeme především z dochovaného díla, u něhož máme právě pro toto klíčové období vzácnou příležitost srovnávat negativy s výslednými pozitivy, můžeme tedy porovnat, co fotograf z kolekce vybral a jak vybraný snímek výřezem či jinak upravil. Dobře je to patrné zejména na snímcích ze svatební cesty, kdy počet vybraných bromolejotisků byl 103 kusů z exponovaných 207 negativů. Tento soubor, největší svého druhu v české fotografii, je pocitovou evokací míst, které spolu novomanželé navštívili a je zároveň i nádherným a monumentálním dárkem své choti. Některé pohledy nebo zachycené situace tak mohly mít i specifický intimní podtext, srozumitelný jen dvojici. Na souboru je dobře patrné, jak Binko zacházel s barevným tónem olejotisku a jaké prováděl výřezy, které byly zřejmě výsledkem dlouhých zkoušek. Josef Binko byl totiž jedním z prvních fotografů u nás, který výřez běžně prováděl pomocí zvětšovacího přístroje, což tehdy nebylo vůbec obvyklé. Binko nepochybně pilně sledoval nejen estetickou problematiku fotografie, ale i různé technické finty, jichž byly tehdejší příručky plné. V krajinářské fotografii kladl velký důraz pochopitelně na seskupení a výraz mraků; je typické, že přítel Ludvík Boháček se ptal: *„Prosím Tě, dej mi recept, jak uděláš takové mraky, něco takového se mně posud nepovedlo. Je k tomu třeba zvláštních desek? Užívám nyní výhradně Perutz [?] a mraky mi posud nevylezly, či je třeba nějakého jiného triku, na který jsem dosud nepřišel? A prosím Tě, co je ten nový aparát za systém, že tak báječně dělá! Napiš mi o tom detailně!“*[31] Binkovu odpověď bohužel nemáme a nevíme tedy, zda k vykouzlení mraků používal filtrů, nebo speciálního fotomateriálu, nebo kombinací obého. Samozřejmě, že technické aspekty věci nemohou překrýt svým významem emotivní obsah Binkových snímků, ale je dobré o jejich uplatňování v Binkově díle vědět. Jsou mimo jiné i důkazem toho, s jakou zodpovědností Binko ke své zálibě přistupoval.

Za první světové války plnila továrna na usně válečné dodávky a byl tam proto dosazen válečný správce. Bratři Ladislav a Josef jako nezbytní odborníci a řada dělníků nemuseli narukovat, ale nejmladší Dušan Binko strávil válku na bojištích. Na tomto místě je nutno zdůraznit, že mezi oběma mladšími bratry bylo zvlášť úzké pouto, které navenek pentlily jejich manželky, které byly sestry, ale byla tu i názorová blízkost. Dušan byl prý obdivuhodně zručný a mimořádně technicky nadaný, ve Starém domě, kde bydlel, měl skvělou „mechanickou dílnu", a zvětšovací přístroj ve fotokomoře bratra byl ostatně především jeho dílem. Pro sebe si zhotovil skioptikon.[32] Také Dušan Binko rád a často fotografoval a na rozdíl od bratra jej více zajímala fotografie jako dokument. Za války musel také Gočár narukovat a jeho manželka Marie žila potom se synkem Jiřím v Krucemburku ve Starém domě.[33]

Slavné říjnové dny roku 1918, které vedly k vyhlášení samostatnosti Československa, strávil Josef Binko podle svých vzpomínek v Praze a velmi aktivně.[34] Naděje spojené se vznikem samostatného státu vedly k plnění četných organizačních úkolů, které ho časově velmi vyčerpávaly. Podílel se například na vybudování Koželužské školy v Hradci Králové, kterou mimochodem navrhl Gočár. Stál na všech podstatných organizačních pozicích domácího koželného průmyslu. Také v továrně se v několika etapách přistoupilo k zásadním rekonstrukcím, modernizaci a zvětšení provozů. 31. května 1923 zemřel jeho otec – Ladislav Binko. Zdá se, že v prvních letech Československé republiky se Josef Binko fotografické práci věnoval mnohem méně než dříve. Je zajímavé, že podobný jev můžeme sledovat u řady dalších fotoamatérů, například u Jaroslava Feyfara, s nímž do určité míry můžeme Josefa Binka porovnávat nejen co se týče odlehlosti místa působení, šíře a významu kulturních zálib, ale i stylu života v letech před první světovou válkou. Jestliže Jaroslav Feyfar přestával ve dvacátých letech fotografovat, protože jej zaujal jiný koníček – rozhlas, byl Josef Binko velmi zaneprázdněn pracovně – organizačními úkoly. Roku 1920 skončil s abonencí posledních dvou fotografických časopisů, z nichž *Wiener Mitteilungen* si pravidelně kupoval od roku 1899. Možná, že určitý nový rozmach jeho fotografické záliby přinesl po roce 1925 kinofilmový fotoaparát Leica, jehož první verzi si podle rodinných vzpomínek Josef Binko hned pořídil, protože mu byly zřejmé jeho výhody. Nová Leica IIIa, která se začala vyrábět od roku 1935, zůstala v rodině dodnes, včetně rozsáhlého archivu kinofilmových negativů, který dokládá, že Josef Binko fotografoval až do počátku padesátých let.[35]

Na konci třicátých let podnik natolik prosperoval, že se musely zřídit sklady vlastního zboží v deseti zemích. Zato v letech druhé světové války výroba téměř ustala a továrnu v podstatě zachránila Baťova firma ve Zlíně prací v úkolu. Tehdy byl zřejmě čas na rekapitulaci, vzpomínání a návrhy. Možná právě proto vznikla zčásti z nových a zčásti ze starých snímků dárková alba pro syny a dceru i jednotlivé fotografie zahrady, rodiny se psem Flušem a okolí Krucemburku. Znovu se zřejmě oživil také zájem o ušlechtilé fotografické tisky.[36]

Nové politické poměry po roce 1948 změnily mnohé. Zejména pro ty, kteří měli nějaký majetek. Koželužna byla znárodněna 28. dubna 1948. O těžkém období – bez stopy hořkosti, jen jako smutné konstatování – vyprávějí mnohé pasáže v dopisech Josefa Binka synu Ivanovi a někdejším přátelům z koželného resortu a takzvaným letním hostům – přátelům a známým, kteří pobývali v Krucemburku „na letním bytě“. Ze společnosti koželužských chemiků k těm nejvýznamnějším náleželi dr. Ivan Růžička, Karel Čáslavský, JUDr. Jaroslav Novák, Jan Pivečka a prof. dr. ing. Václav Kubelka, z „letních přátel“ pak bývalý konzul v Turecku ing. Jan Novák, Robert Rakušan, Jan Vrba, někdejší konzul ve Francii Miloš Šafránek (otec Anny Fárové) a ing. Ladislav Němec, jehož syn, pozdější režisér, trávil prý coby dítě ve společnosti Josefa Binka ve fotokomoře mnohé chvíle.

V zimě 1953 přestala temná komora asi poprvé plně sloužit svému účelu, protože byla jedinou prostorou ve velkém domě, kde se dalo udržet teplo a tudíž tam přebývat. Až do konce života nový režim rodinu rafinovaně trápil takzvanými nedoplatky na majetkových dávkách a posléze i vyvlastněním vily se zahradou.[37] Josef Binko zvlášť těžce nesl úmysl státu provést ve vile stavební úpravy a zmáhal ho pocit, že *„všechno kolem, co jsme za celý život vytvořili a udržovali, s takovou láskou – dnes pomalu podléhá zkáze“.*[38] Ve všeobecném marasmu všude kolem lze přesto v dopisech Josefa Binka dětem a přátelům nalézt slova útěchy a naděje. Ing. Novákovi, bývalému konzulovi ve Francii, jednomu z někdejších „letních přátel“, 20. prosince 1953 píše Binko k Vánocům: *„Ale nemyslete prosím, že naříkám, naopak, celé moje nitro je přímo naplněno nadějí na lepší časy, nadějí, že zas budu zdráv, že Vás zde na jaře znova uvítáme, a že si ještě jednou vynahradíme všechen ten smutek, který nás nyní přímo zaklopil, a že celé lidstvo se zase zbaví té hrůzy nejistoty, kdy člověk se zase stane člověkem, kdy lež bude lží, a právo a čest se zase stanou prostou samozřejmostí... Dnes zní bohužel takovéto úvahy skoro absurdně, ale zač stál by ten život – bez naděje?“*[39]

V dopise Františku Petrovi, malíři a restaurátorovi, Binko 3. dubna 1957 píše: *„Jinak žijeme již v úplné odloučenosti od okolního světa, a pomalu jsem již odvykl lidem. Sice pilně čtu, studuji dějiny hudby a umění vůbec, a těším se, že snad bude letos příznivější léto, abychom se zase otužili a připravili na další život. Doufáme, ba věříme pevně, že se dočkáme ještě lepších časů a to nás sílí – třebaže již žádných plánů při našem věku zásadně neděláme a žijeme více ve vzpomínkách. Zvláště si rád vzpomínám na doby plného národního rozkvětu, a děkuji Pánubohu, že mi bylo popřáno onu dobu prožíti v plné životní síle. Co jen jsem užil koncertů v Praze, ve Vídni, osobní známosti s tolika, dnes slavnými, umělci, spisovateli, výtvarníky, kolik galerií po skoro celé Evropě jsem prochodil...“*[40]

Syn Ivan se ještě za otcova života snažil o zabezpečení otcovy fotografické pozůstalosti, kterou na výzvu ing. Karla Paspy při jejich náhodném setkání nabídl v roce 1958 darem Národnímu technickému muzeu.[41] Ing. Karel Paspa, člen Spolku Národního technického muzea, v srpnu 1959 Krucemburk navštívil. Dopis, který mu 31. 8. 1959 po návštěvě Ivan Binko napsal, je důležitým pramenem k poznání stavu fotokomory a fotografického archivu na sklonku života Josefa Binka: *„Po Vašem odjezdu jsem urovnal celou laboratoř, dnes jsou v jedné skříni všechny fotografické přístroje, v druhé zařízení pro projekci a diapozitivy. Všechny negativy jsou pohromadě a všechny pozitivy jsou pohromadě. Prohlédl jsem zběžně diapositivy, nejsou ještě zachváceny skoro vůbec plísní, jsou však poněkud zvlhlé a rozlepují se. ... Negativy jsou většinou v dobrém stavu, též nejsou z největší části ještě poškozeny plísní, potřebují asi jen očistit opocení skel, pokud jsou na deskách. Negativy z cest jsou na filmech z Cupida a jsou bezvadné. U aparátů jsem kožené části vyčistil. Posbíral jsem všechny práce provedené nepřímými positivními technikami a s dědečkem neb podle negativů je zkatalogisoval. Jsou nyní všechny uloženy u dědečka v jeho pokoji ve skříni, aby se nestaly obětí plísně. Kopie seznamů jsem si uschoval, originály jsou přiloženy přímo vždy v příslušných deskách, které jsem na jednotlivé cykly udělal. To je vše, co jsem za dovolenou stačil udělat. Bylo by zapotřebí provést důkladnější katalogisaci negativů. Negativy z cest jsou katalogisovány dědečkem přímo velmi přesně, negativy z Vysočiny a rodinné však někdy jen přibližným údajem a někdy neskatalogisovány.“*

Díky zachovalé korespondenci Ivana Binka s Karlem Paspou můžeme rekonstruovat postup dalších, poněkud tristních jednání o předání fotografického archivu a zařízení fotokomory včetně fotopřístrojů.[42] Během těchto jednání 11. února 1960 Josef Binko zemřel. Syn Ivan poté v září dopravil na svůj náklad dar do Národního technického muzea v Praze.[43]

Osudů fotografů podobných osudu Josefa Binka bylo v naší zemi mnoho. Žádný z nich však po sobě nezanechal takové množství precizních ušlechtilých fotografických tisků. Josef Binko krásu nacházel v hudbě, na procházkách lesem a při četbě knih. V prostých, jednoduchých sceneriích, v souhře stromů, mraků, kupek sena, terénních záhybech a kopcích Vysočiny. Jako by si známý výrok o architektuře a zmrzlé hudbě poopravil tak, že fotografie je zmrzlá hudba. Odráží i evokuje pocity a nálady, vyvolává starou náladu a pocit, stejně jako fixuje vzpomínku. Hudbou a fotografováním se zaměstnávaly – a zároveň rekreovaly – dva nejpodstatnější smysly: sluch a zrak. Vjemy se v mysli protínaly ve zvláštní jednotě a souladu. Josef Binko neměl potřebu dávat v názvech snímků najevo svou sečtělost, vzdělanost, hudební rozhled, přisuzovat jim další hlubokomyslné významy. Názvy jeho fotografií jsou prosté, orientační, bez symbolického podtextu. Jistě i proto, že on skutečně fotografoval především pro sebe a své nejbližší, nezáleželo mu na úsudku anonymního obecenstva, nebojoval o uznání jako umělec. *„Chtěl jsem vás jen zabezpečit,“* píše v třicátých letech svým dětem o továrně a svém snažení. *„Trochu té muziky, četby a fotografování jsou tak světlé chvilky v té všeobecné mizérii,“* psal v roce 1912 přítel Boháček.[44] A jeho slova jsou myslím dobře platná i pro pocity adresáta. V osobnosti Josefa Binka vidíme ty nejlepší vlastnosti čistého fotografického tvoření a můžeme se ptát, proč člověk vůbec fotografuje. Nikoli pro tvorbu uměleckého díla, ne pro uznání společnosti, ne pro kšeft. Dílo Josefa Binka, v podstatě velmi nerafinované, přehledné a jednoduché, ukazuje, že Josef Binko fotografoval pro svou vnitřní radost z krásy světa. Jeho fotografování bylo především hledáním krásy v mnoha podobách: krásy přírody na Vysočině, krásy architektury měst, krásy uvnitř lidí, které poznal, krásy zážitku svatební cesty. Asi to zní dnešním uším banálně a „nekunsthistoricky“ prostě: Binkovy objektivy se snažily hledat, zachycovat a díky specifickým vlastnostem fotografie uchovávat krásu. Tento mnohokrát a z různých úhlů definovaný pojem zní zde snad až příliš jednoduše. Já jsem však přesvědčen, že jeho hledání bylo pravým smyslem Binkova fotografování.

Poznámky

1 Viz Janáček, J.: *700 let Krucemburku – Křížové*, Krucemburk 1966, rukopis.
Jako mistr koželužský se poprvé uvádí Martin Skřivan roku 1690. Srov. též Kynčl, J.:
Průvodce Krucemburkem s rodinnými kronikami, Krucemburk 1918.

2 Binko, Josef: *Paměti koželužny v Krucemburku*, Krucemburk 1956. Strojopis o patnácti stranách
je uložen v kopiích u příbuzných. Dále je zde nazýván jen *Paměti...* Viz též Vomela, P.: Historie
koželužny v Krucemburku, *Obecní noviny Domov*, č. 14, 18. 12. 2002.

3 *Paměti...*, s. 3.

4 Antonín Skřivan (1818 Krucemburk – 1887 Praha), ředitel Skřivanovy obchodní školy v Praze,
byl tvůrcem českého obchodního názvosloví. Předčasně zesnulý Gustav Skřivan
(1831 Krucemburk – 1866 Praha) byl první český profesor matematiky na pražské polytechnice,
mimořádný člen Královské české společnosti nauk. Zasloužil se o budování výuky matematiky
na českých vysokých školách. Viz *Ottův slovník naučný*, 1903, 23. díl, s. 313–314.

5 Augustin Skřivan (1805–1869) byl významnou osobností krucemburského života. V letech
1850–1867 byl purkmistrem a právě on navrhl užívat původní název obce Krucemburk namísto
zkomoleného Krucburk. Byl bratrem Antonína Skřivana a otcem Gustava Skřivana. Viz též Binko,
Ivan: *Ze života Augustina Karla Skřivana a Gustava Skřivana*, rukopis.

6 *Paměti...*, s. 9.

7 *Paměti...*, s. 6.

8 *Paměti...*, s. 8–9.

9 Dopisy Ludvíka Boháčka se dochovaly u Evy Kolářové. Celá korespondence z let 1909–1914 je
prodchnuta láskou k příteli a zprostředkovaně přináší i četné zajímavé údaje o Binkově fotografické
zálibě. V dopisu ze 14. 1. 1913 Boháček připojuje seznam notového materiálu o 104 položkách,
které svému příteli od roku 1907 poslal. Část not se zachovala v rodinách ing. Jana Binka a Heleny
Binkové.

10 Josef Binko byl až do konce života členem Společnosti Antonína Dvořáka v Praze. Stojí za zmínku,
co napsal 29. 11. 1958 v souvislosti s Dvořákem příteli Janu Vrbovi o Zdeňku Nejedlém: „*...považuji jej
za zrádce všeho národního cítění a za podlou povahu.*"

11 *Paměti...*, s. 10.

12 Jedná se o negativ označený č. 3 – záběr „partie při pramenech řeky Doubravky". Viz seznam
„Z pozůstalosti J. Binka předaný negativní materiál na skleněných deskách" o dvanácti stranách,
který je v majetku ing. Jana Binka. Seznam vznikal zřcjmč péčí Ivana Binka v letech 1958–59
za součinnosti Josefa Binka. Není uspořádán chronologicky, obsahuje čísla negativů dle
jednotlivých formátů a popis záběru. Někdy bývá uvedeno i přesné datum vzniku snímku,
z datovaných je nejstarší záběr ze 16. 7. 1895 (zahrada se špejcharem v Krucemburku). Čísla 1–2,
nadepsaná letopočtem 1895 a označená jako „původní číslování", byly záběry na vyhořelý mlýn
v Krucemburku. Bohužel tyto převážně skleněné negativy formátů 9 × 12 cm, 13 × 18 cm, 18 × 23,5
cm, panoramatické 10 × 15 cm, stereo 7,5 × 9 cm, 9 × 9 cm a 6 × 4,5 cm, vše v dřevěných krabicích
a bedýnkách, se ztratily. Viz dále pozn. 24.

13 Dopis Ivanu Binkovi datovaný 10. 10. 1958 je u Evy Kolářové.

14 V knihovně (dnes u ing. Jana Binka) jsou vedle asi třiceti fotografických publikací ročníky
Photographische Rundschau und Mitteilungen (1912–1920), Vogelovy *Photographische Mitteilungen*

(1900–1911), Lechnerovy *Wiener Mitteilungen* (1899–1920), *Photographische Rundschau* (1908–1911), Wachtlův *Der Amateur* (1905–1908), *Kamera Kunst* (1909–1912), *The Studio* (1905–1906). Nechybí ani pět ročníků českého Fotografického věstníku (1894–1899). Pokud se publikací týče, jedná se o velmi reprezentativní průřez fotografickou literaturou kolem roku 1900 (nejmladší tituly – *Bromöldruckverfahren* a *Oeldruck und Bromöldruck* – byly vydány v lctcch 1913 a 1915). Všcchny knižní tituly jsou v němčině. Také knihy dokazují, že Josef Binko získával teoretickou fotografickou průpravu převážně koncem 90. let 19. století.

15 Dopis Ivanu Binkovi datovaný 10. 10. 1958.

16 *Paměti...*, s. 8 (na stejném místě jsou i další dvě citace).

17 V roce 1910 měl Krucemburk 216 domů a 1616 stálých obyvatel. Viz Binko, Ivan: *Data obce Krucemburk od založení podnes*, rukopis, nedatováno.

18 V dopisu z 8. 11. 1945 Obchodní a živnostenské komoře v Praze ve věci přijetí funkce náměstka generálního ředitele pro obor kožedělný podává Josef Binko přehled svých životních dat a vypočítává své nové (nebo obnovené) funkce. Dopis je v majetku Evy Kolářové. Přesnější rekonstrukce dat působení je obtížná, protože starý spisový materiál k činnosti továrny na usně v Krucemburku byl po jejím znárodnění zničen.

19 Josef Štursa navrhl roku 1904 rodinnou hrobku Binků v Krucemburku. Josef Gočár nejprve navrhl úpravu fasád, průčelí a interiérů novostavby nejstaršího z bratrů Ladislava. Tato takzvaná Bílá vila byla postavena v letech 1907–1908.

20 Jak vyplývá z dopisu Ivana Binka Karlu Paspovi z 31. 8. 1959, unikátní vertikální zvětšovací přístroj byl zřejmě krátce po roce 1950 darován Janu Pěničkovi z Krucemburku čp. 196, kde byl také složený na půdě Ivanem Binkem nalezen. Byl nepoškozený, pouze objektiv Tessar „je zvlhlý a potřeboval by přetmelit". V dopisu Ivan Binko Karla Paspu prosí, aby zmíněného muže Národní technické muzeum (dále jen NTM) požádalo o předání přístroje.

21 Dušan Binko také sám fotografoval. Jak vyplývá z korespondence Dušana Binka s jeho budoucí chotí z let 1911–12, byly pro něho „největším dárkem" fotografické papíry. Vedle záběrů z Vysočiny sc například zachoval komplctní soubor snímků z válečného období, kdy č. 1 nese datum 15. 7. 1914 a č. 383 datum 1. 2. 1917. Jde o snímky z Itálie, Podkarpatské Rusi a Haliče. Viz dále pozn. 32.

22 Z cesty podniknuté ve dnech 13. –29.(?) 5. 1910 se dochovalo v Uměleckoprůmyslovém museu (dále jen UPM) 207 filmových negativů formátu 9 × 12 cm, z nichž vznikl cyklus 103 tónovaných bromolejotisků, uložených jako celek v NTM. Jednotlivé bromolejotisky z tohoto cyklu jsou též uloženy v rodinách příbuzných.

23 Viz *Photographische Rundschau und Mitteilungen* 48, 1911, č. 17. Jednalo se převážně o záběry z přírody v okolí Krucemburku. Krátce poté bylo pět snímků Josefa Binka publikováno v ročence *Die Photographische Kunst im Jahre 1911* na s. 81, 86, 88, 93, 94 (vydavatel M. Mazuren, Photograph-Verlagsgesellschaft m.b.H., Halle A. D. S). Jednalo se o snímky s názvy V lese, Ves, Břízy, Portrét a Podzimní večer.

24 Skleněné negativy souvislé řady z let 1895–1909 formátů 9 × 12 a 13 × 18 cm a z doby pozdější různých formátů, jakož i diapozitivy Josefa Binka bohužel nejsou v současné době k nalezení. Byly spolu se soupisem připraveny k předání do NTM, ale k tomu podle záznamů v NTM nedošlo. Vzhledem k tomu, že filmové negativy z let 1909–1914 předal do UPM Rudolf Skopec, nabízí se hypotéza, že Skopec měl z důvodu zájmu o sepsání Binkovy monografie k dispozici i skleněné

negativy a diapozitivy. Snadněji přenositelné filmové negativy v počtu téměř 3000 kusů přinesl do UPM, převoz asi 15 bedýnek se skly však již neuskutečnil a ty mohly vzít zasvé na půdě Skopcova domu v Čimicích. Je doloženo, že na půdě Skopcova domu skutečně množství skleněných negativů bylo. Významným dokladem o struktuře a počtu záběrů vytvořených před rokem 1909 je podrobný seznam, který se nachází v majetku ing. Jana Binka (viz pozn. 12).

25   Dopisy Františka Kavána a koncept dopisu Josefa Binka paní Kavánové jsou nedatované, ale je zřejmé, že pocházejí převážně z let první světové války. Jsou v majetku Evy Kolářové. Negativy Josefa Binka zobrazující Kavánův dům, vytvořené 21. 5. 1914, jsou uloženy v UPM.

26   Josef Binko v dopisu synu Ivanovi z 10. 10. 1958. Ivan Binko předtím 4. 10. psal otci o bohatství „německých měst na diapozitivech, jež zmizela za války ze světa". Dopisy jsou v majetku Evy Kolářové. U ing. Jana Binka je soupis 729 diapozitivů po jednotlivých devíti krabicích. Ze soupisu vyplývá, že diapozitivy tvořily výběr ze zahraničních cest, počínaje cestou svatební v květnu 1910 a konče výletem do Německa v srpnu 1913. 177 diapozitivů tvořily dále záběry z Vysočiny, Prahy a českých měst.

27   V dopisu z 29. 11. 1958 Janu Vrbovi. Dopis je uložen u Evy Kolářové.

28   Josef Binko podnikl „Německou cestu" na trase Norimberk, Rothenburg, Ulm, Mnichov, Salzburg, Königsee ve dnech 3.–12.(?) září 1912. Z cesty se dochovalo (dnes v UPM) 241 negativů formátu 9 × 12 cm, z nichž vznikl cyklus 43 bromolejotisků s názvem Rothenburg 5. 9. 1912, který je uložen jako celek v NTM. Jednotlivé listy zůstaly také v rodině. Osm snímků z tohoto cyklu bylo publikováno v časopisu *Photographische Rundschau*, 1913 (č. 20, 21, 23) a tři v ročence *Die Photographische Kunst im Jahre 1913* na s. 114, 115, 116.

29   Doklad o koupi je v majetku ing. Jana Binka. Vedle objektivu Novar používal Binko jetě Tessar, „dělal" prý ale „příliš tvrdé snímky, neosvědčil se" (citace ze soupisu věcí určených k předání do NTM). Všechny předměty z Binkovy pozůstalosti mají v NTM přírůstkové číslo 14 / 18. 01. 1963. Pokud jde o inventární čísla fotopřístrojů, Icarette 6 × 6 cm má 26 869, Cupido 9 × 12 cm má 26 870, Kunstler Camera 9 x 12 cm má 26 871, neoznačený cestovní přístroj anglického typu na formát 13x18 cm má inv. č. 26 872, Kodak Cartridge No. 2 na 6 × 9 cm má 26 873 a boxík na 3 × 4 cm má inv. č. 26 874. Kvalitní cestovní komora pro formát desek 13 × 18 cm, pocházející z doby kolem roku 1895, je vyobrazena v knize Jiřího Jandy: *Kamery obskury. Fotografické přístroje z let 1840–1940*, Praha, Národní technické muzeum 1982, na s. 58 pod č. 36.

30   Z dopisu dr. Ivanu Růžičkovi z 18. 12. 1950. Dopis je uložen u Evy Kolářové.

31   Dopis Ludvíka Boháčka Josefu Binkovi datovaný 19. 2. 1912. Oba přátelé si technické zkušenosti s fotografováním vyměňovali poměrně často. Například dopisy Ludvíka Boháčka z 28. 3., 26. 5. a 31. 5. 1913 se poměrně detailně zabývají vlastními zkušenostmi z tvorby olejotisků a vhodnými pomůckami. 28. 3. 1913 Boháček přítele prosí o návod k Höchheimerovu gumotisku, který předpokládal zvětšovací přístroj, který Boháček rovněž měl.

32   Většina památek po Dušanu Binkovi je v držení dr. Simony Binkové, včetně projekčního přístroje vlastní konstrukce na formát diapozitivů 9 × 9 cm.

33   Starý dům, kde žil Dušan Binko, měl č. p. 69.

34   *Paměti...*, s. 11.

35   Ruličky s kinofilmovými negativy, pečlivě evidované, jsou v majetku ing. Jana Binka. Na stejném místě jsou i zvětšeniny k některým vybraným záběrům.

36   Album *Vánoce 1942*, které je jakousi evokací zážitků roku, je v majetku MUDr. Věry Bouškové.
      Obsahuje jeden olejotisk, ostatní jsou zvětšeniny. Kolekci celkem 20 kusů Binkových snímků
      (včetně dvou bromolejotisků) získala v letech 1999 a 2000 Moravská galerie v Brně. Obsahovala
      také portfolia *Podzim* a *Jaro na naší zahradě*, datovaná 29. 5. 1944, která jsou chronologicky posledním
      dokladem Binkových reprezentativních zvětšenin (223 × 173 a 234 × 173 mm). Z mladší doby jsou dále
      jen kontakty a zvětšeniny malých formátů.

37   Výměry, rozhodnutí, zrušení rozhodnutí, nová rozhodnutí, korespondence, nedoplatky, rozsudky
      lidového soudu, odvolání, protest – to jsou bolestné ukázky státní mašinerie 50. let, přičemž se
      táhly od 10. 8. 1950 až do posledních dnů života Josefa Binka. Je až neuvěřitelné, že Generální
      prokuratura na základě odvolacích dopisů Ivana Binka z 5. 1. 1956, postoupených Prezidentské
      kanceláři a Ministerstvu financí, posléze podala protest proti výměře a navrhla ji zrušit, což se
      20. 9. 1956 skutečně stalo. Typické je, že vzápětí došlo k odvetě: Národní výbor v Křížové rozhodl
      18. 2. 1957 o vystěhování vdovy po Dušanu Binkovi ze Starého domu, kde žilo několik pokolení
      předků, a posléze rozhodl o exekuci domu Josefa Binka, tzv. Červené vily. 11. 1. 1960 vyzval finanční
      odbor v Chotěboři o exekuční zástavní právo pro 23 000, – Kčs; přesně za měsíc potom Josef Binko
      zemřel. Při projednávání dědictví finanční odbor navrhl, aby movité i nemovité věci byly přikázány
      státu.

38   Z dopisu synu Ivanovi 14. 1. 1957. Dopis je uložen u Evy Kolářové.

39   Z dopisu ing. Janu Novákovi z 20. prosince 1953. Dopis je uložen u Evy Kolářové.

40   Dopis je uložen u Evy Kolářové.

41   O setkání s ing. Karlem Paspou, referentem na Státním úřadu pro vynálezy, dne 3. 10. 1958, napsal
      Ivan Binko otci 4. 10. 1958. Paspa Binka v rozhovoru označil „za jednoho zc zakladatelů české
      obrazové fotografie“. Syn sdělil, že je v Krucemburku zachována „skoro úplná kolekce Vašich
      olejových tisků, pigmentových tisků, diapositivů a negativů, úplné ročníky starých německých
      fotografických časopisů, stará dřevěná komora, Petzwaldův portrétní objektiv atd. Nejhorší je
      to ovšem s ceníky a katalogy, ty již zub času odklidil.“ V dopise syn otci, jemuž vykal, pokračuje:
      „Nepověděl jsem panu ing. Paspovi ani všechno, co se u Vás nachází, že máte provedeny v krásných
      olejových tiscích celé cykly, jako cestu po Jadranu, stará německá města, Lübeck, Rothenburg, jež
      snad již ani neexistují, cyklus českých chalup velké folkloristické ceny, velkou část německých měst
      na diapositivech, jež zmizela za války ze světa, dokumentární cykly fotografií stavby průmyslových
      závodů na negativech… Myslím však, že bude velmi překvapen, až uvidí, co je u Vás všechno
      ukryté…“. Dopis je v držení Evy Kolářové. Josef Binko v odpovědi souhlasil, aby syn zahájil oficiální
      jednání s Národním technickým muzeem.

42   9. 8. 1960 píše ing. Karel Paspa Ivanu Binkovi: „Stydím se za muzeum, ačkoliv za ty průtahy
      nemohu, a jako externí spolupracovník celkem nemám moc vlivu. Sám jsem často urgoval, ale
      bezvýsledně. Upřímně a důvěrně: v muzeu je jakýsi chaos v názorech i v práci.“ V tomtéž dopise
      prosí ing. Paspa Ivana Binka: „Prosím Vás, až budete pořádat listinný materiál, uschovejte všechny
      doklady a korespondenci týkající se fotografie, i stvrzenky na nákup materiálu a pod.“ Ve stejném
      dopise ing. Paspa opětovně píše, jako již několikrát předtím, že by rád napsal o Josefu Binkovi
      monografii, a to do známé edice Umělecká fotografie nakladatelství Odeon. „Podaří-li se to, budu
      pak od Vás potřebovat i mnohá data osobní a ten listinný materiál, který by se v muzeu za nynější
      situace nezvěstně zaběhl“. Dopis je v držení Evy Kolářové.

43   „Soupis předmětů věnovaných zesnulým p. J. Binkem z Křížové Národnímu technickému museu
      v Praze" o třech stranách je v držení ing. Jana Binka. Položky 1–7 představují fotografické přístroje,
      8–18 „Přístroje a pomůcky pro positivní procesy", položky 19–29 „Příslušenství temné komory".
      Oddíl IV. obsahoval 729 kusů diapozitivů formátu 9 × 12 cm, oddíl V. obsahoval početně ne ve všech
      položkách určené „Fotografické obrazy", minimálně však 206 kusů a tři položky označené jako
      „Různé". „Negativy skleněné a filmové ve formátech 9 × 12–13 × 18 cm a 6 × 6 cm, náležející k daru,
      nebyly dosud podrobně popsány a roztříděny. Jakmile bude tato práce dokončena, budou předány
      museu se zvláštním soupisem. Jedná se o několik set kusů, z nichž je třeba vyřadit všechny snímky
      rodinného charakteru." V protokolu je dále uvedeno, že „Předměty a materiál... byl převzat dne
      22. 4. 60 zástupcem Národního technického musea s. M. Malíkem a za expertisy ing. K. Paspy,
      zabalen a připraven k odvozu ČSAD, který se dle možností dopravního podniku uskuteční
      v nejbližší době. Konečné potvrzení o příjmu jednotlivých předmětů do správy NTM bude písemně
      potvrzeno po inventarizaci předmětů v NTM". Podepsáni jsou Ivan Binko a M. Malík. Převoz věcí
      se poté uskutečnil na náklady Ivana Binka 21. 9. 1960. Faktem ovšem je, že negativy a zřejmě ani
      diapozitivy nikdy do NTM nedorazily. Zápisy v inventurních knihách v NTM se o nich nezmiňují.
      Také k převozu připravená kolekce „Fotografických obrazů" se zřejmě zmenšila a malá část zůstala
      v rodině. Považuji za pravděpodobné, že si některé snímky vypůjčil Rudolf Skopec, který možná
      začal sám uvažovat o sepsání monografie Josefa Binka. Osm Binkových gumotisků a olejotisků
      bylo vystaveno v listopadu 1961 v Domě umění města Brna na výstavě Dějiny fotografie II, kterou
      uspořádal právě Rudolf Skopec. Zcela jistě měl Rudolf Skopec u sebe Binkovy klíčové negativy na
      filmech, neboť právě on je daroval kolem roku 1975 Uměleckoprůmyslovému museu v Praze. Viz
      též pozn. 24.
44   Ludvík Boháček Josefu Binkovi 19. 2. 1912. Dopis je uložen u Evy Kolářové.

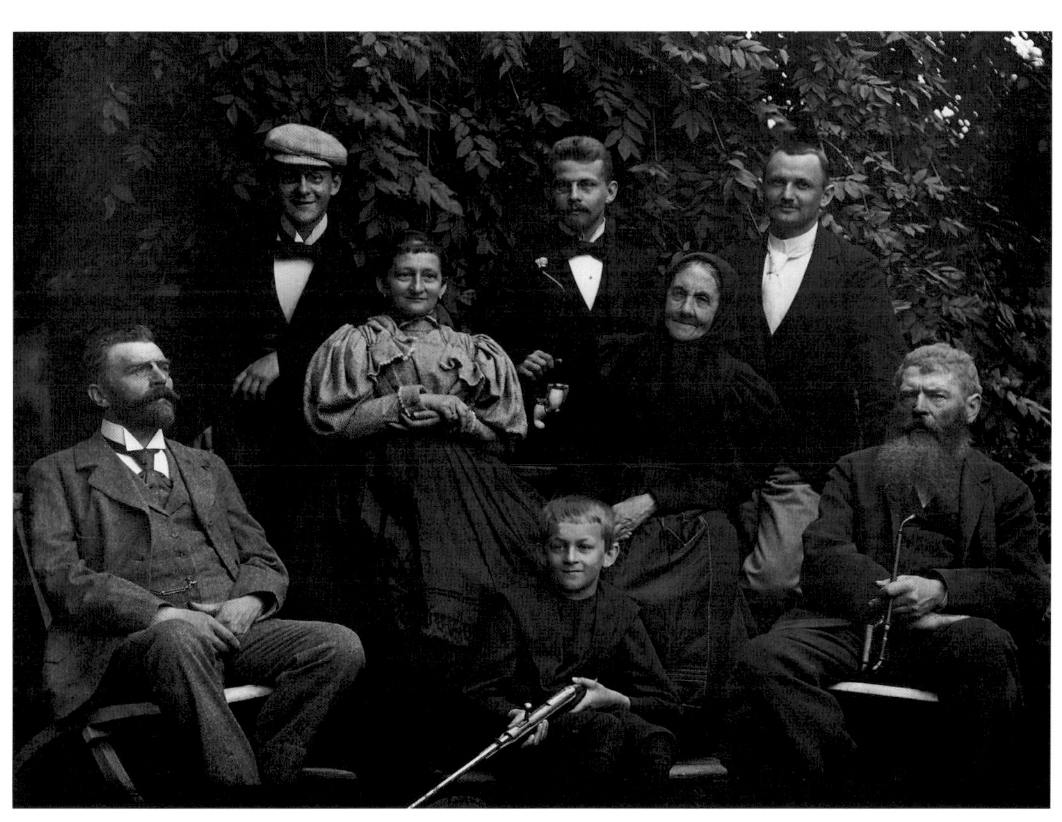

1 **Self-portrait with the family / Autoportrét s rodinou** 1891–92

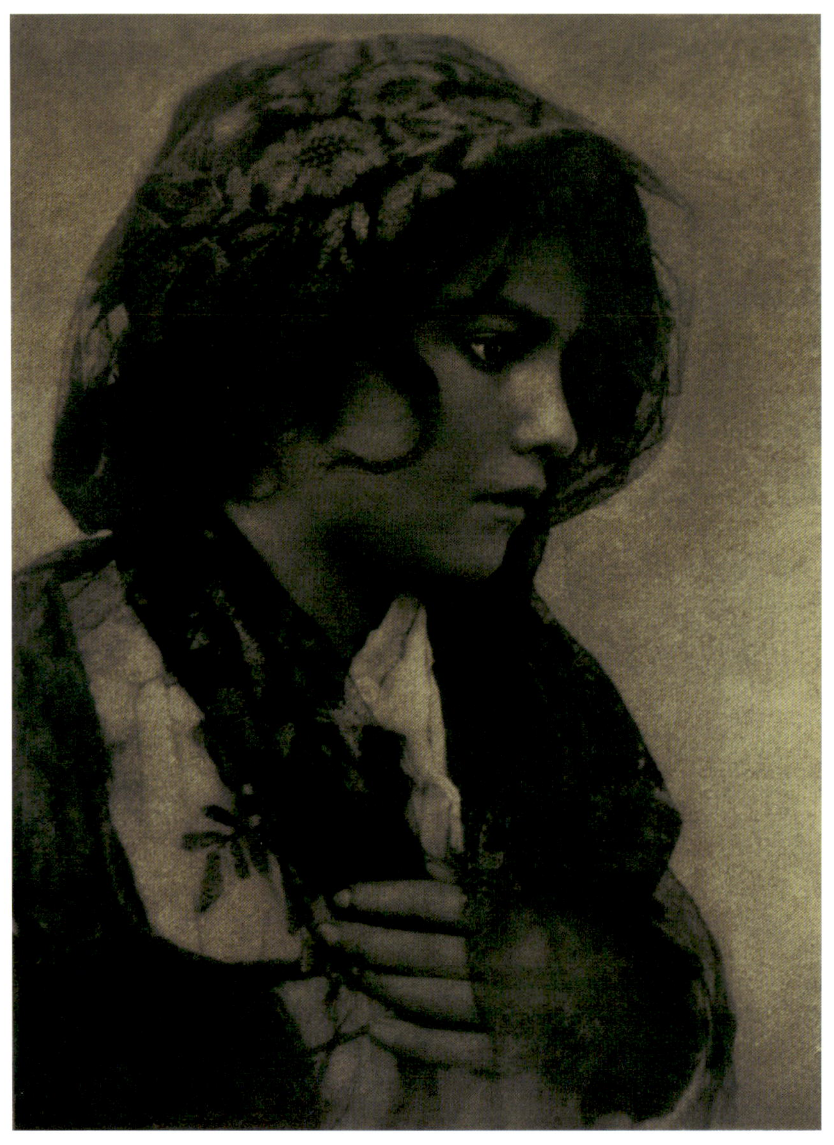

2 **Portrait of a girl** / **Portrét neznámé dívky** c. 1898

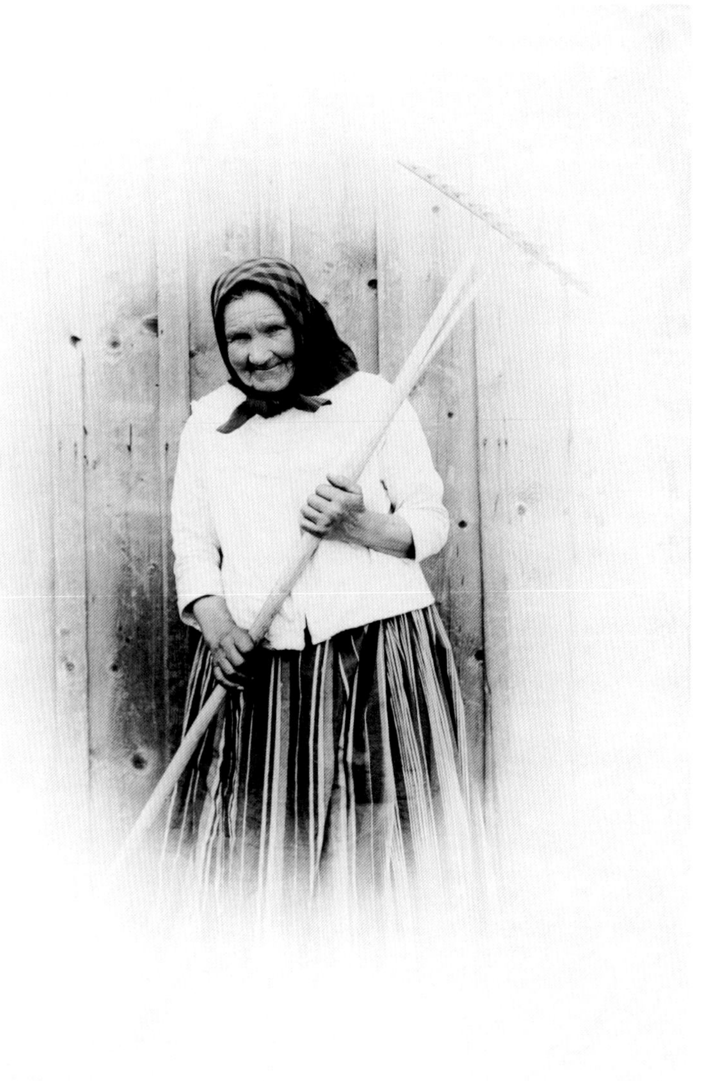

3 **A woman with a rake / Žena s hráběmi** c. 1891

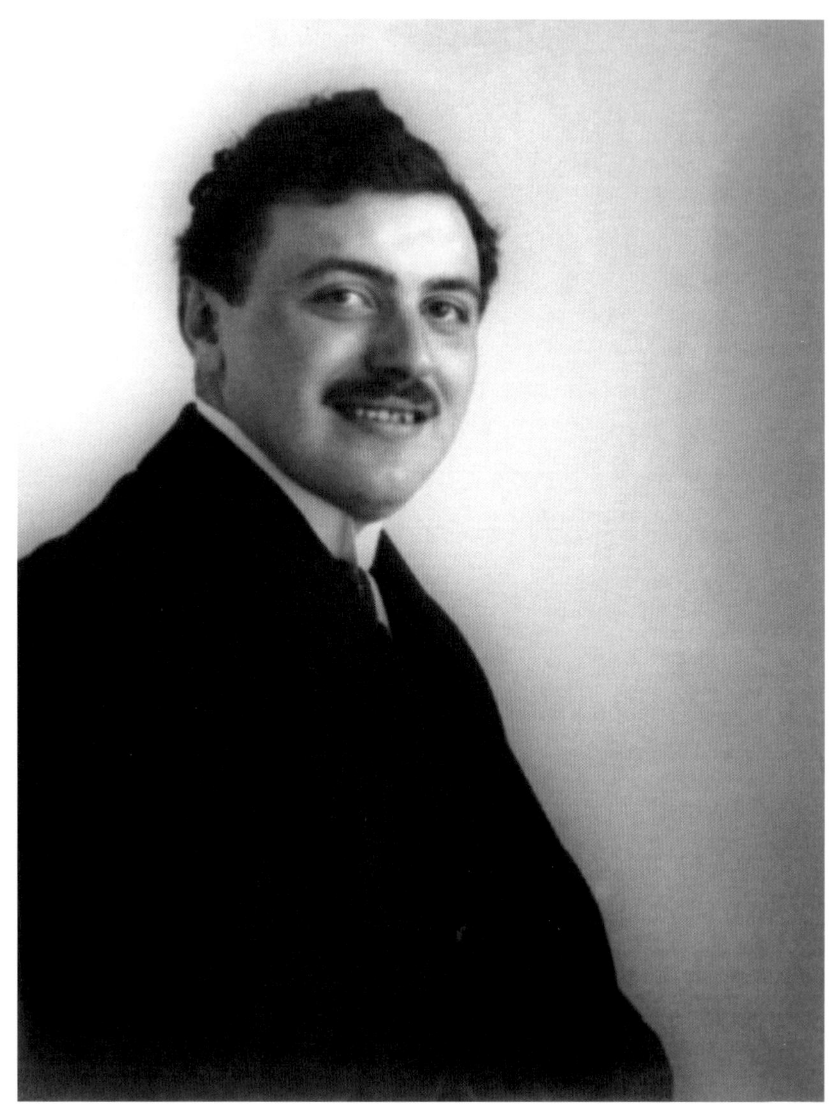

4 **Ludvík Boháček** c. 1907

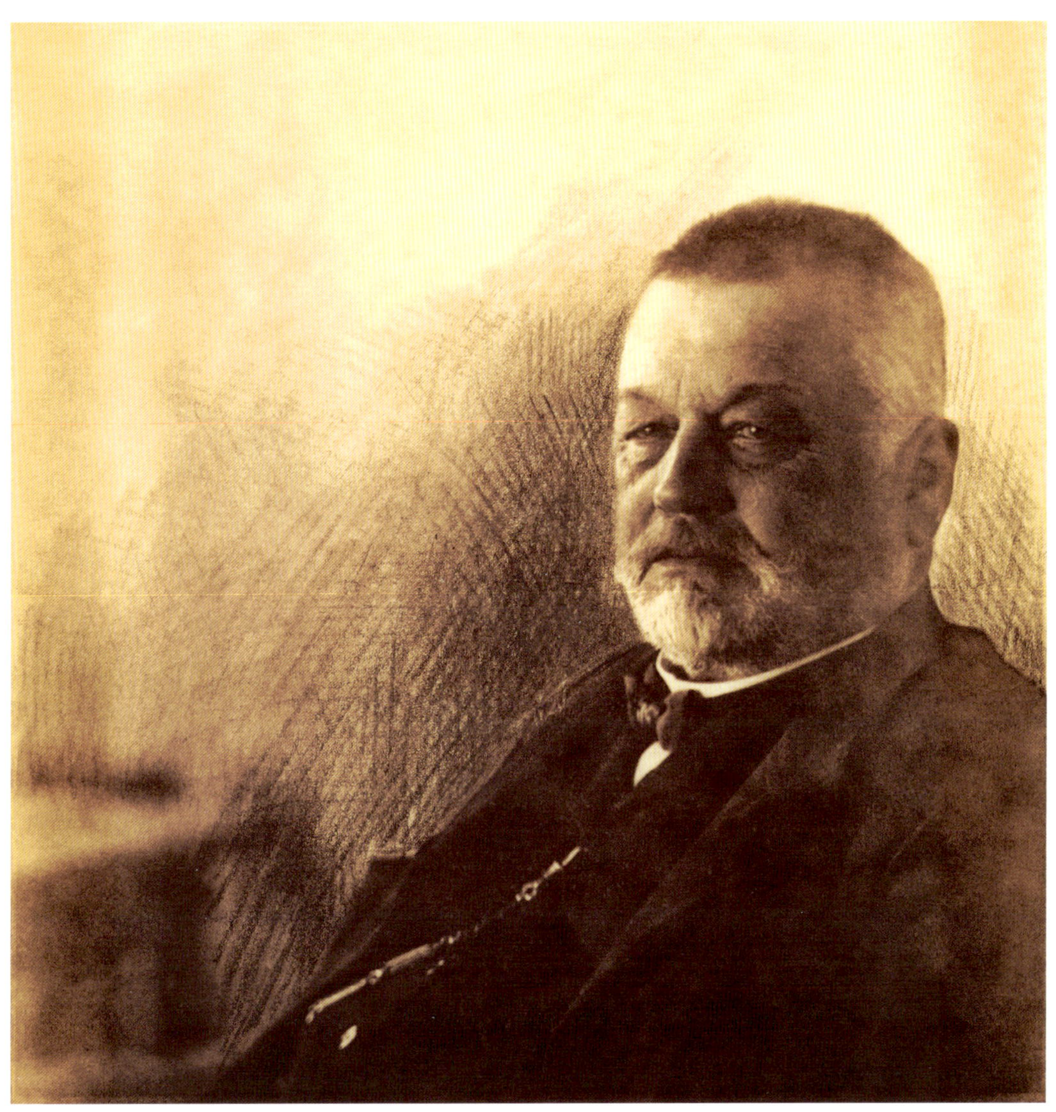

5 **Josef Chlad** 1909–10

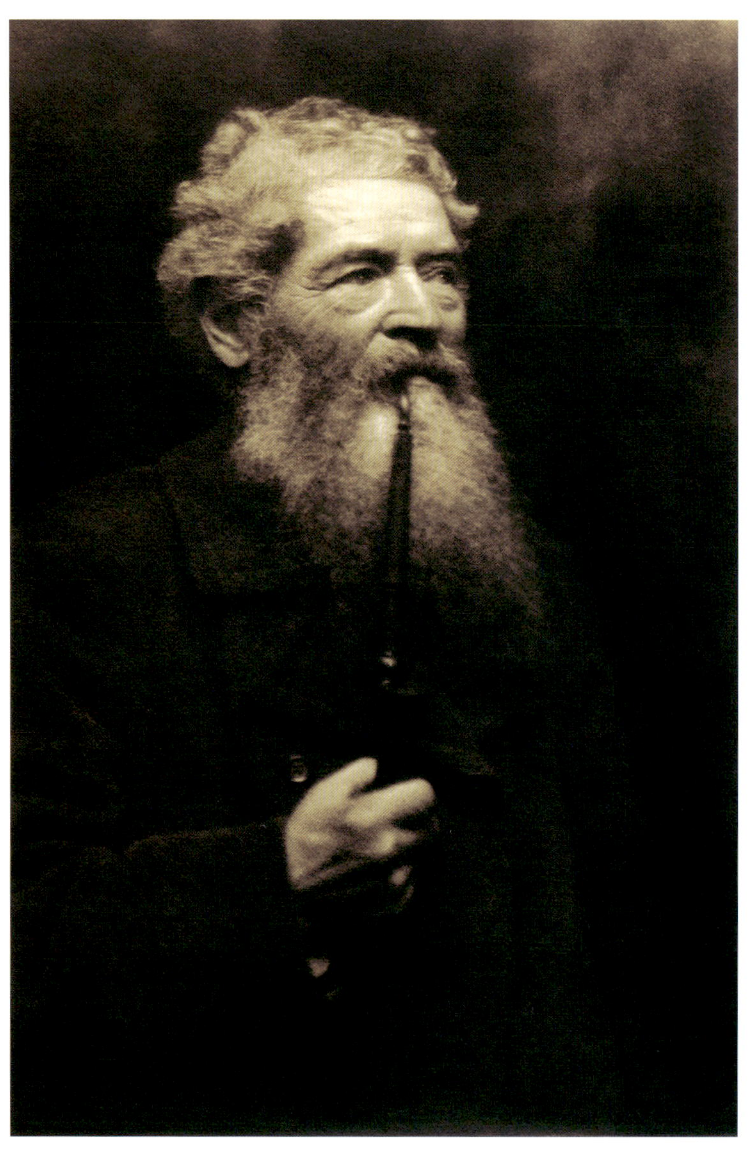

6 **Eduard Binko** c. 1900

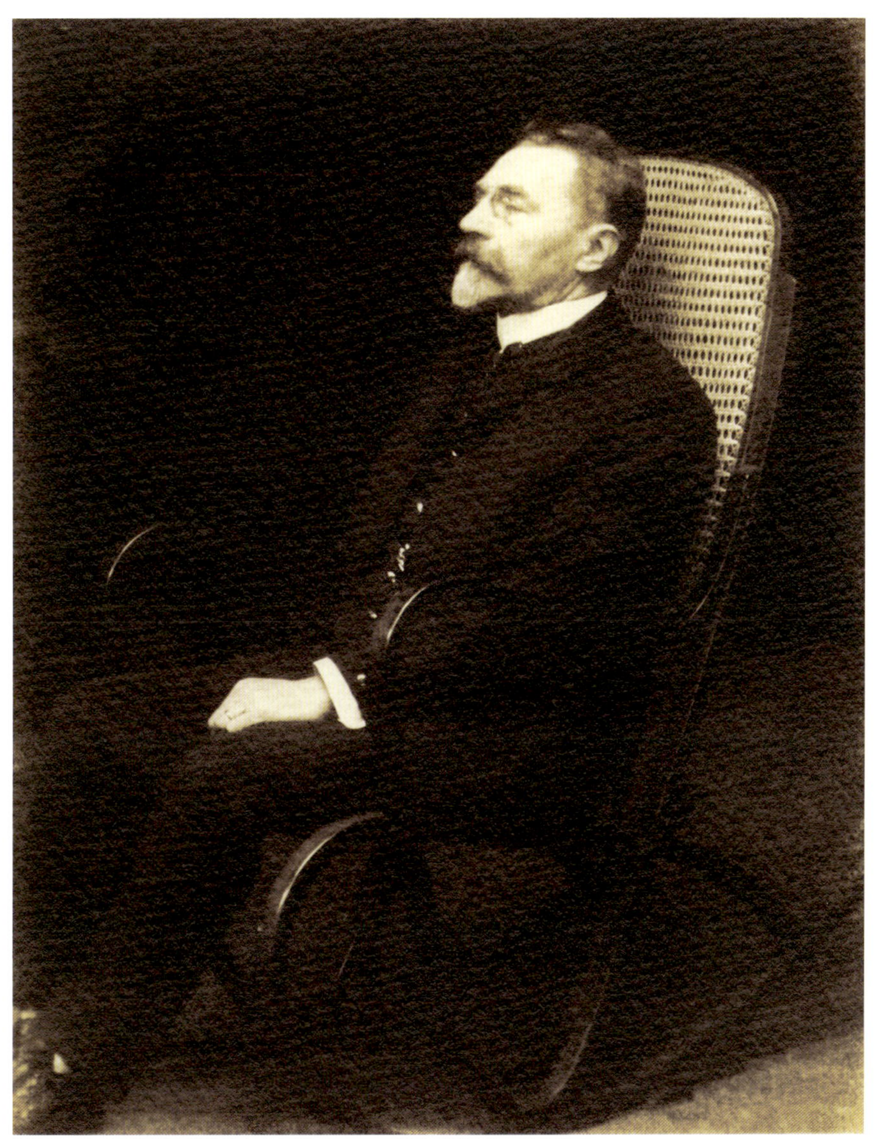

7 **Ladislav Binko** c. 1900

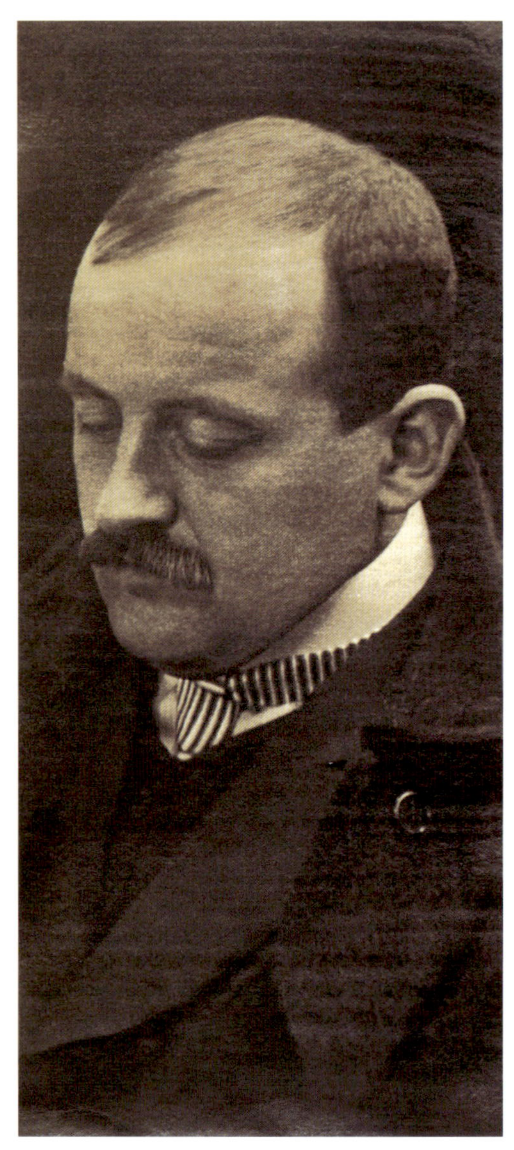

8 **Ludvík Boháček** c. 1911

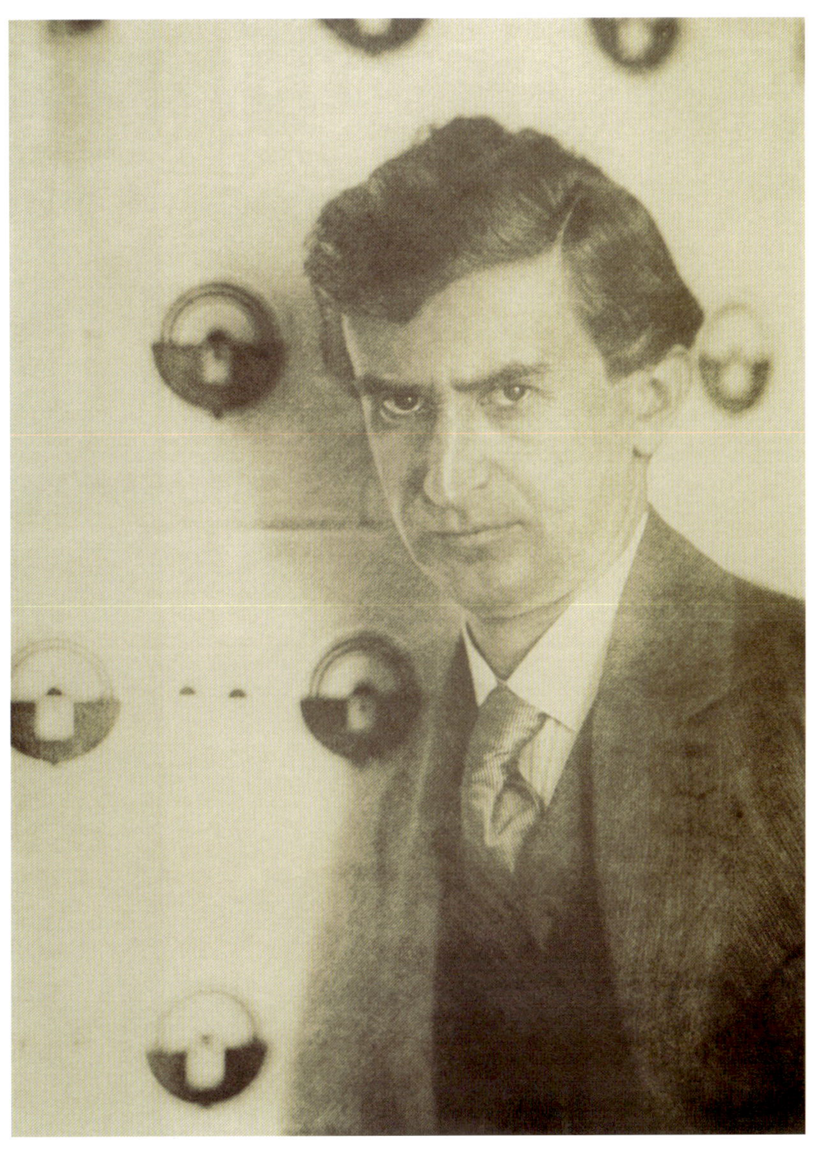

9 **Josef Gočár** 1909–10

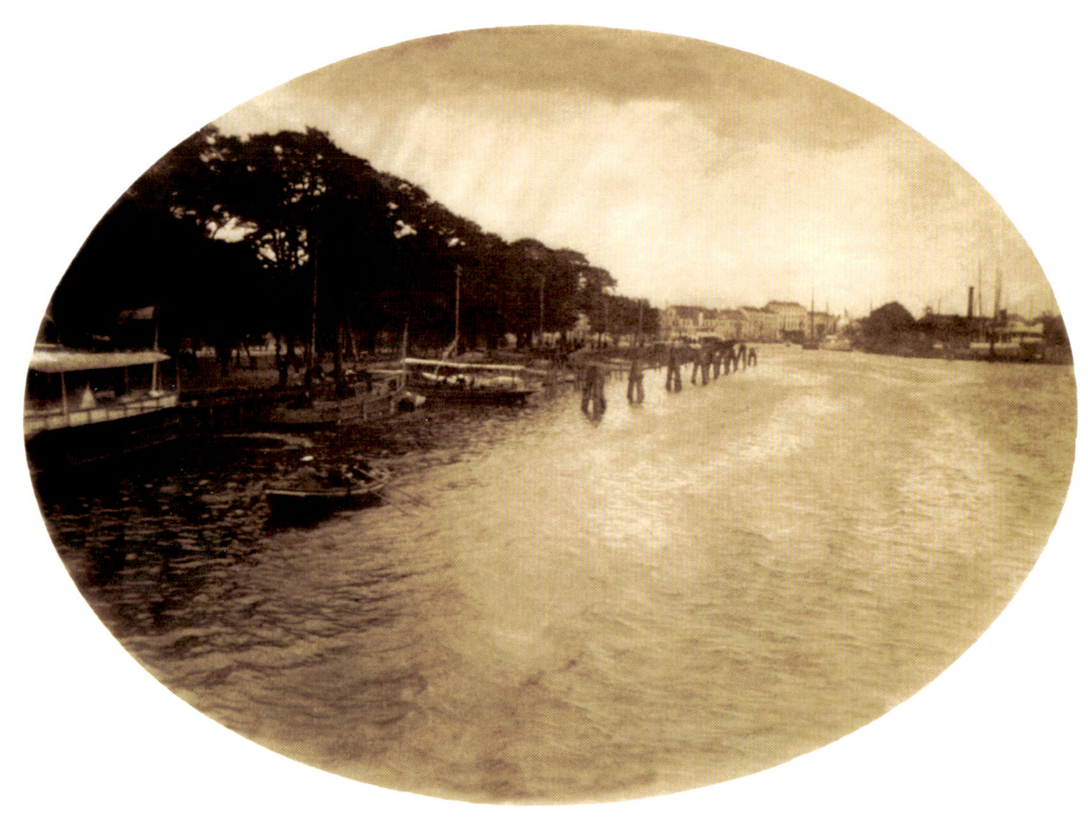

10 **Unidentified harbor / Přístav na nezjištěném místě** c. 1898

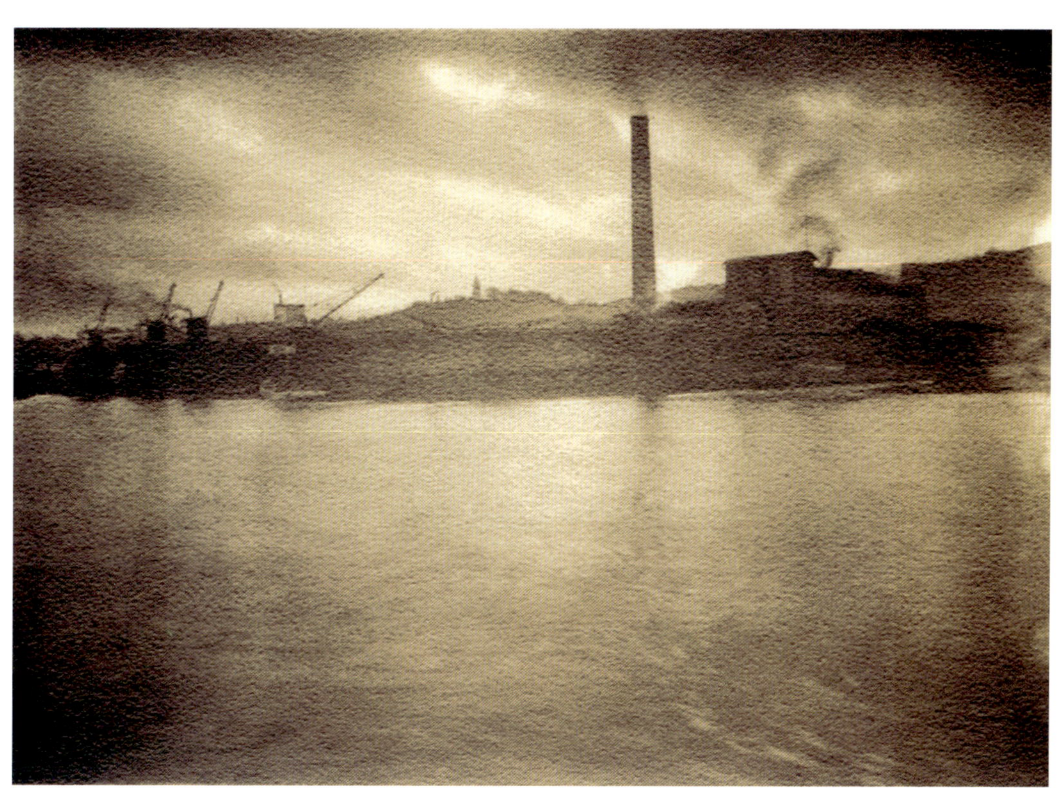

11 **Riverside industrialization / Industrializace u řeky** c. 1900

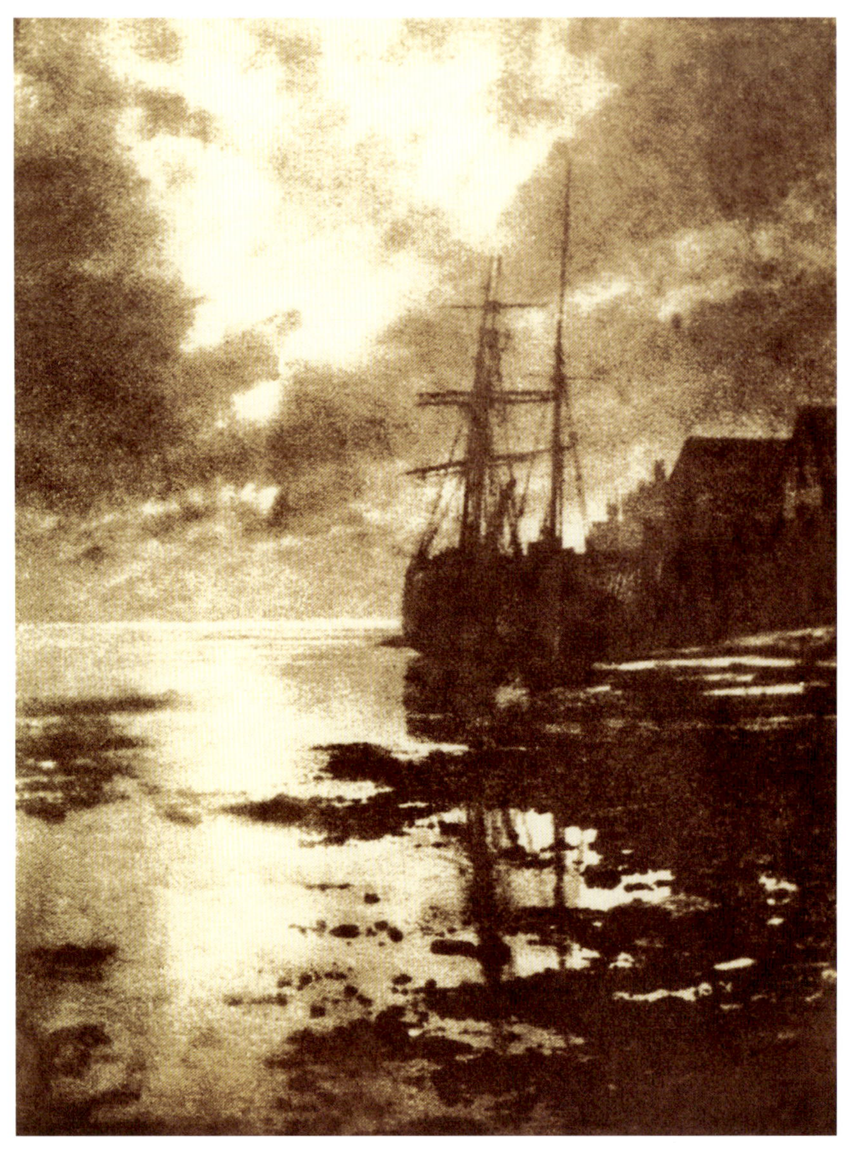

12 **Near the sea / U moře** c. 1900

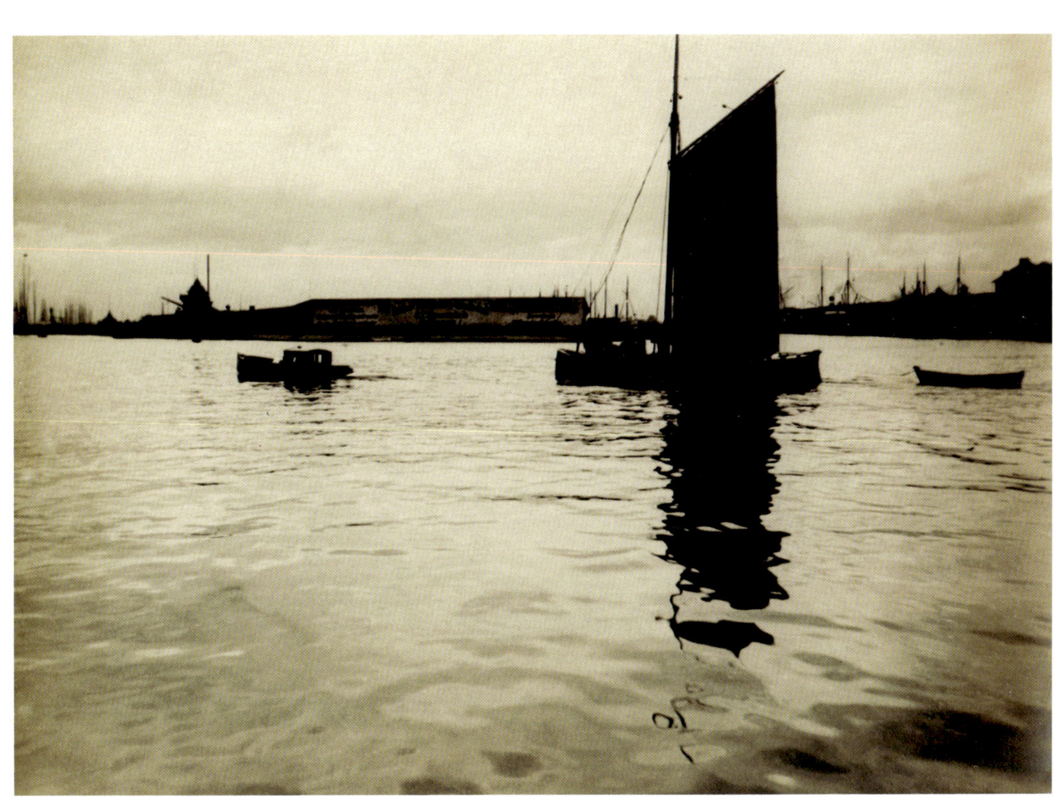

13 **Seaside mood / Nálada u moře** c. 1904

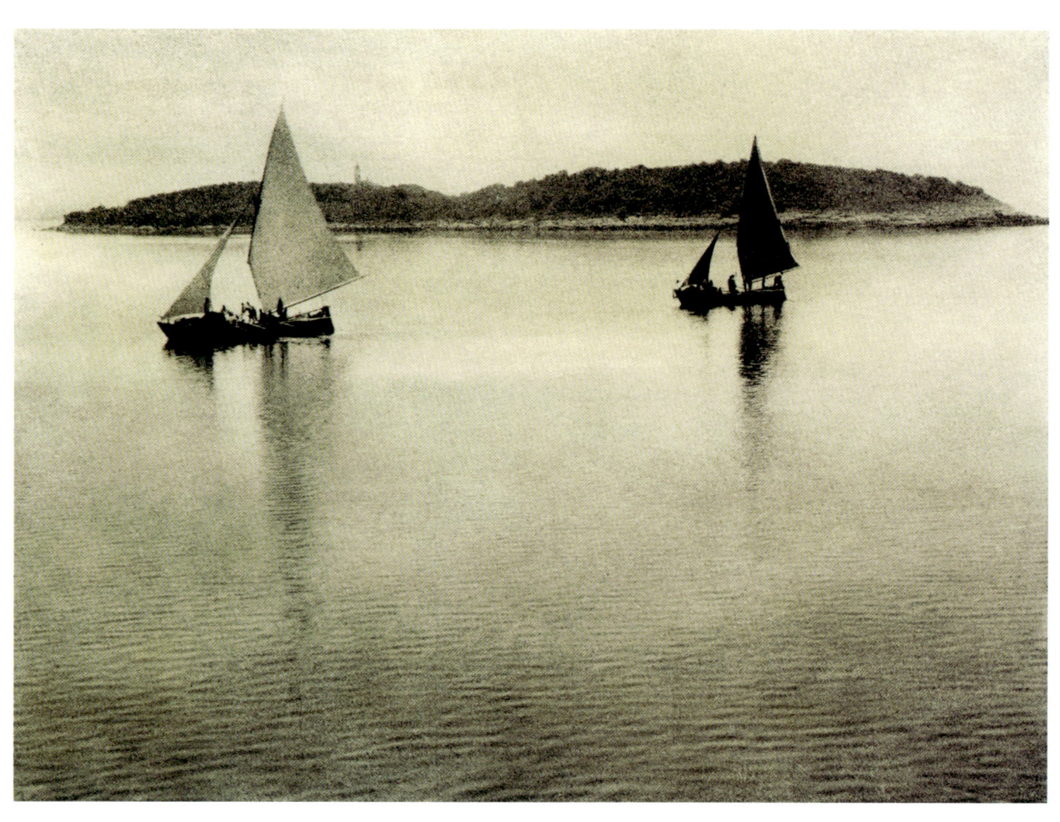

14 **The sea near Miramare Castle / Moře poblíž Miramare** 1910

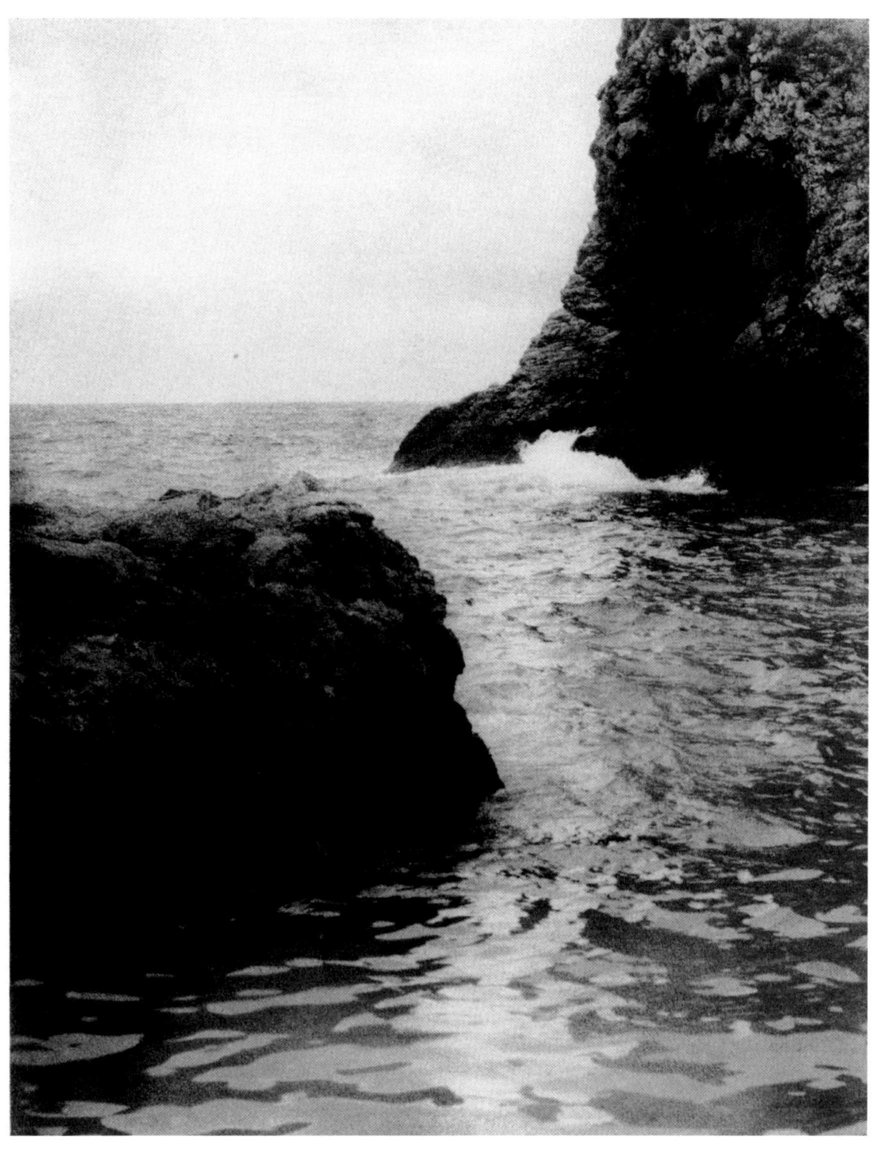

15 **The Sea at Pula / Moře u Puly** 1910

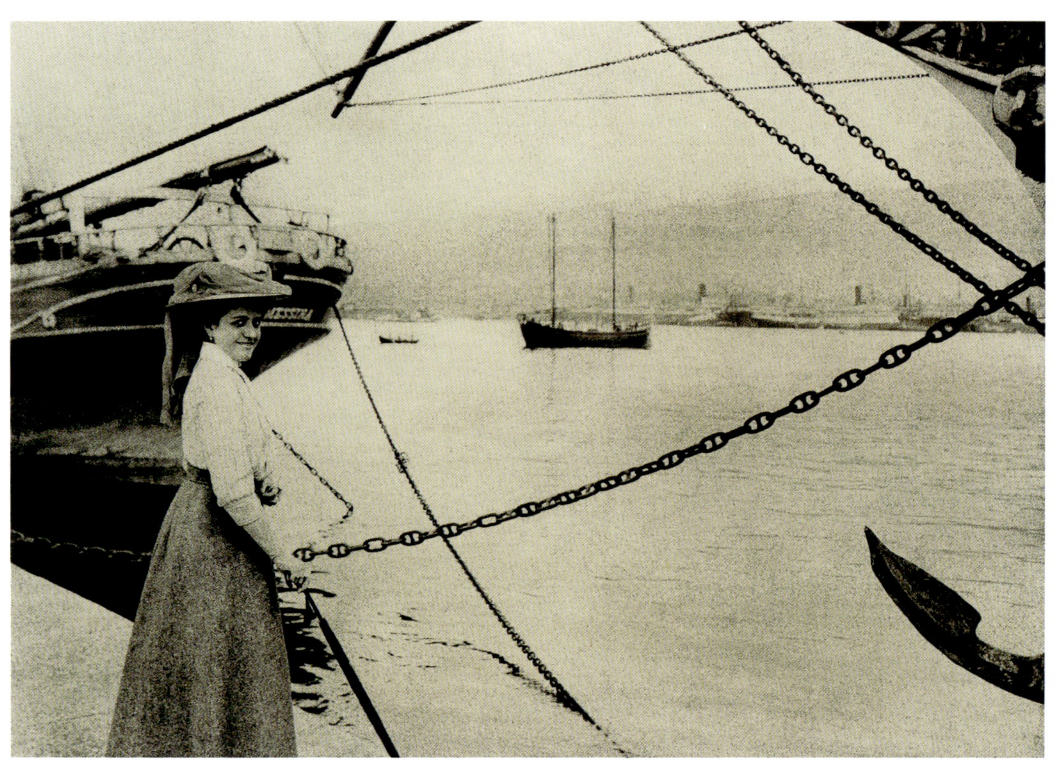

16 **Between Ships / Mezi loděmi, Trieste** 1910

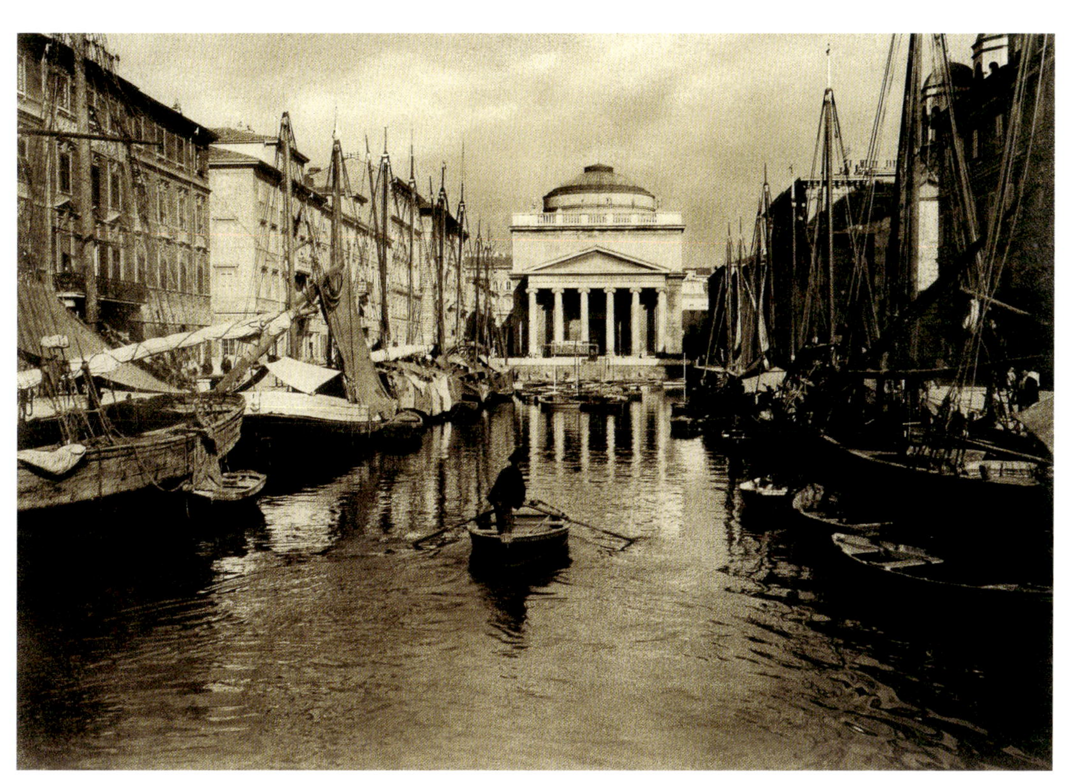

17 **Canal Grande II / Kanál Grande II, Trieste** 1910

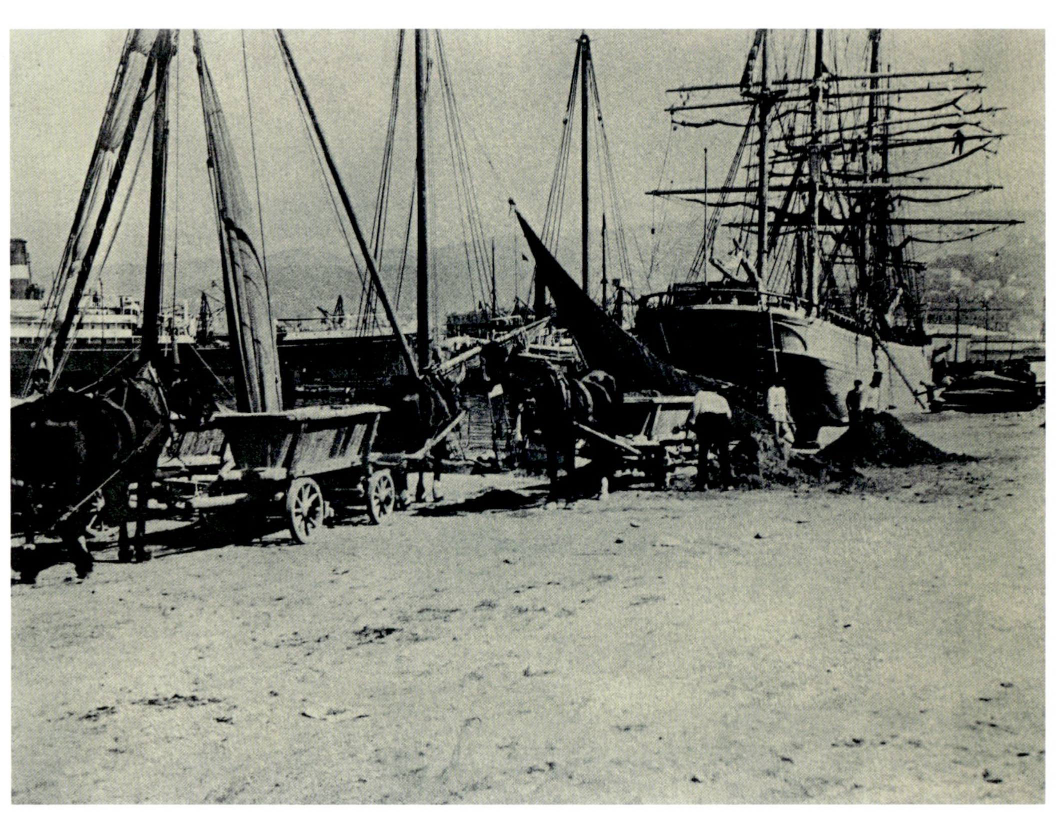

18 **The Quay San Carlo / Molo San Carlo, Trieste** 1910

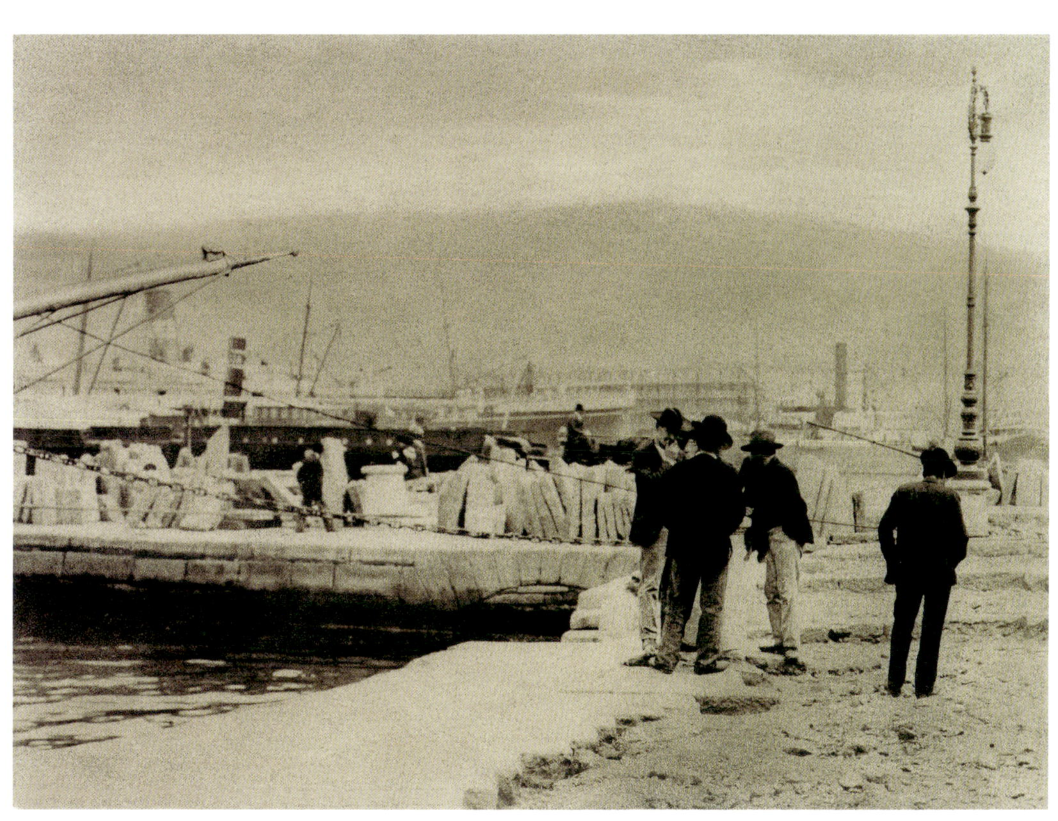

19 **The Quay / Molo, Trieste** 1910

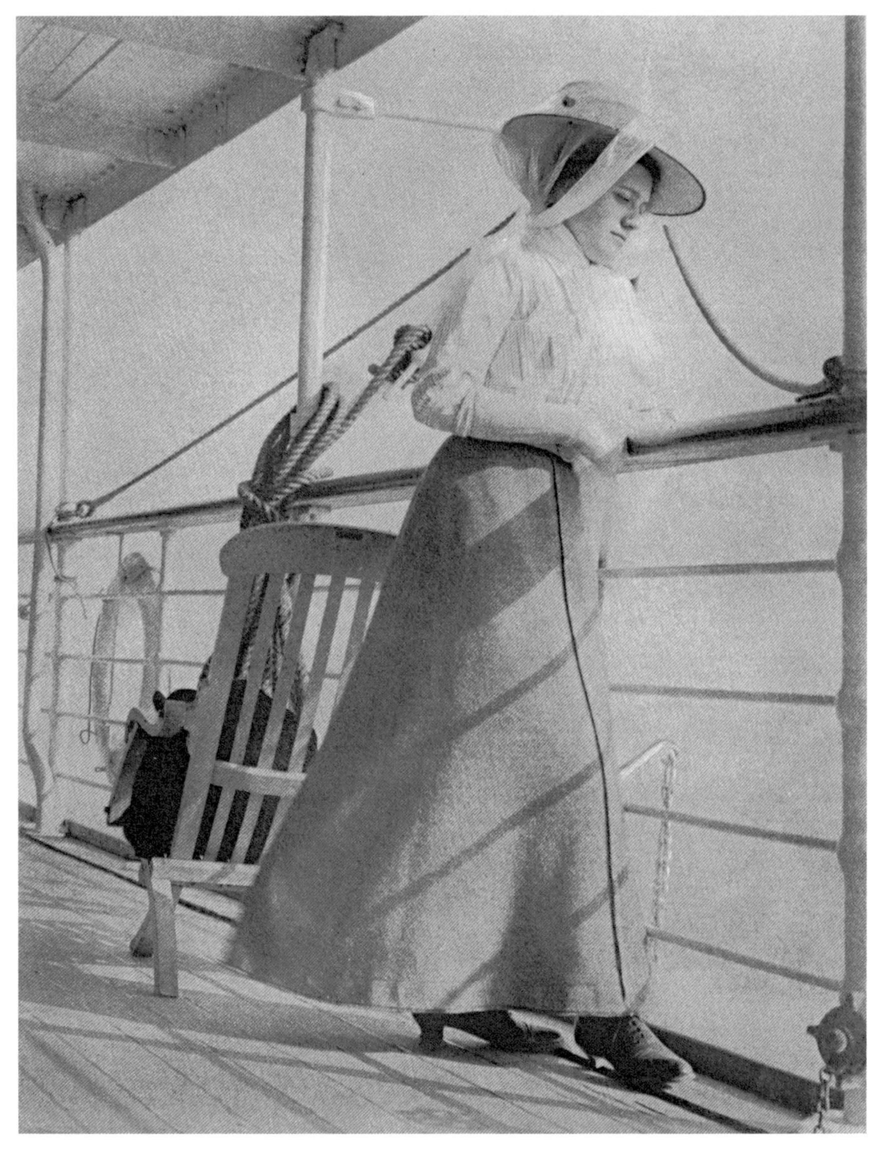

20 **Binko's wife on the *Baron Gautsch*** / **Manželka na parníku Baron Gautsch** 1910

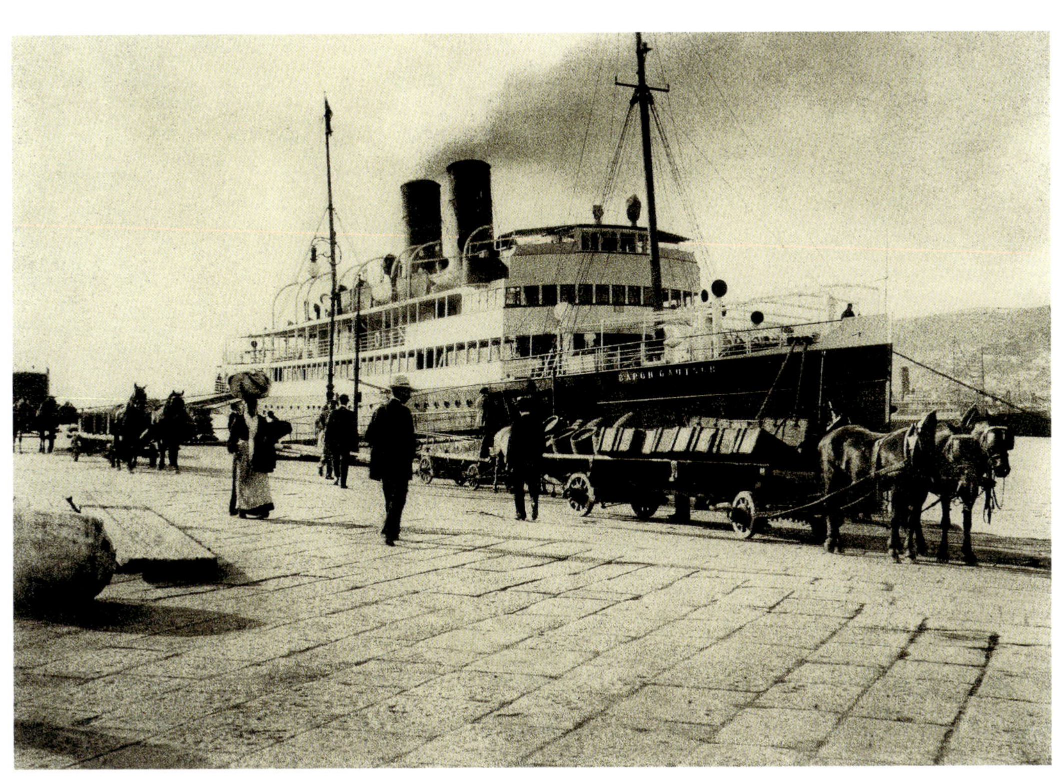

21 **The *Baron Gautsch* / Parník Baron Gautsch, Trieste** 1910

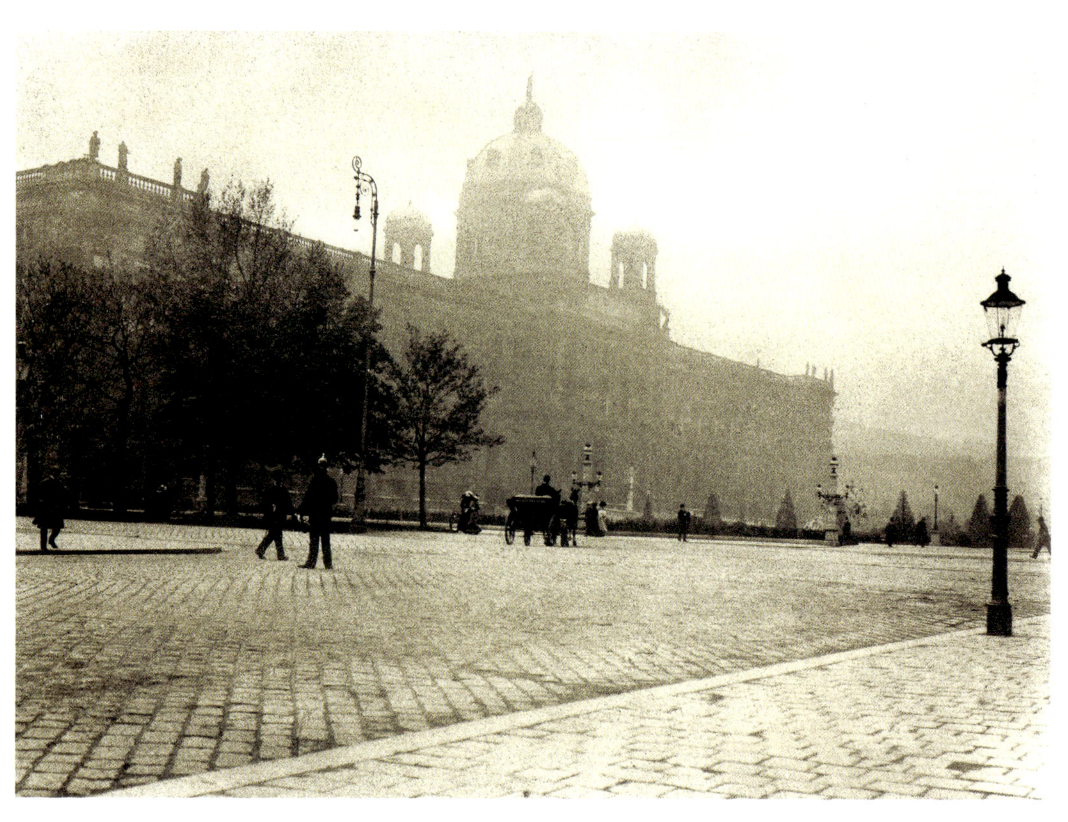

22 **Kunsthistorisches Museum, Vienna / Vídeň** 1910

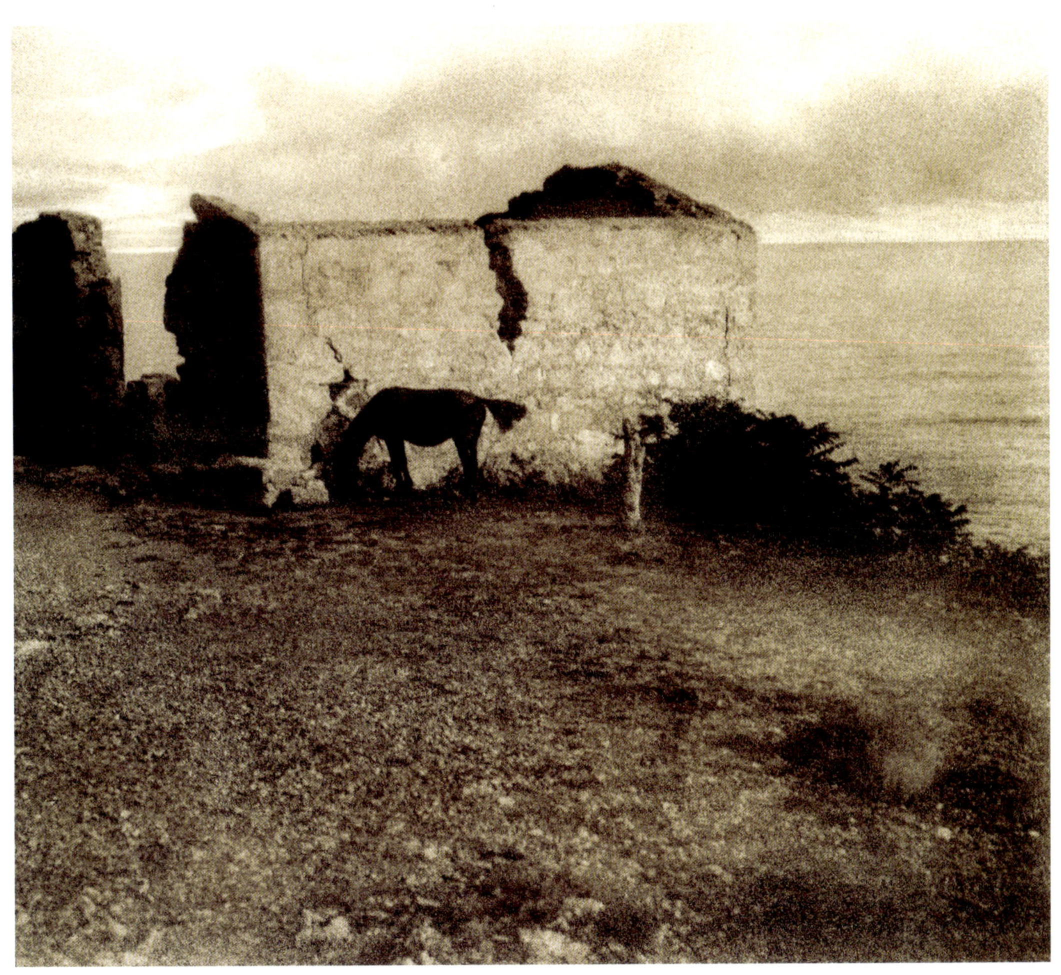

23 **San Giacomo, Ruins / zbořeniště** 1910

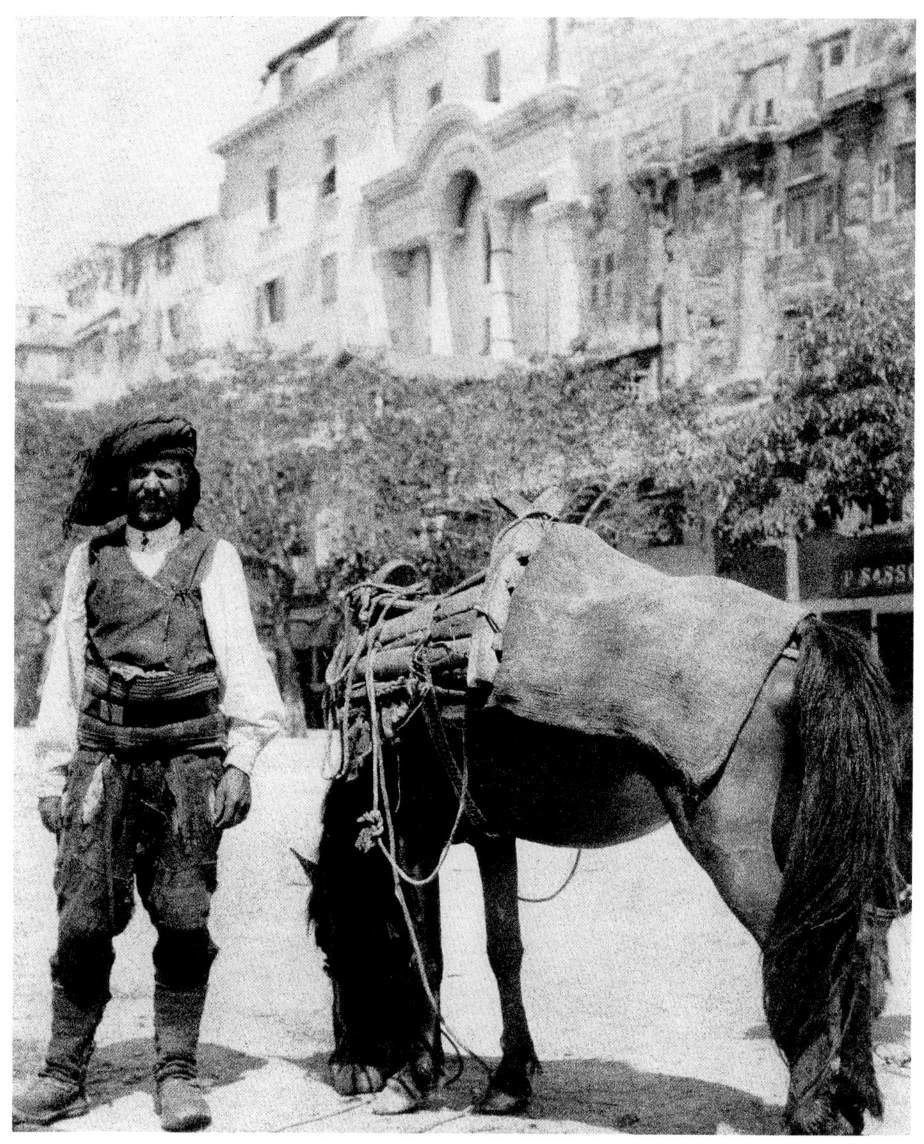

24 Diocletian's Palace / Diokleciánův palác, Split (Spalato) 1910

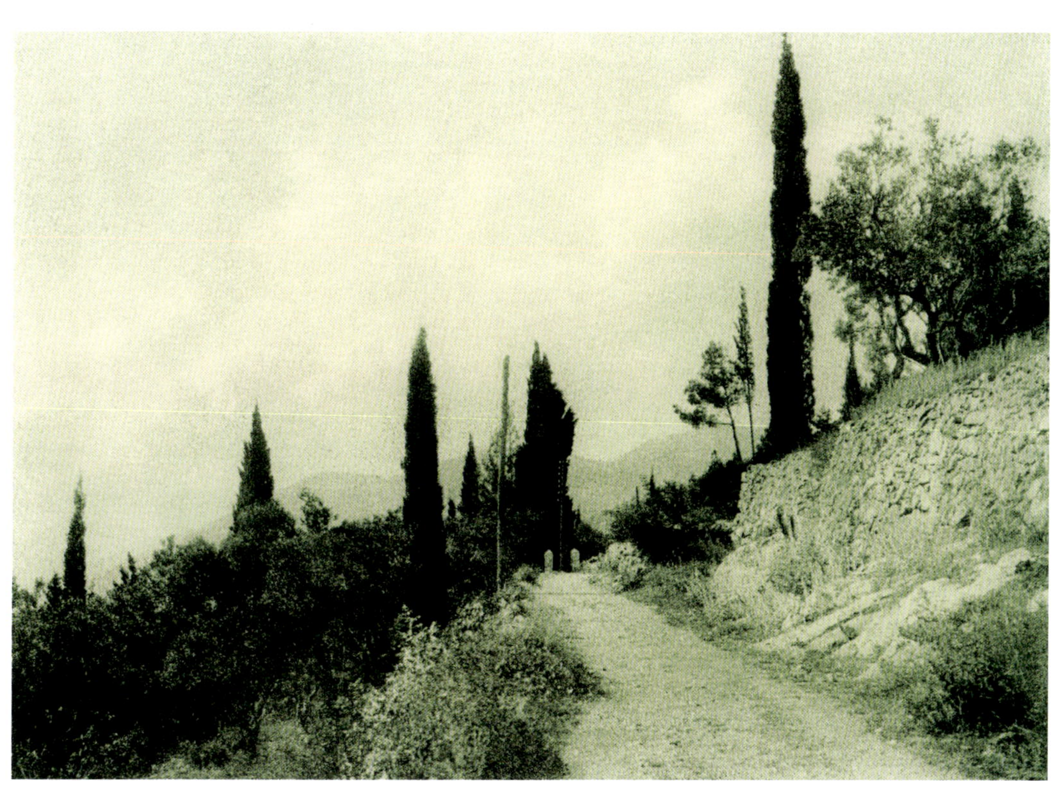

25 **Excursion to Lopud Island / Výlet na Lopud** 1910

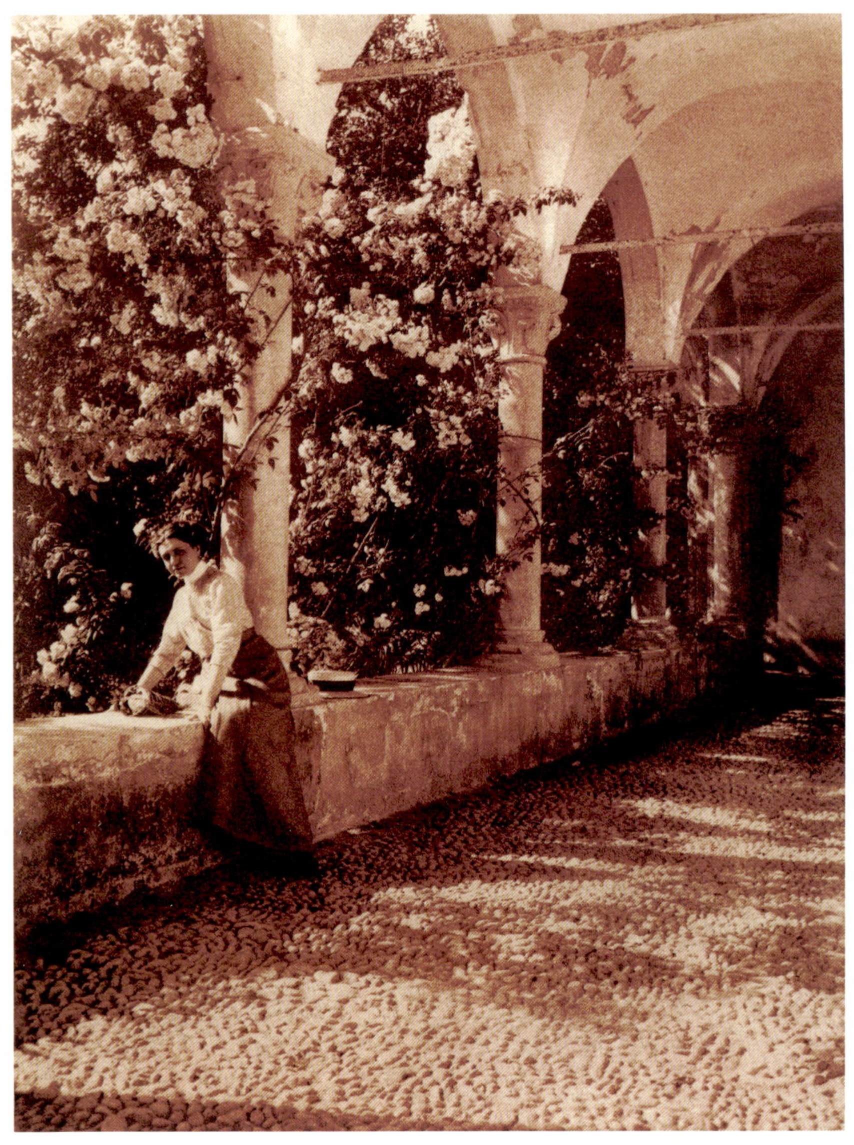

26 **Binko's wife by some rose bushes / Manželka u růží, Lokrum** 1910

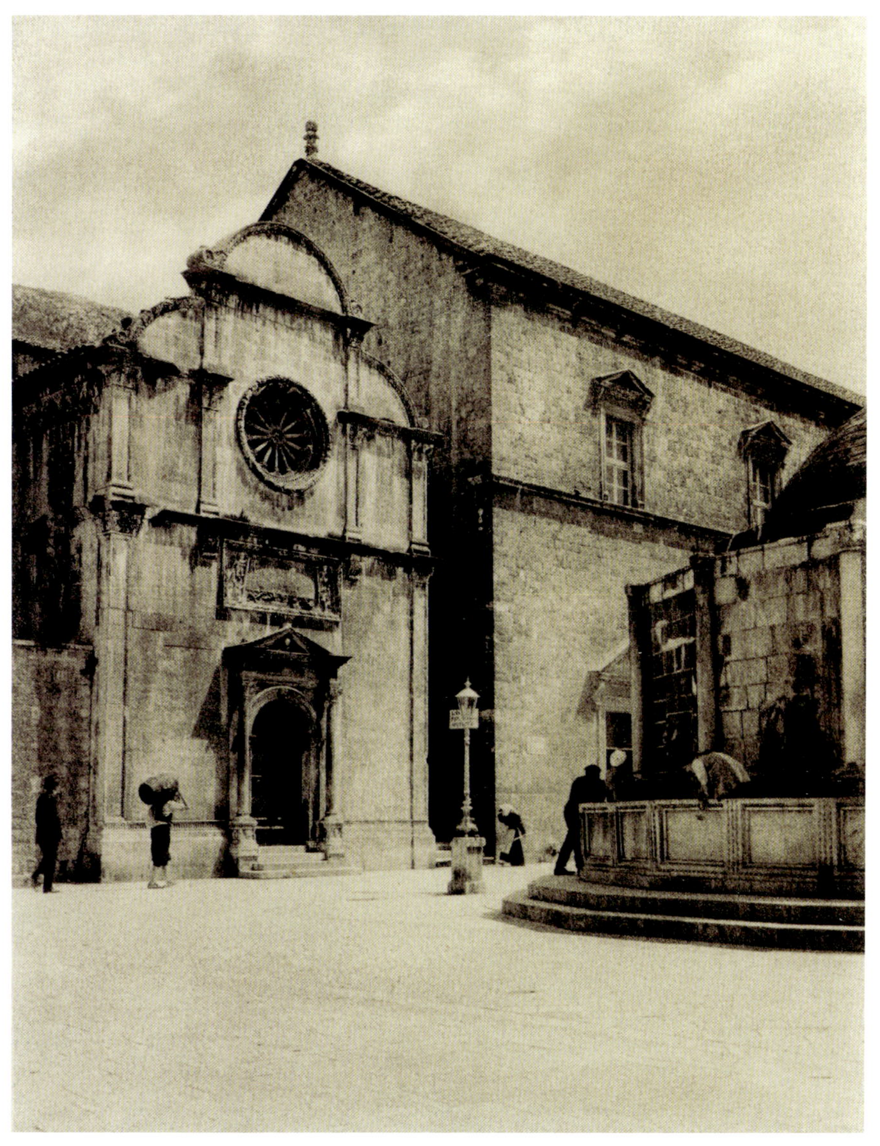

27 **Chapel of St. Saviour / Kaple sv. Salvátora, Dubrovnik** 1910

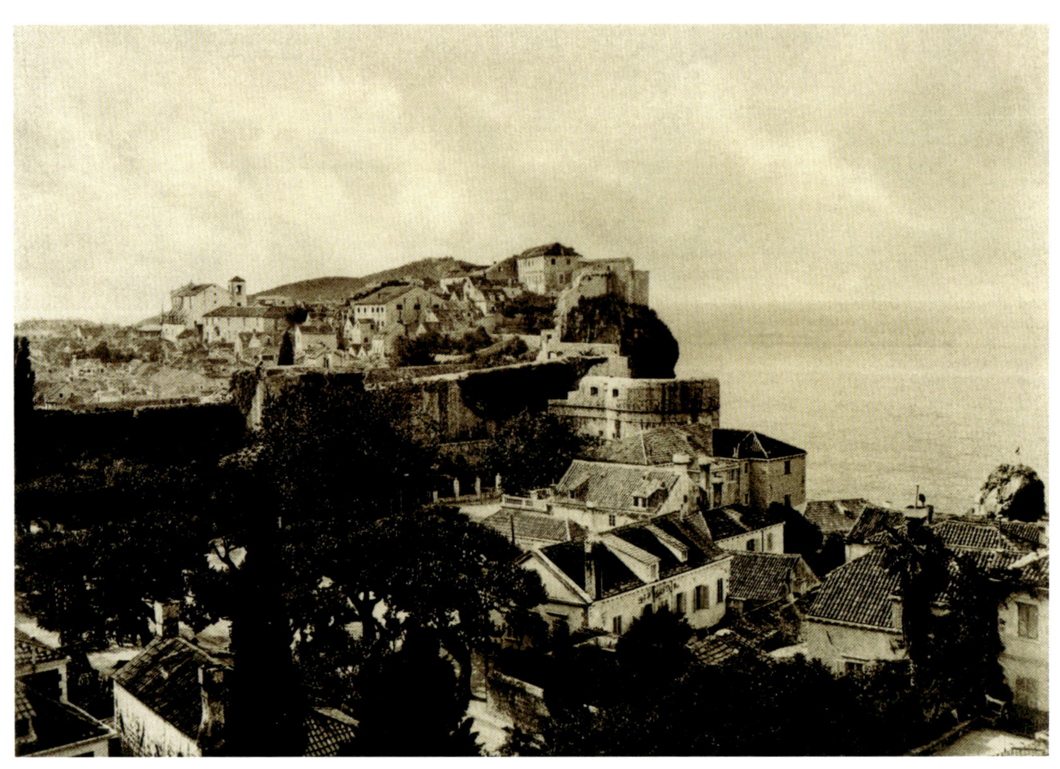

28 **A View from a Window I / Pohled z okna I, Dubrovnik** 1910

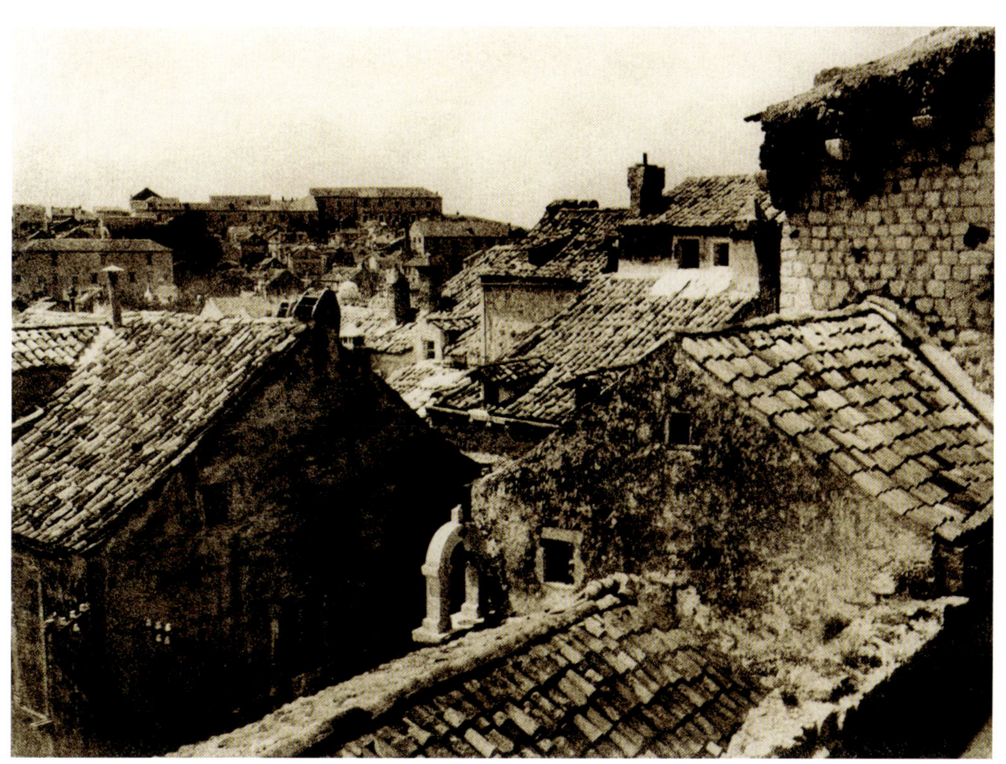

29 **Roofs III / Střechy III, Dubrovnik** 1910

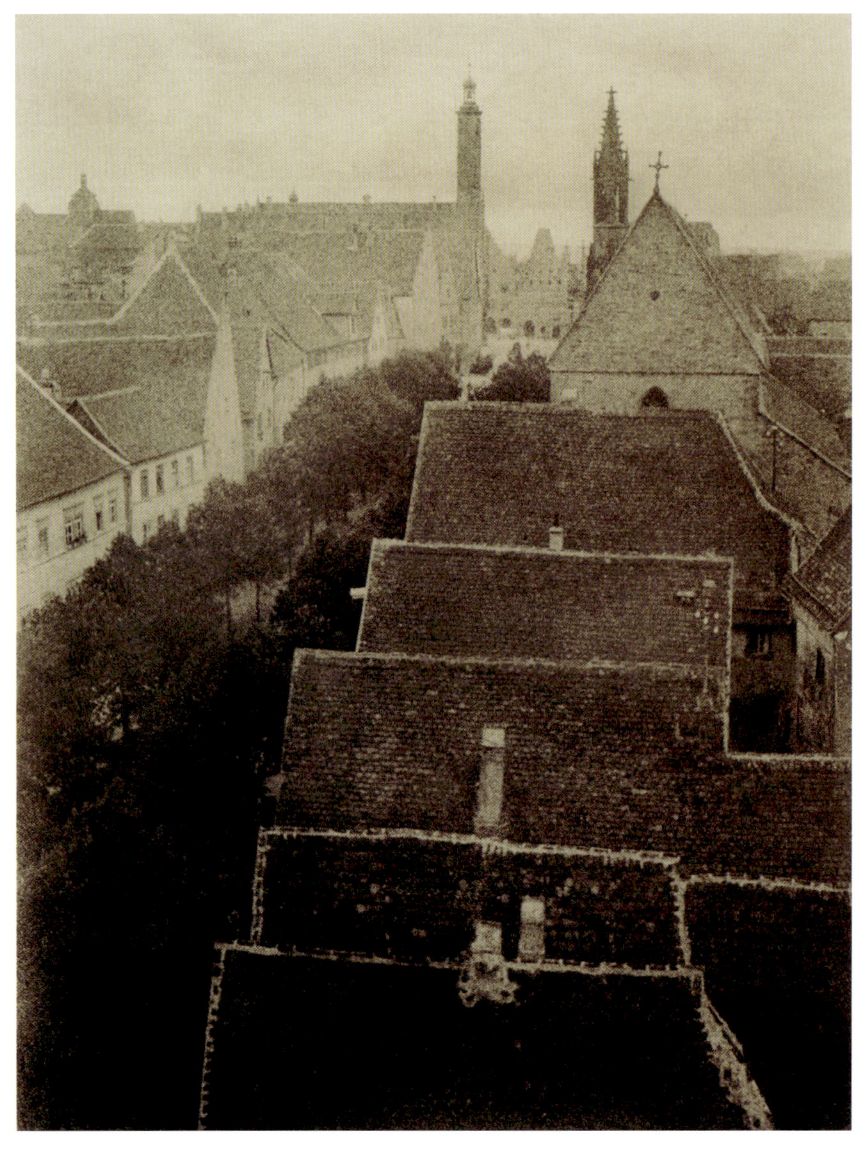

30 **Rothenburg with the Burgtor II / Pohled na Rothenburg z věže Burgtoru II,** 1912

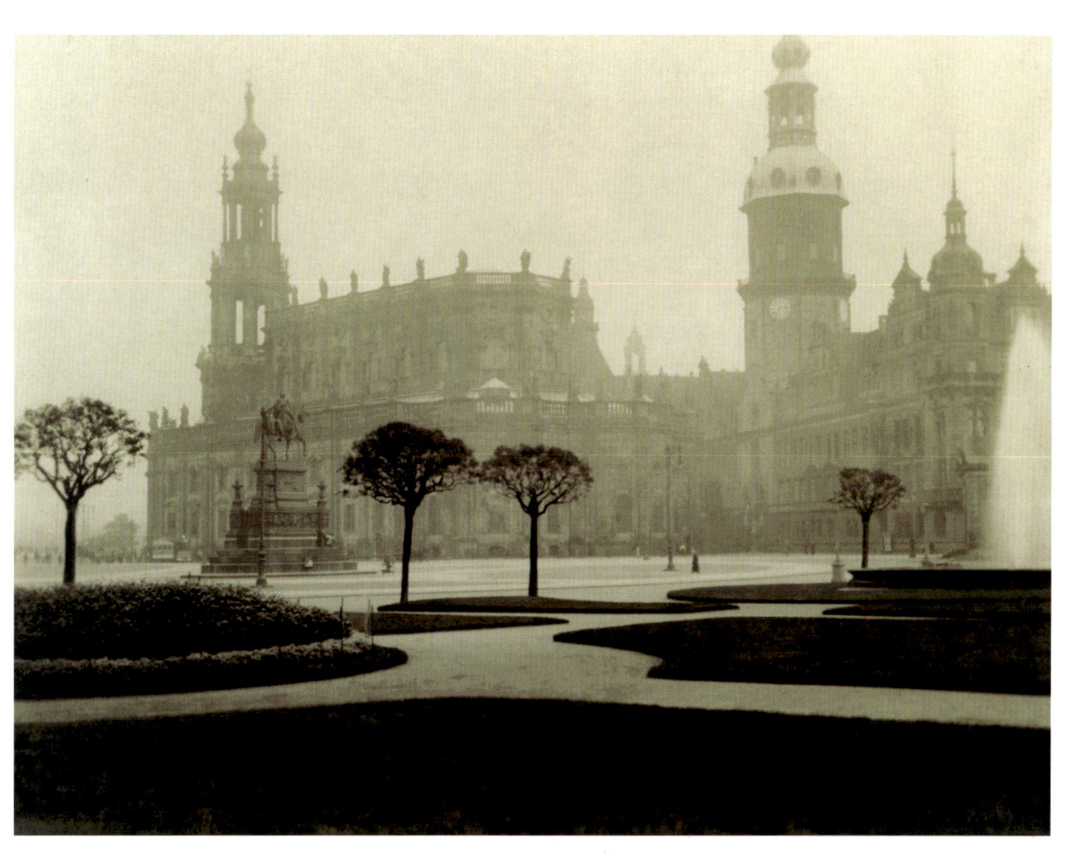

31 **Dresden / Drážďany** 1912

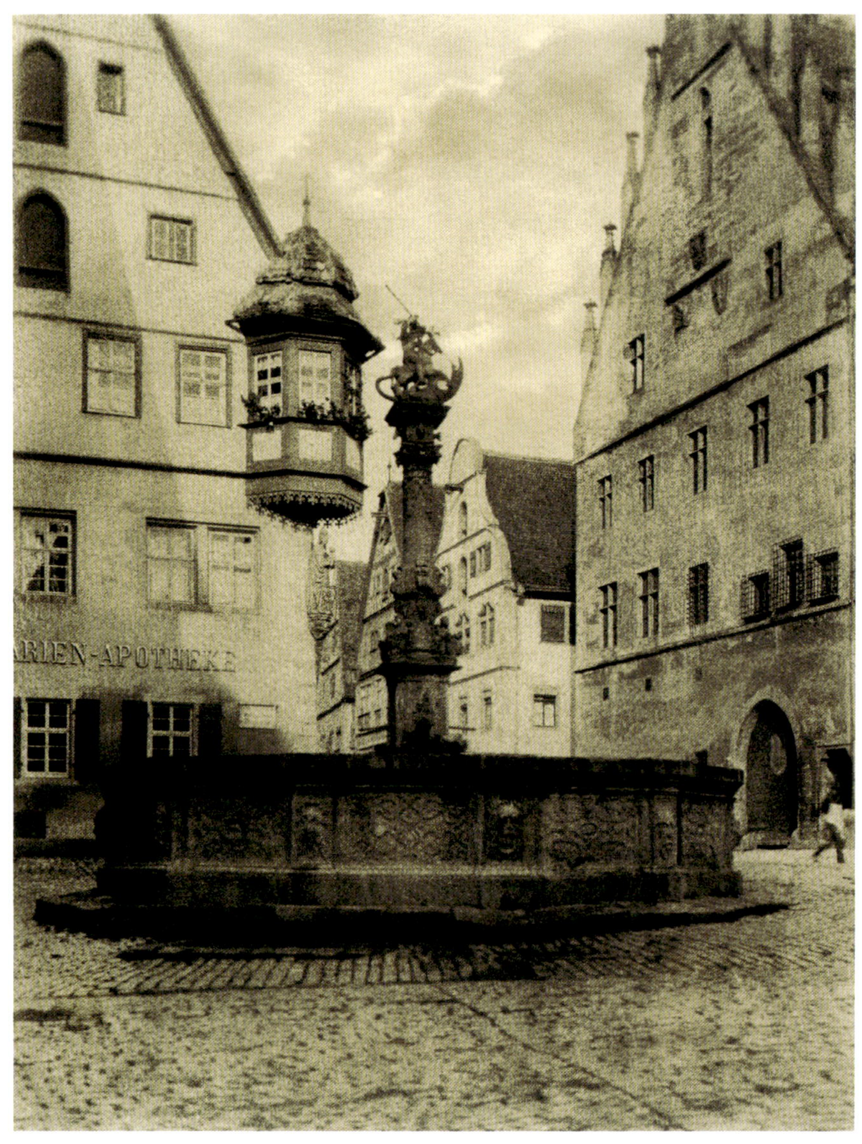

32 **Herterichsbrunnen, Rothenburg** 1912

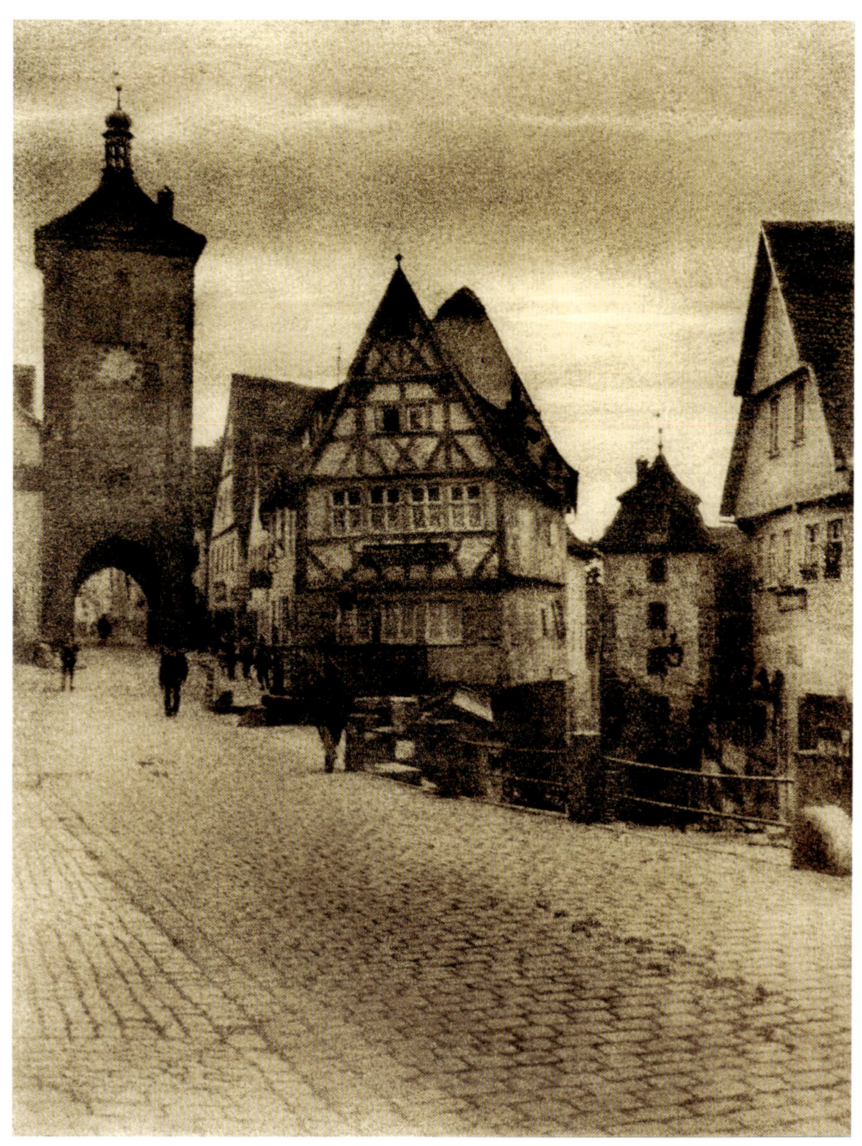

33 **Plönlein, Rothenburg** 1912

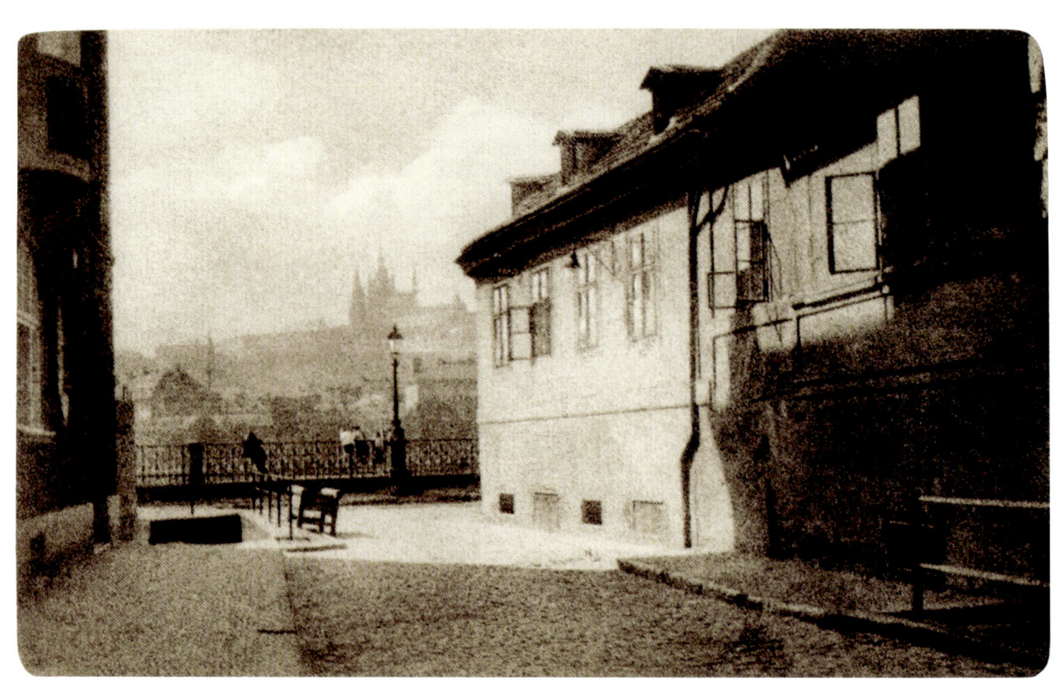

34 **Platněřská ulice (Platnergasse), Prague / Praha** 1910–14

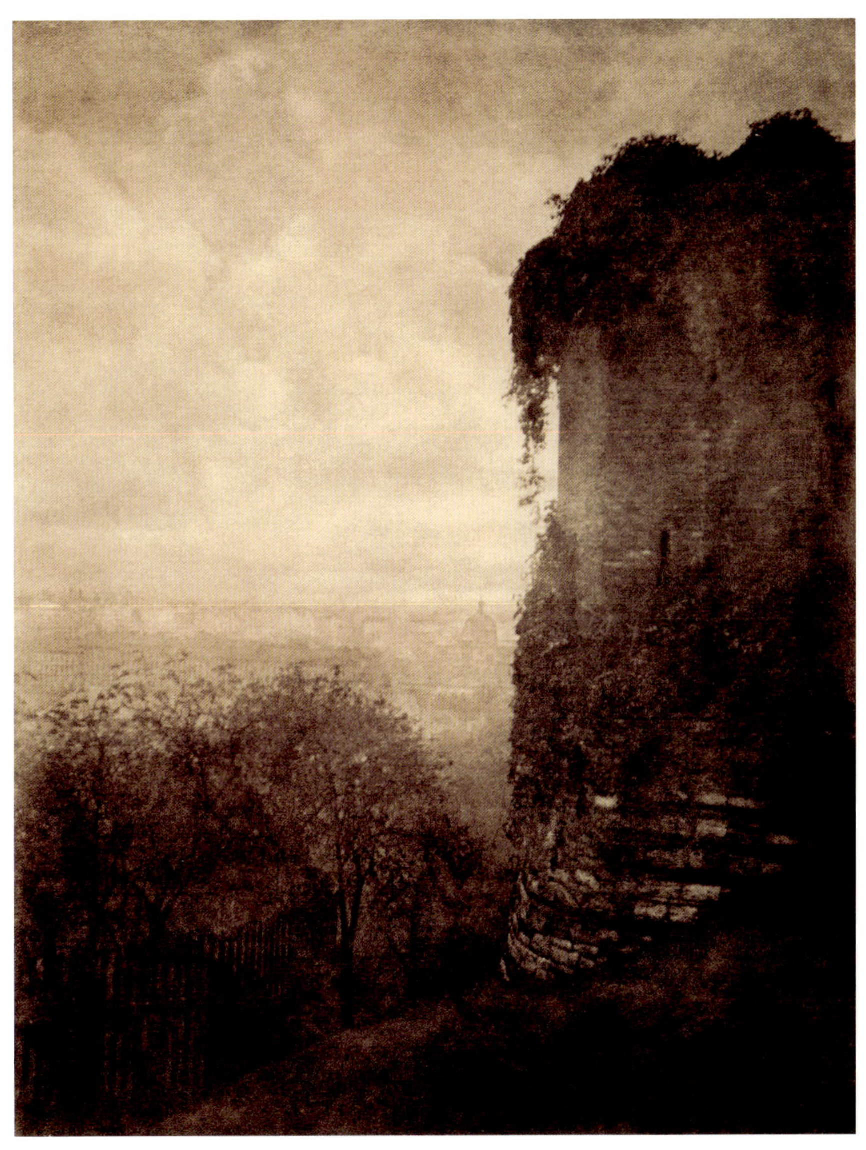

35 **Red Sky in the Morning / Ranní červánky** 1906–14

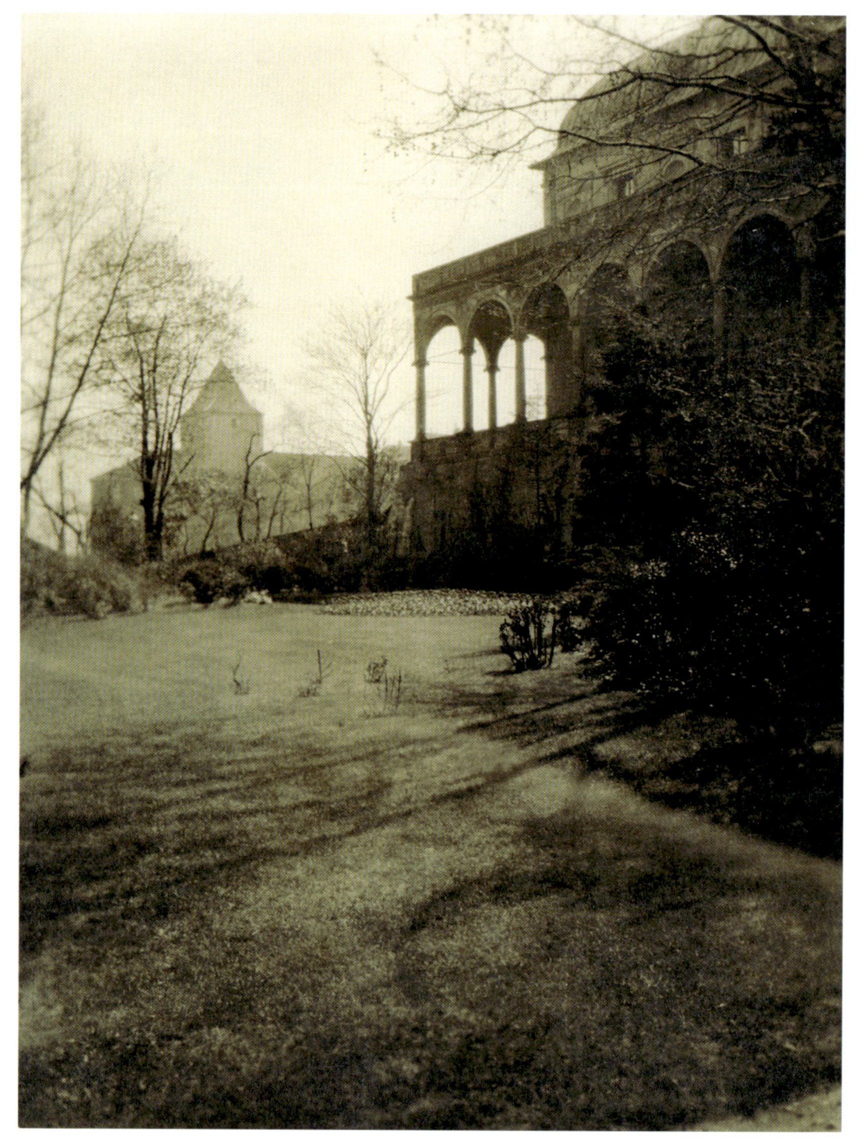

36 **Queen Anne's Summerhouse / Letohrádek Královny Anny, Prague / Praha** 1906–20

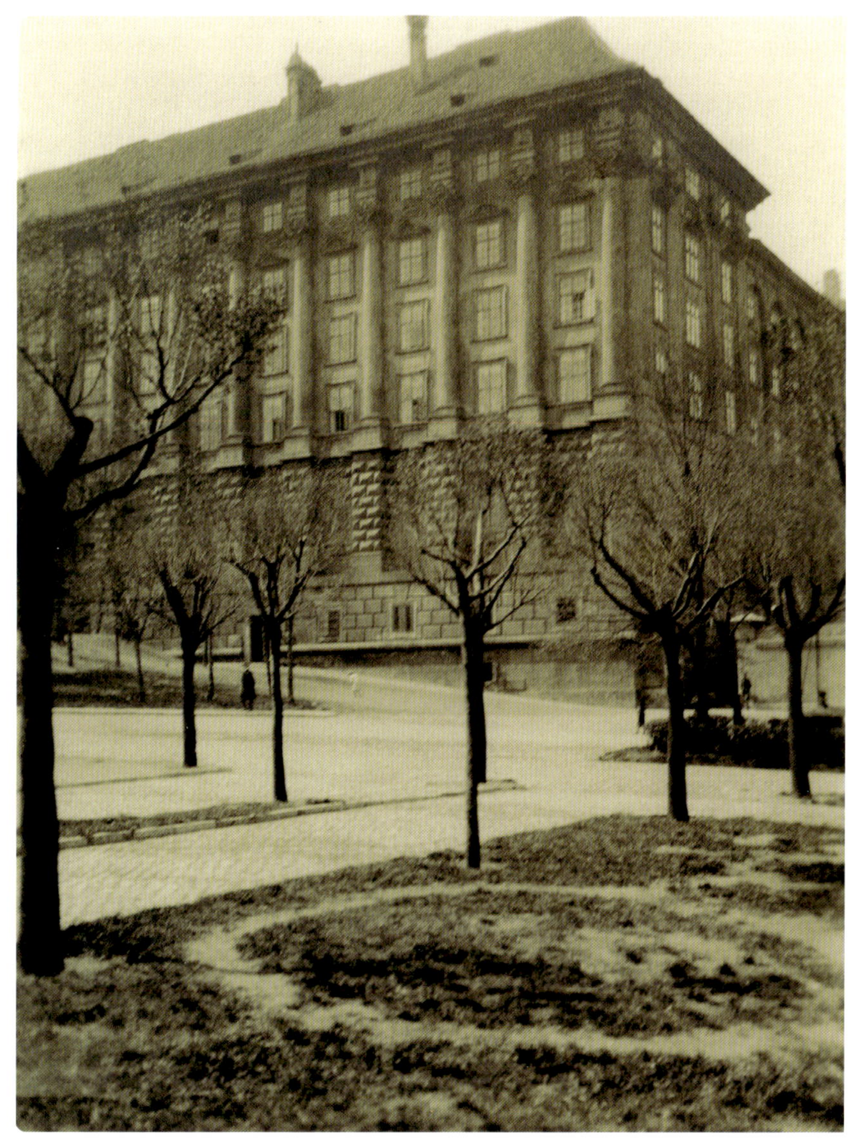

37 **Czernin Palais / Černínský palác, Prague / Praha** 1906–20

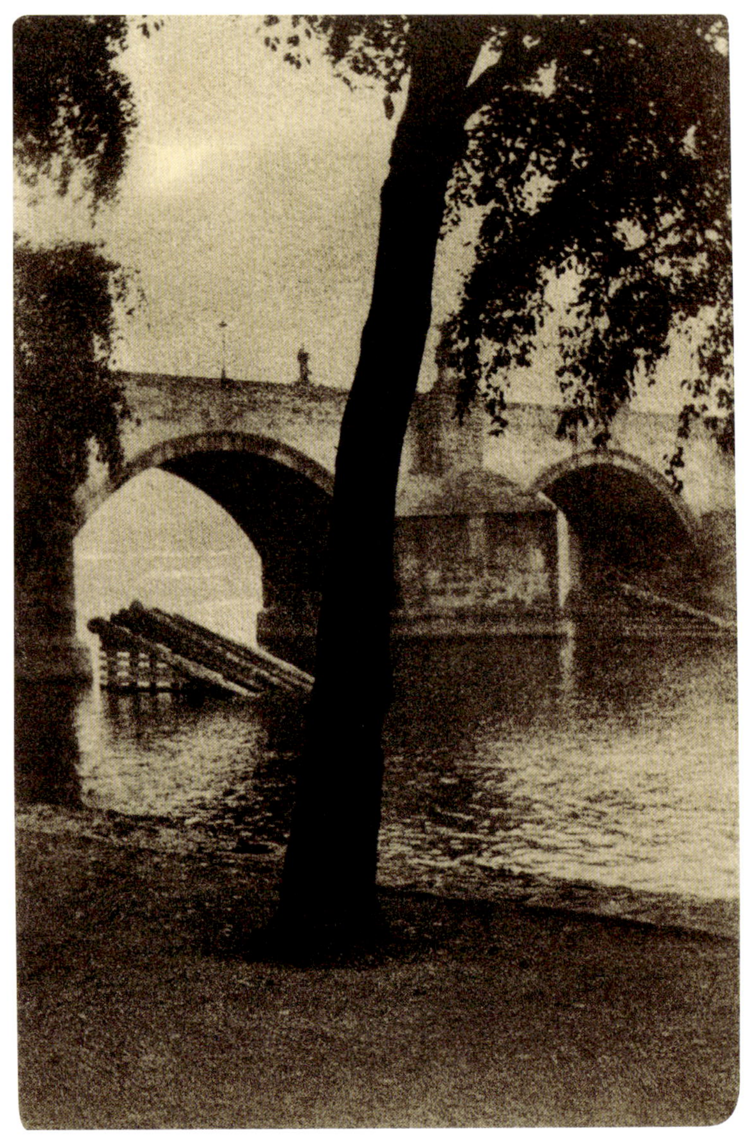

38 **Charles Bridge from Kampa / Karlův most z Kampy, Prague / Praha** 1906–14

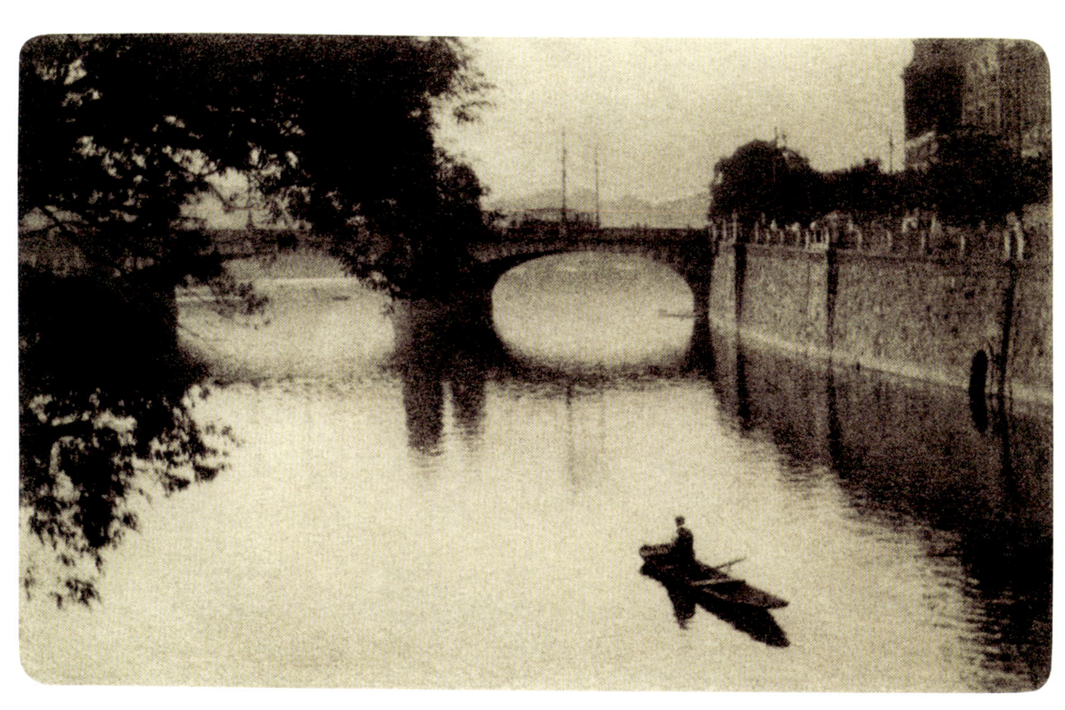

39 **Francis I Bridge / Most Františka I, Prague / Praha** 1906–14

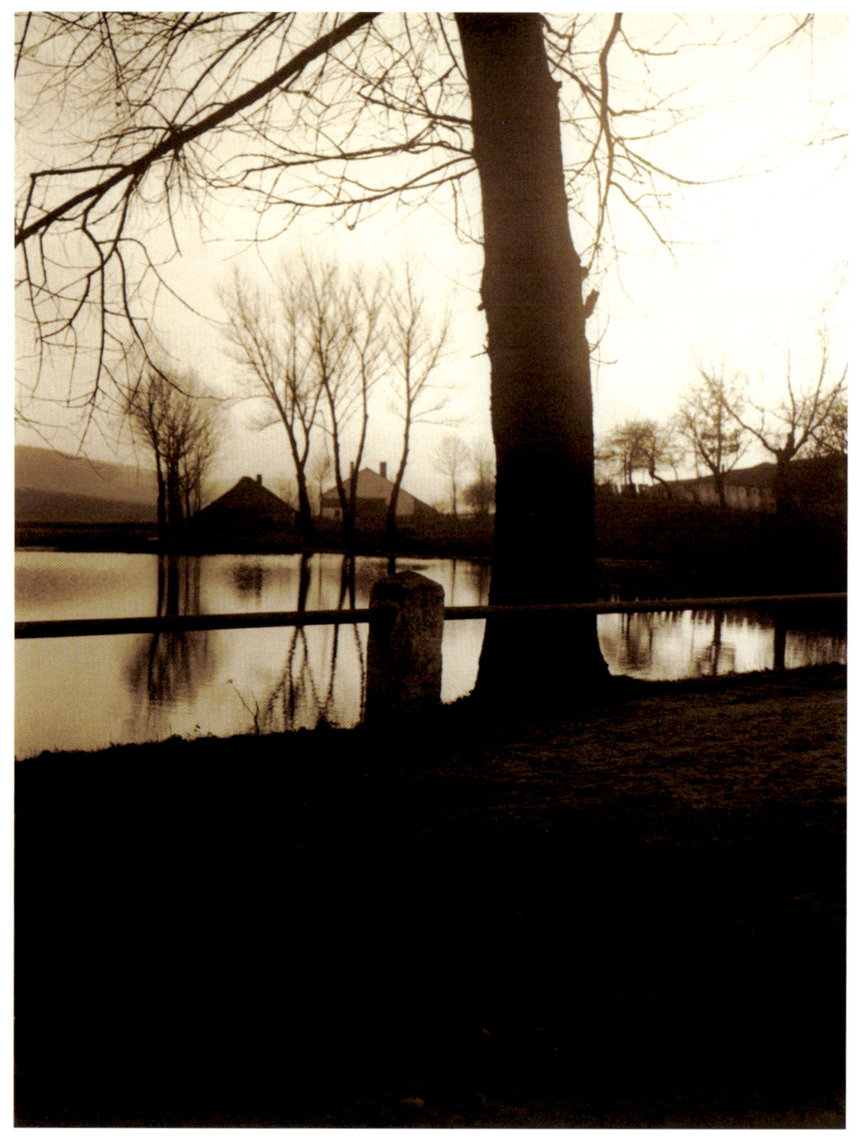

40 **The Mill pond, Krucemburk / Mlýnský rybník v Krucemburku** undated / nedatováno

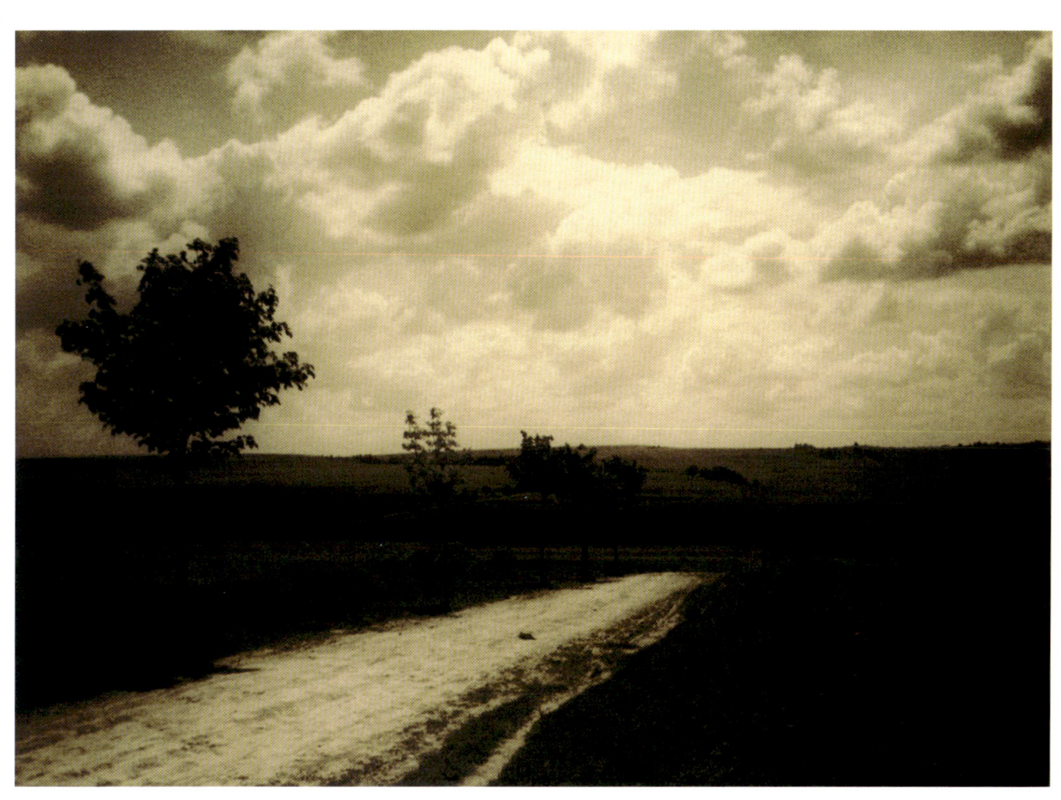

41 **The road from Krucemburk to Hluboká / Silnice z Krucemburku do Hluboké** 1910–14

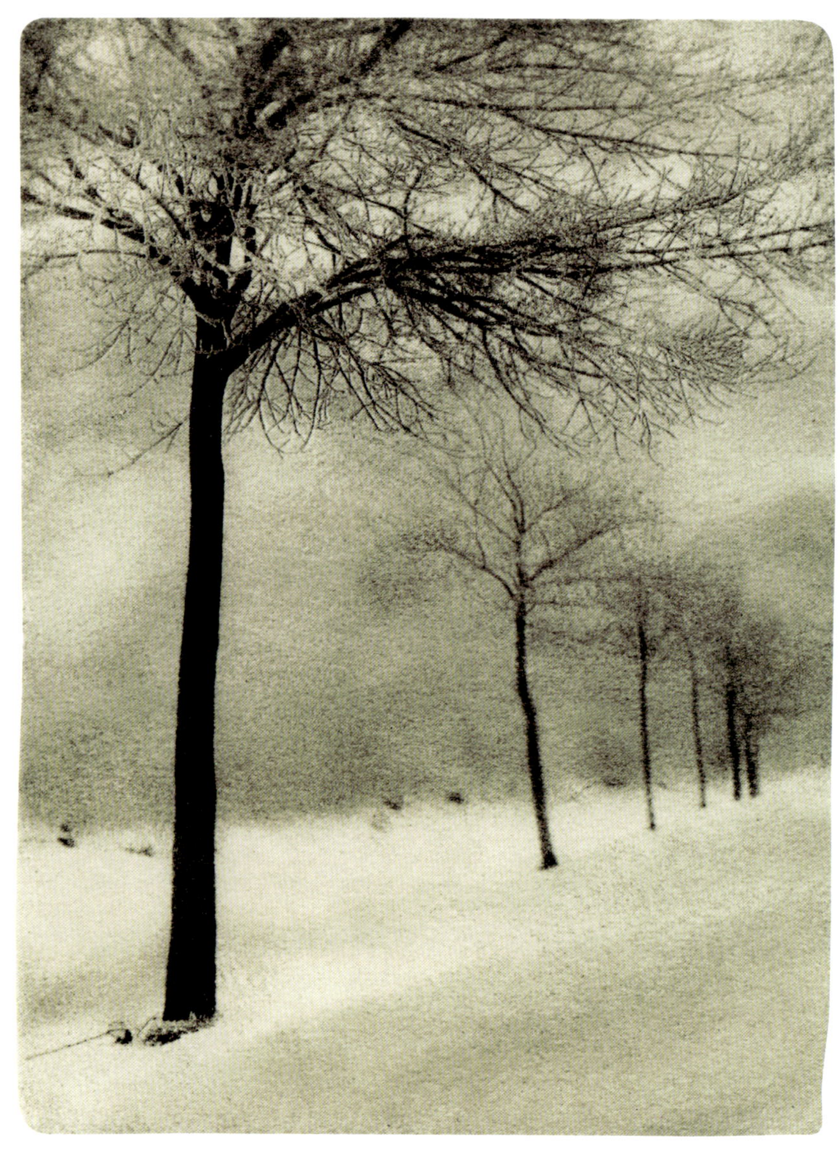

42 **The way to Škrdlovice / Cesta do Škrdlovic** 1910–14

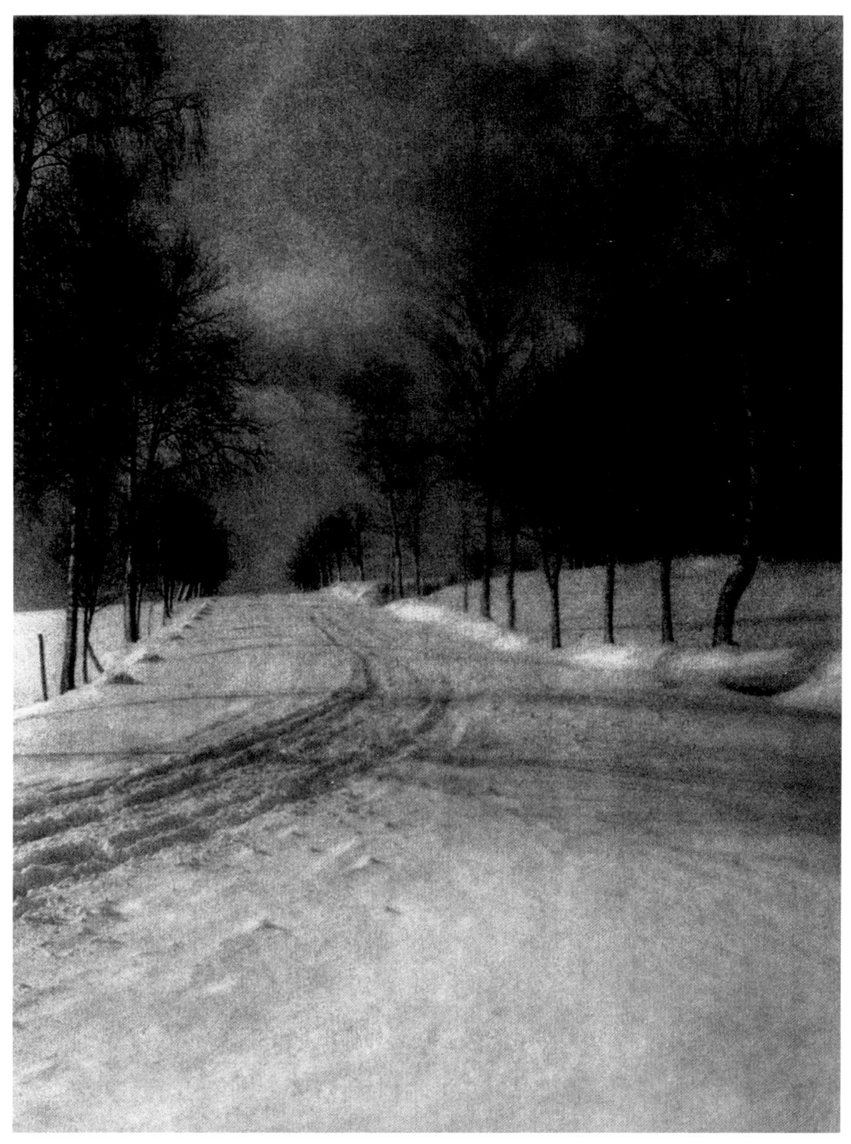

43 **Road in Winter / Silnice v zimě** 1909–11

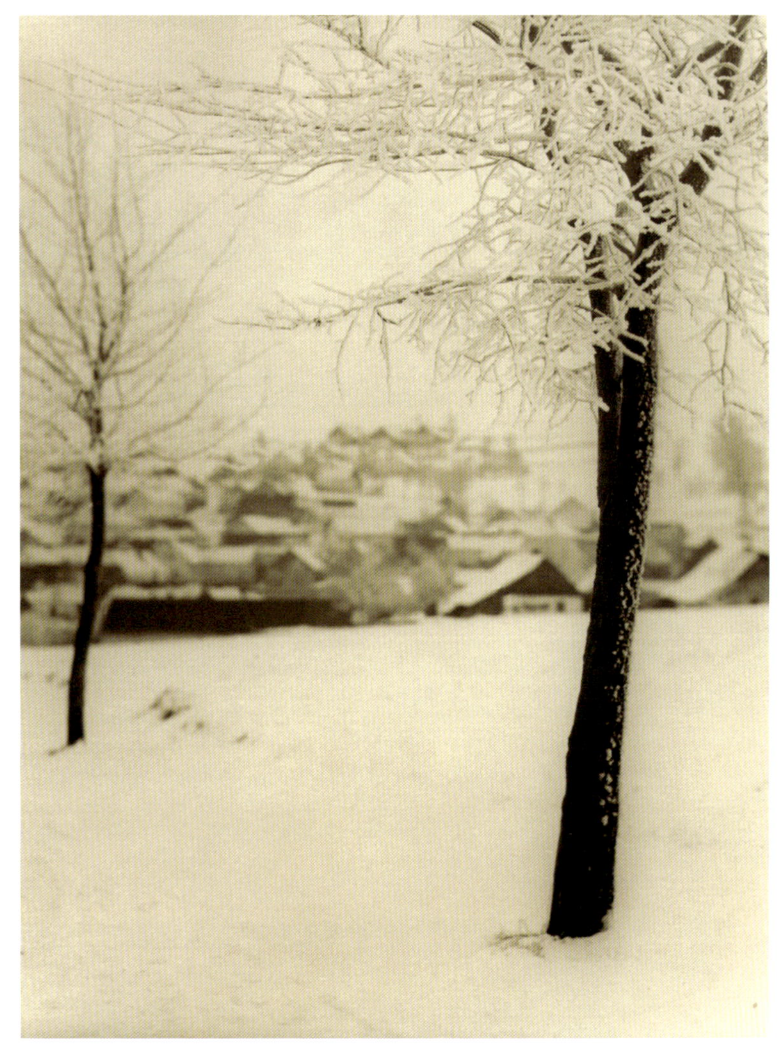

44 **Krucemburk in winter / Krucemburk v zimě** 1910–14

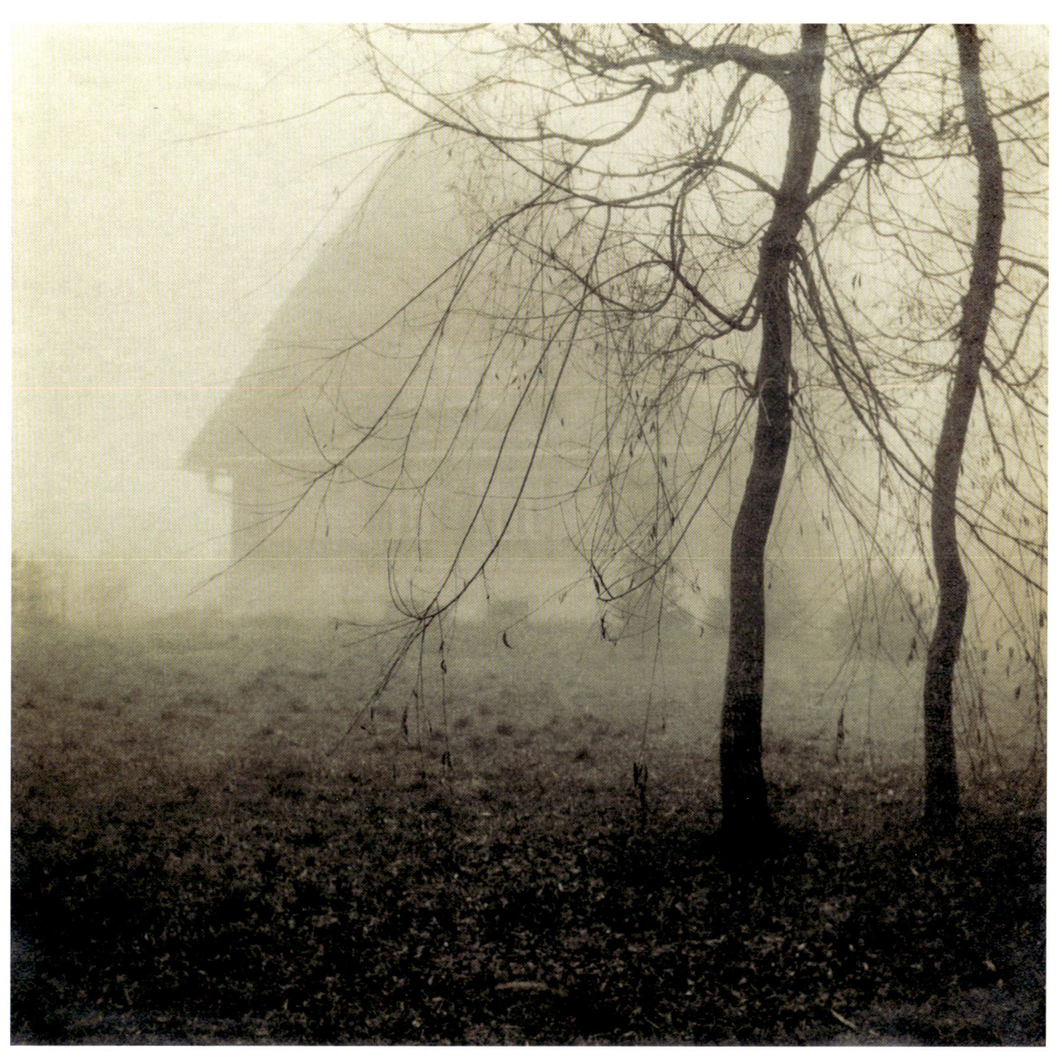

45 **In the garden of the villa / Na zahradě vily** 1911–12

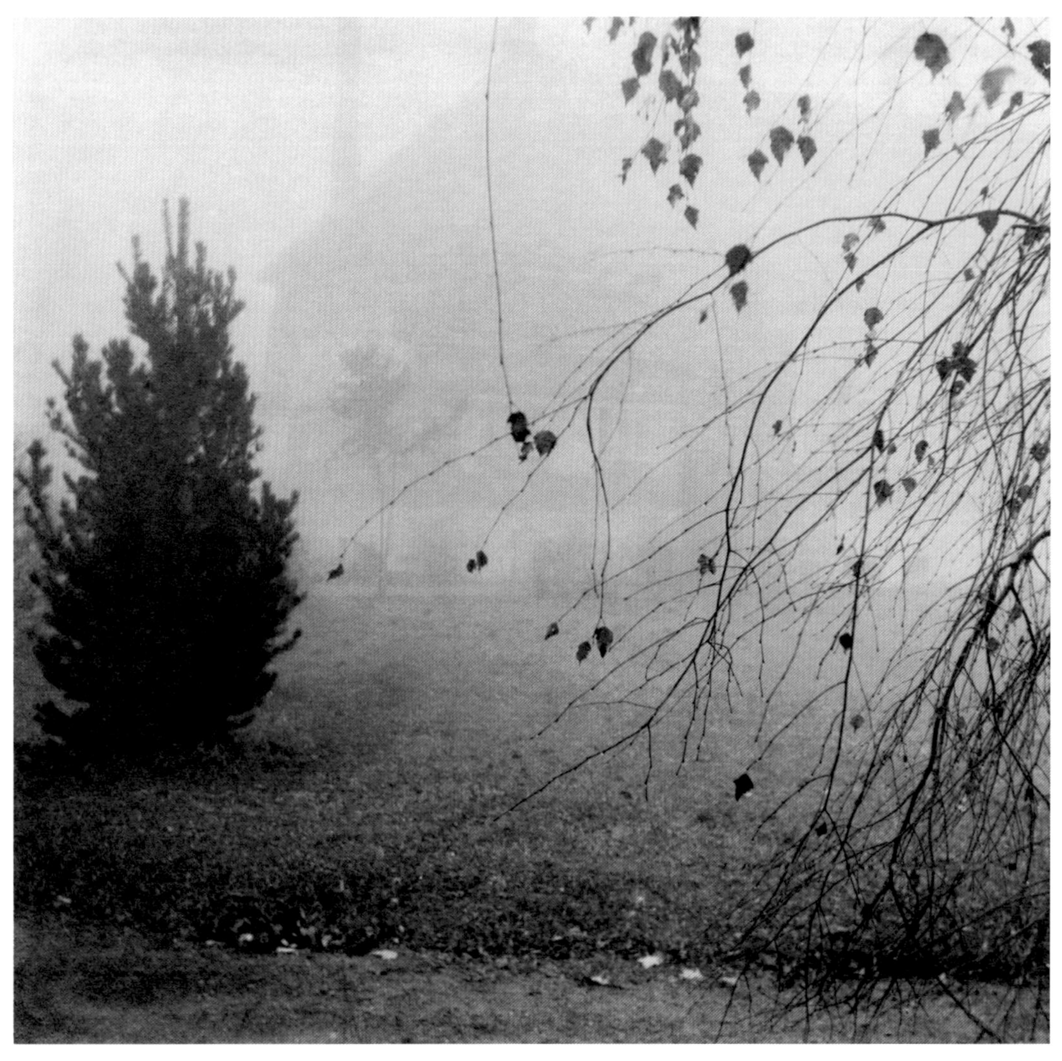

46 **In the garden of the villa / Na zahradě vily** 1911–12

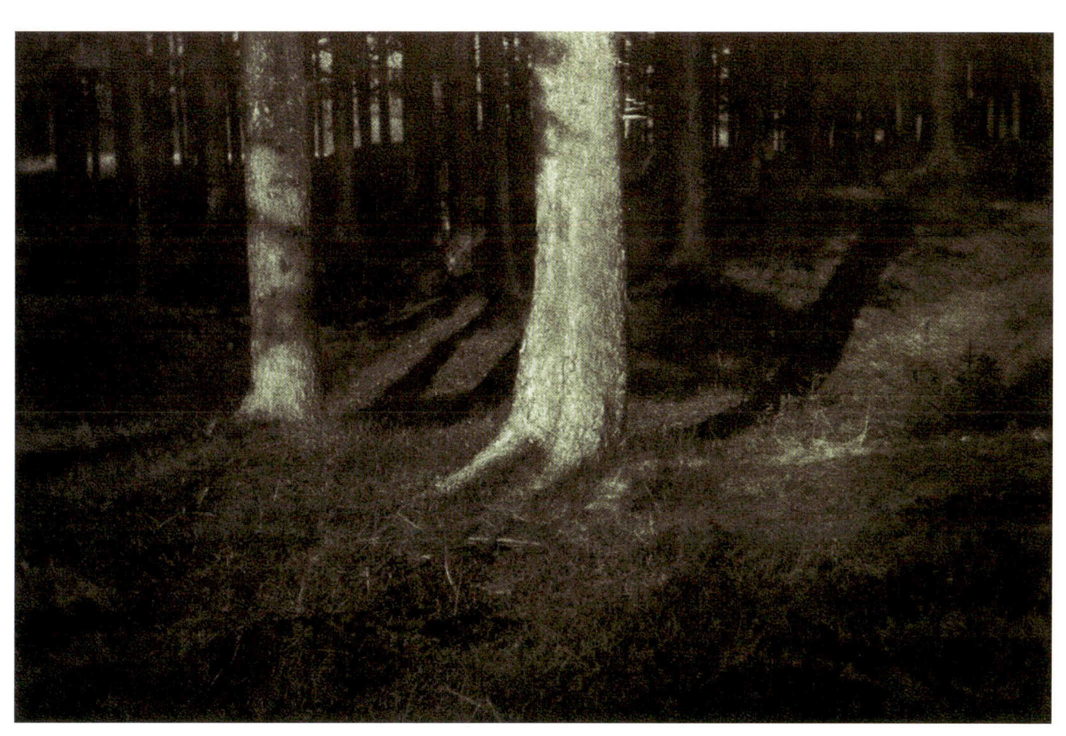

47 **In the Woods / V lese** 1909–11

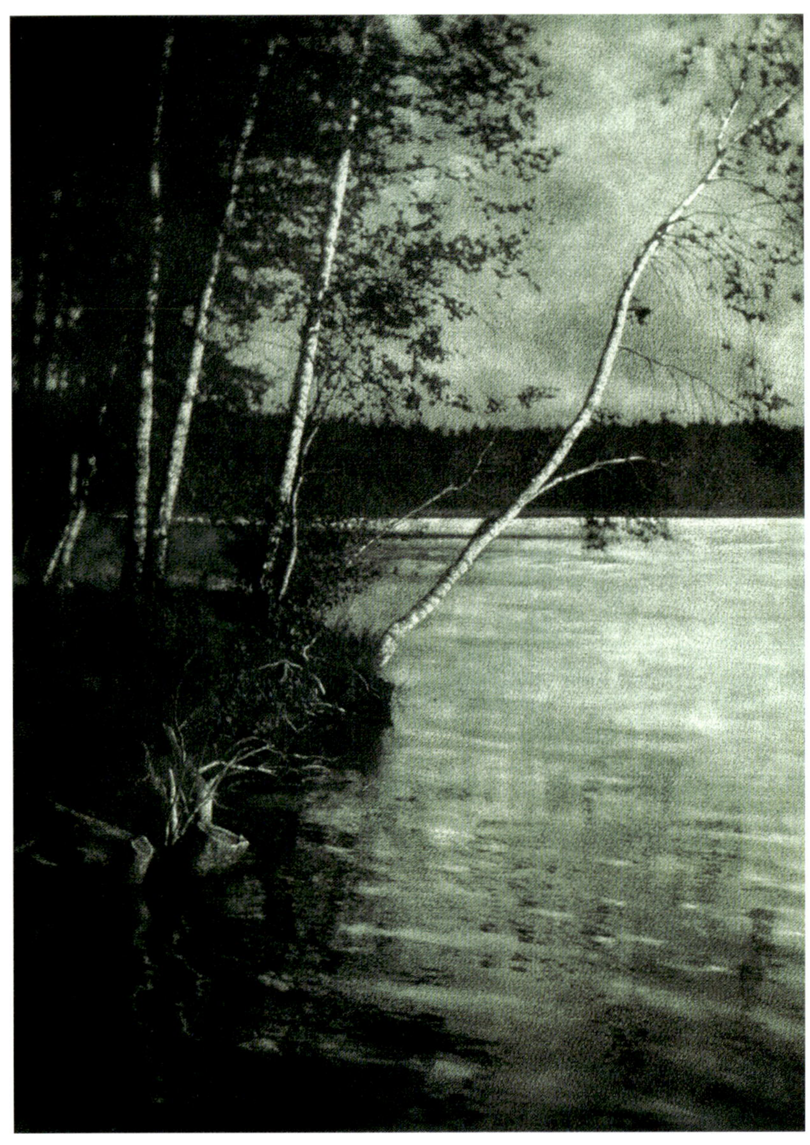

48 **Dusk on the Pond / Soumrak na rybníku** 1909–11

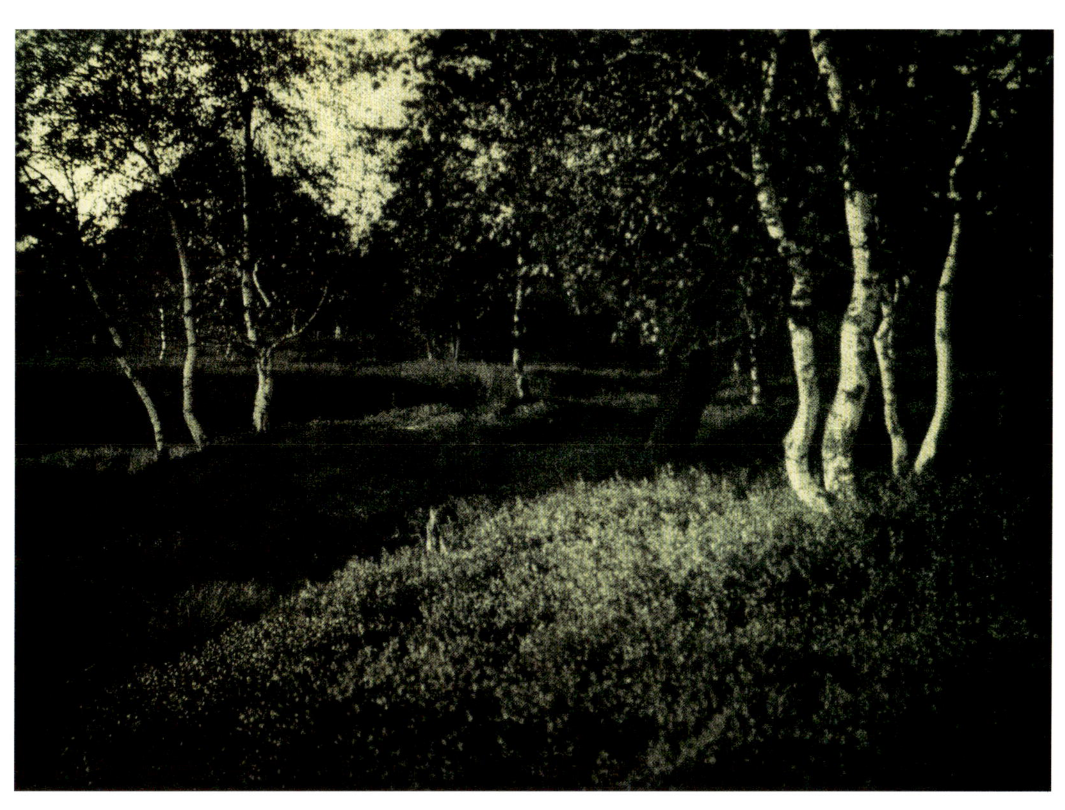

49 **Birch trees in the woods / Les s břízami** 1909–12

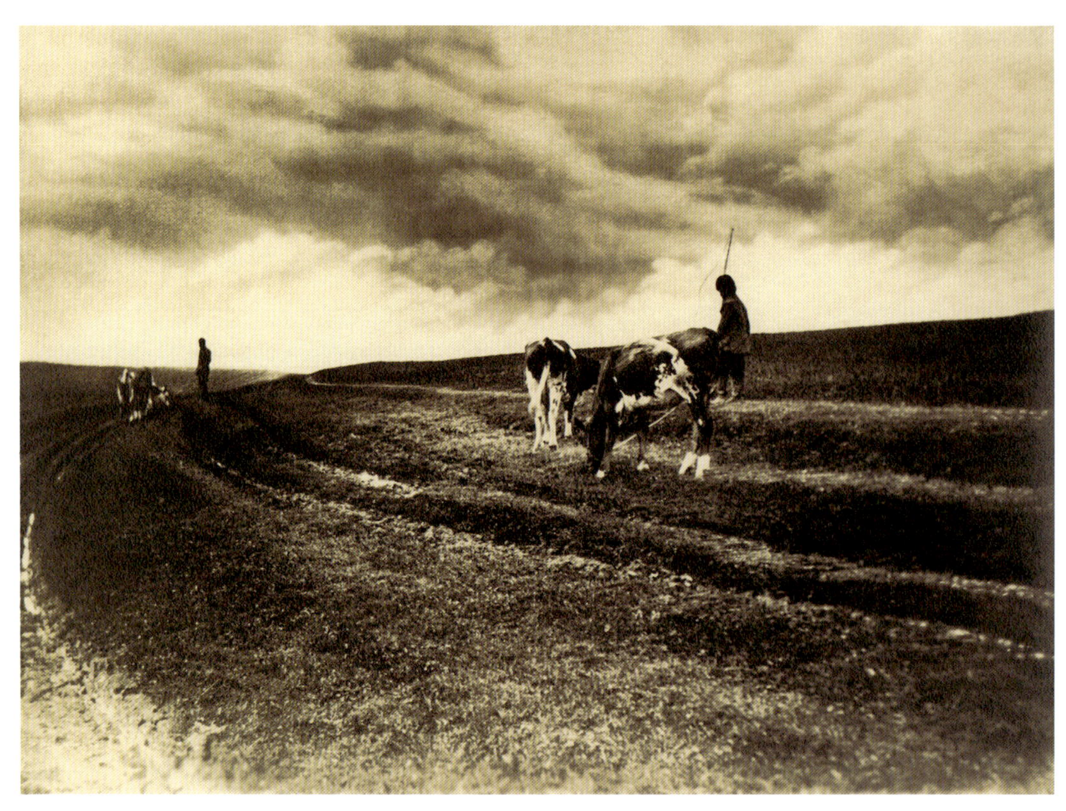

50 **In the pasture / Na pastvě** 1906–11

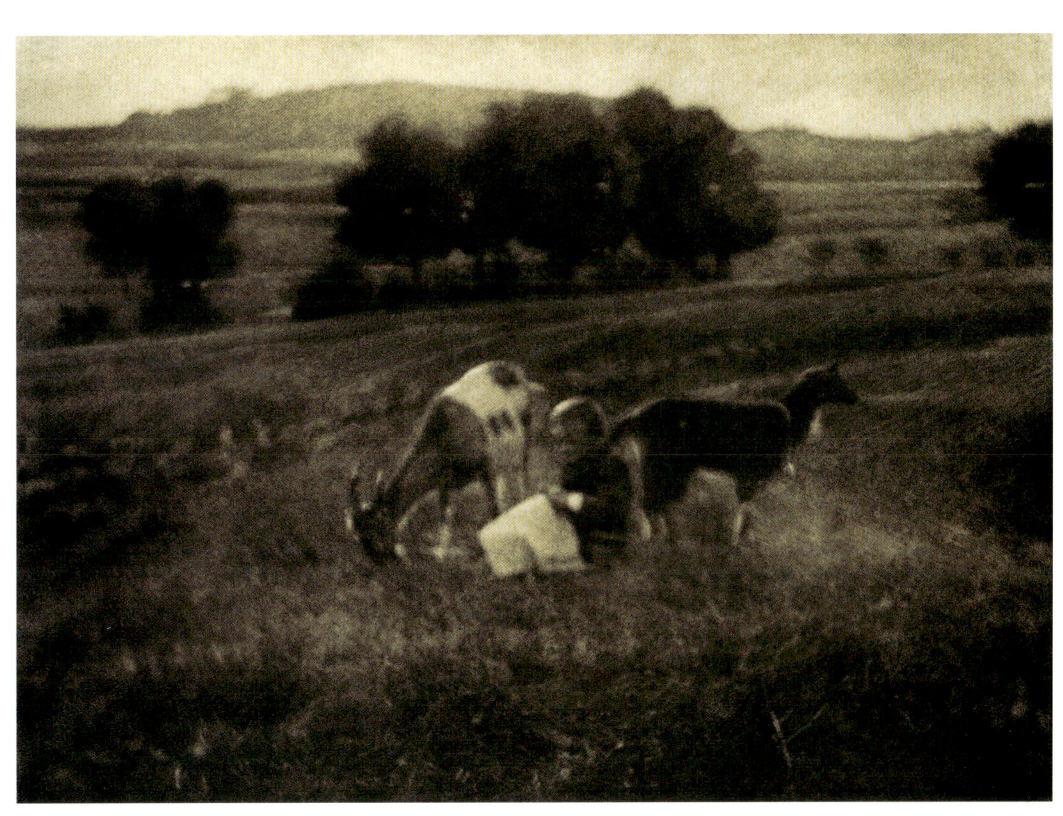

51 **Goats / Kozy, Nové Město** 1906–11

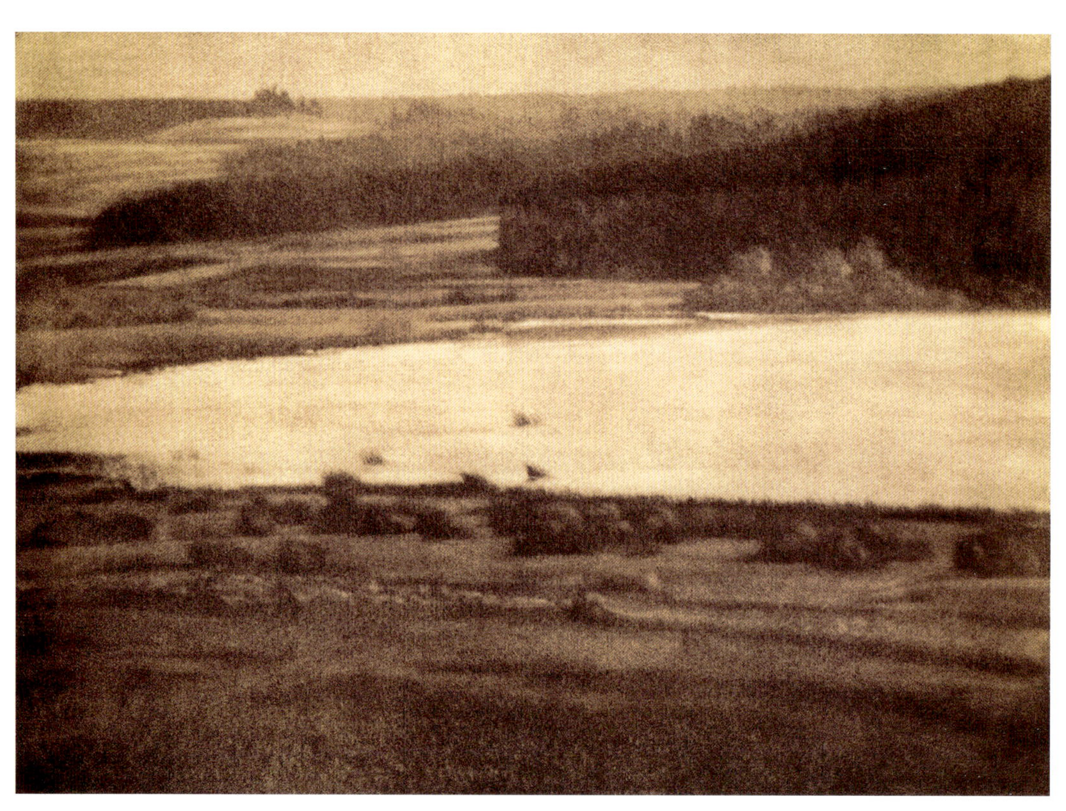

52 **The Řeka pond / Rybník Řeka** 1906–11

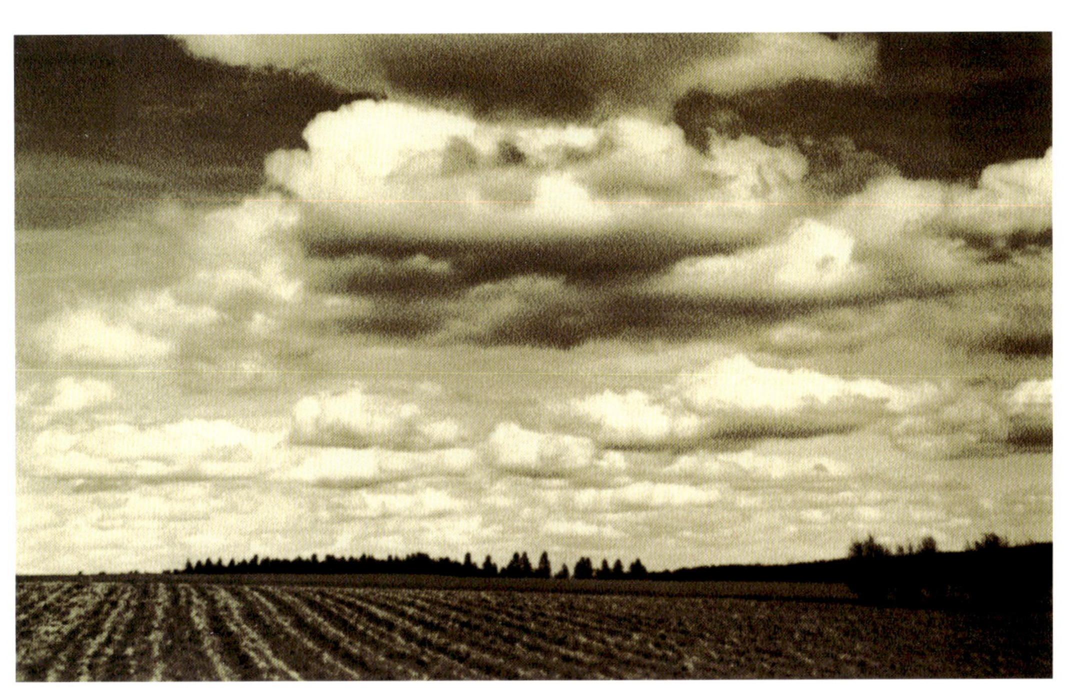

53 **Clouds in the Highlands / Mraky na Vysočině** 1906–12

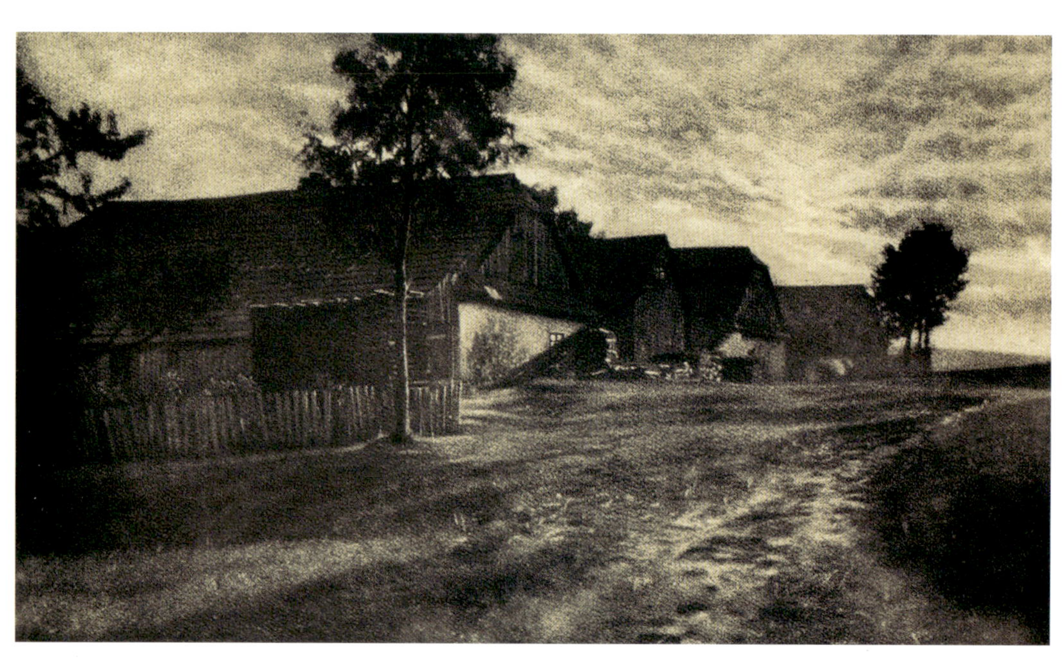

54 **Morning Mood / Ranní nálada** 1909–11

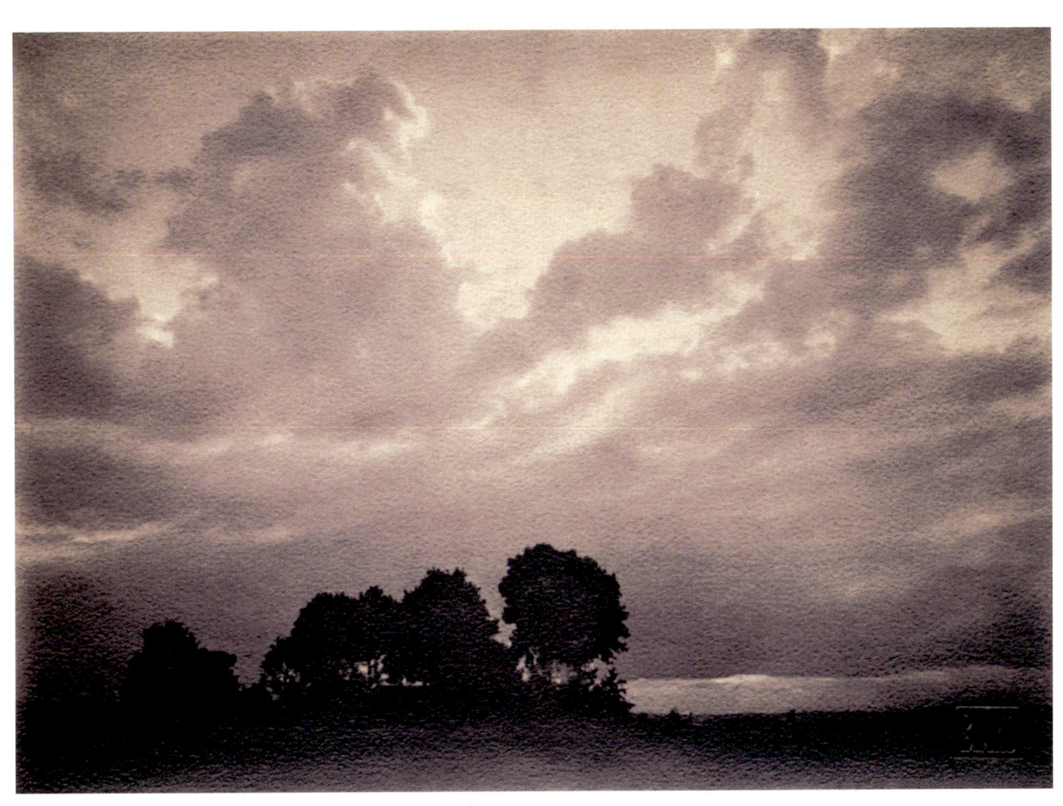

55 **In the Highlands / Na Vysočině** 1909–12

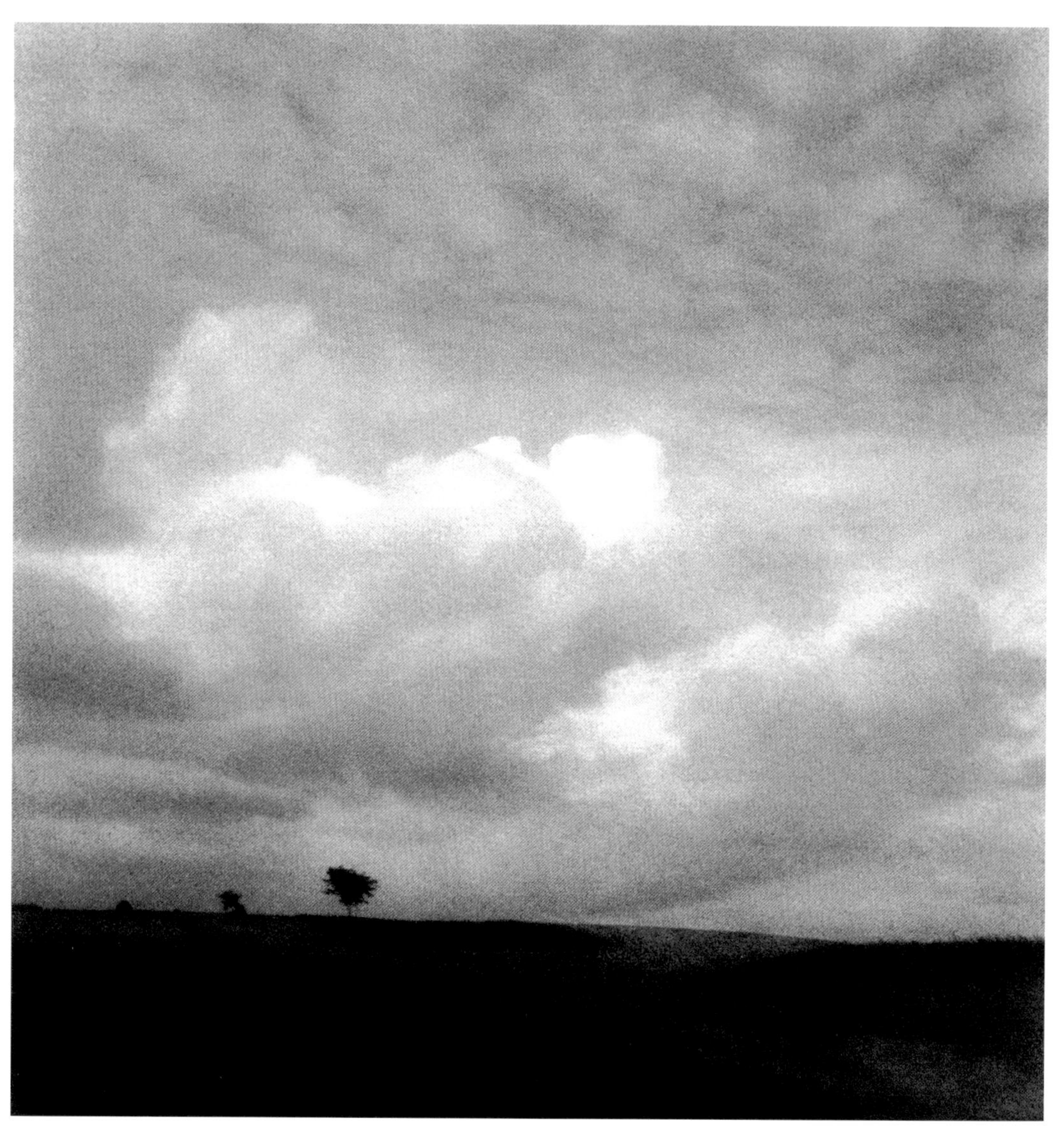

56–57 **Cloud study / Studie mraků** 1910–14

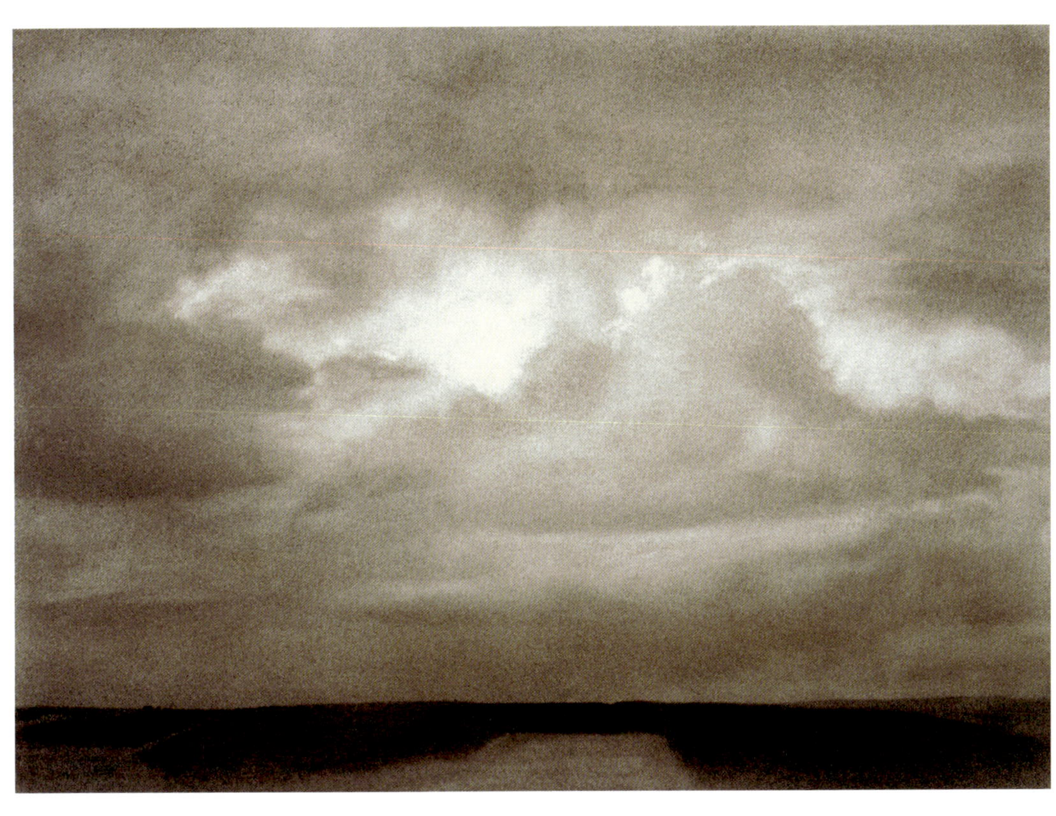

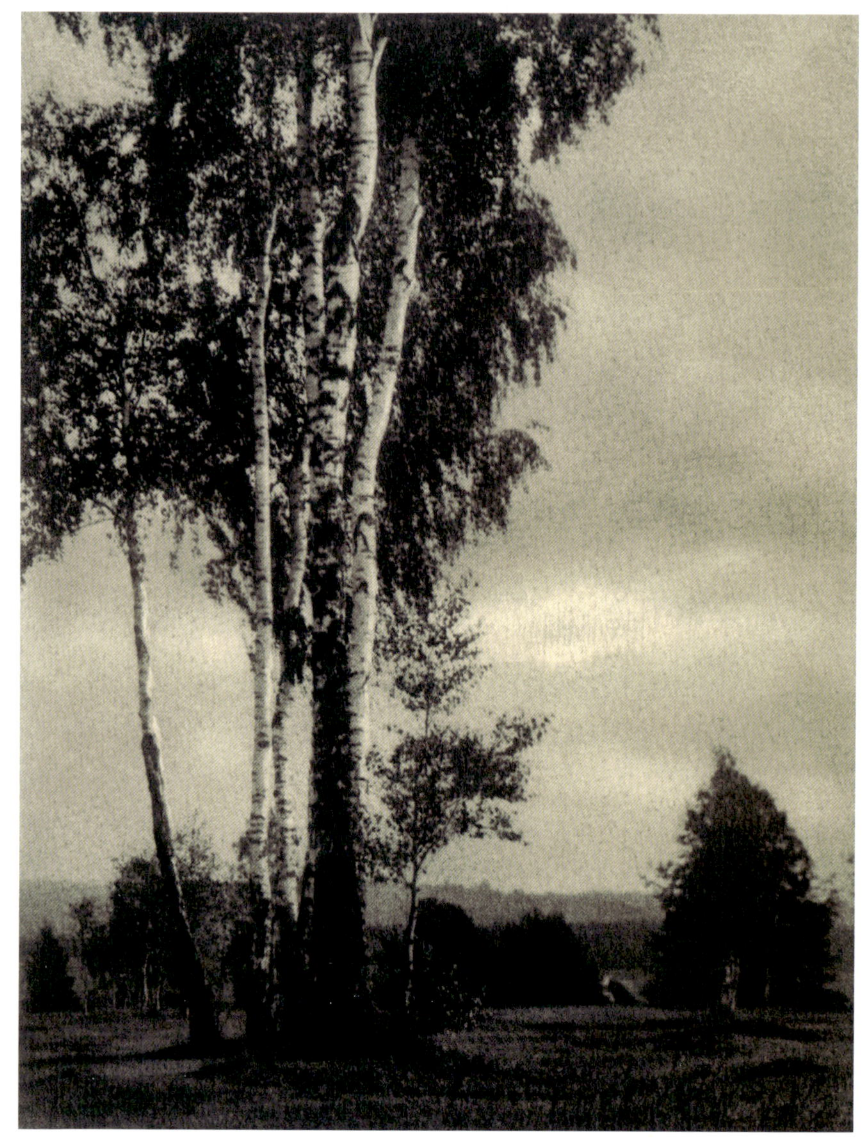

58 **Birch Trees in Jasná Pole / Břízy v Jasných Polích** 1910–14

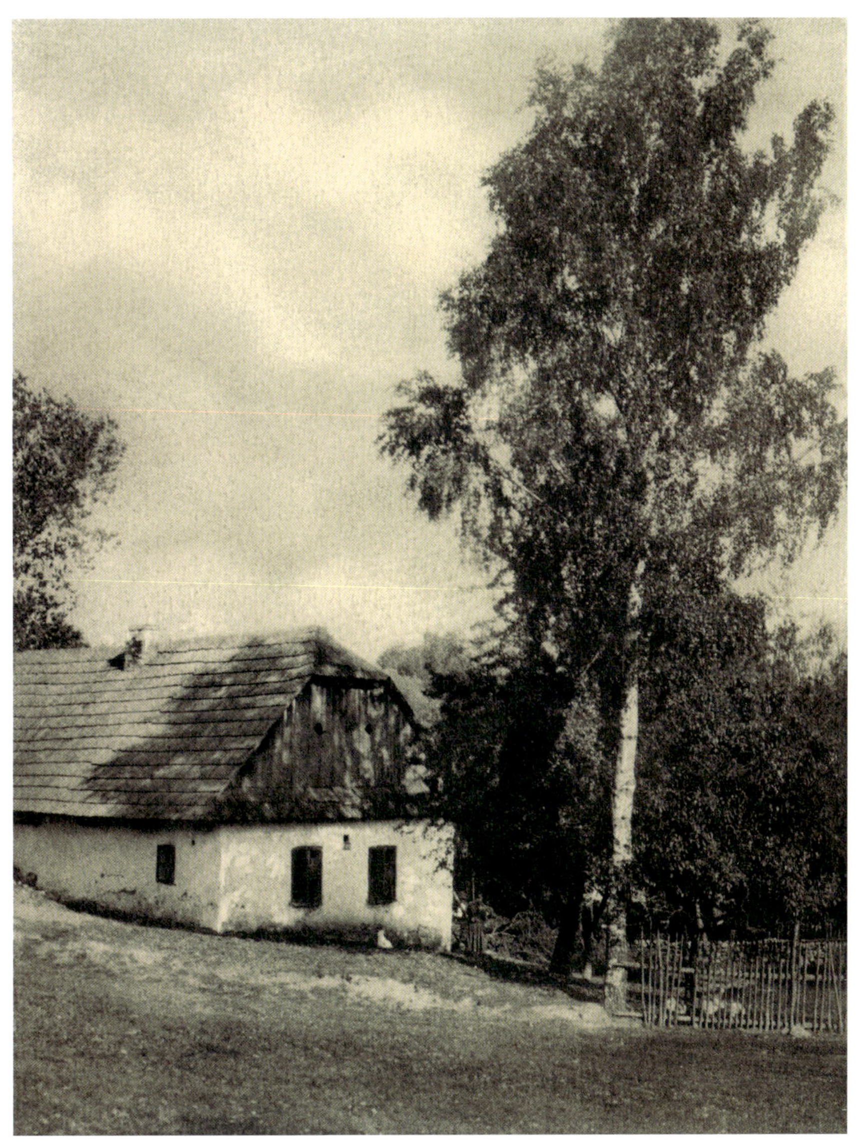

59 **Vítanov** 1911–14

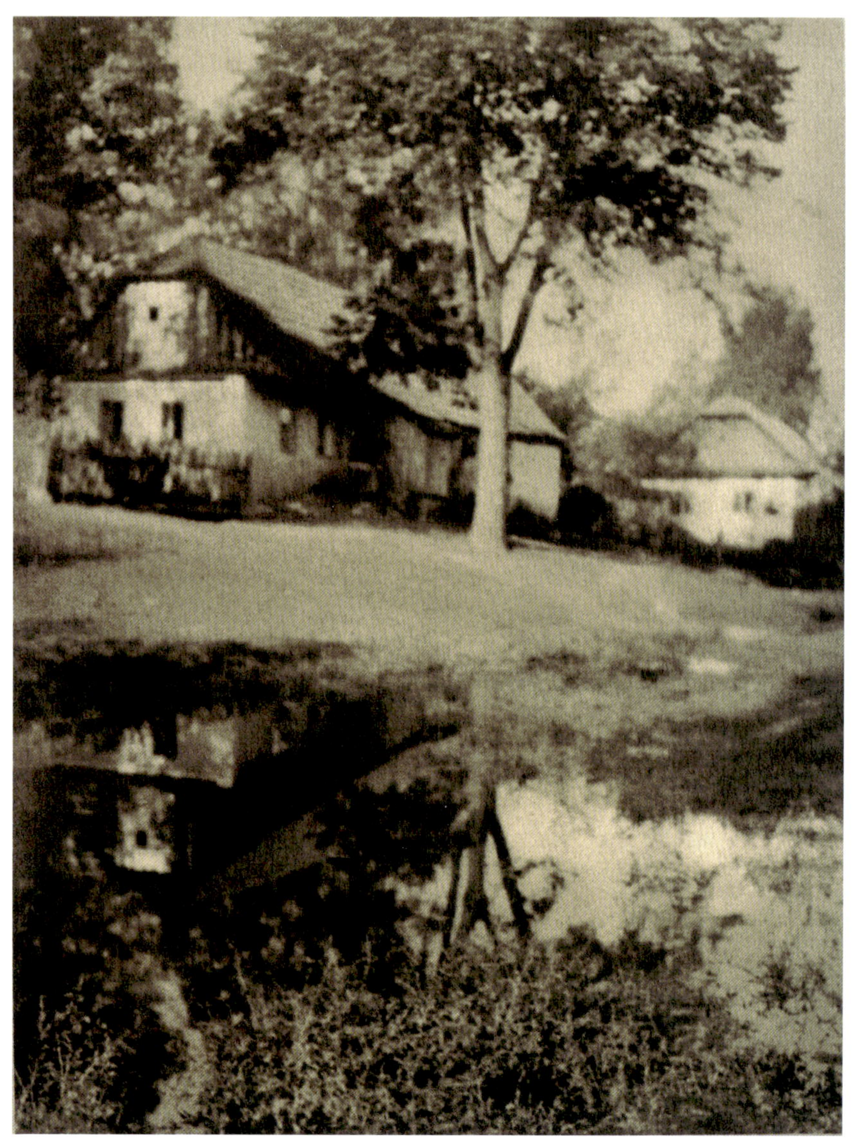

60 **Vítanov** 1911–14

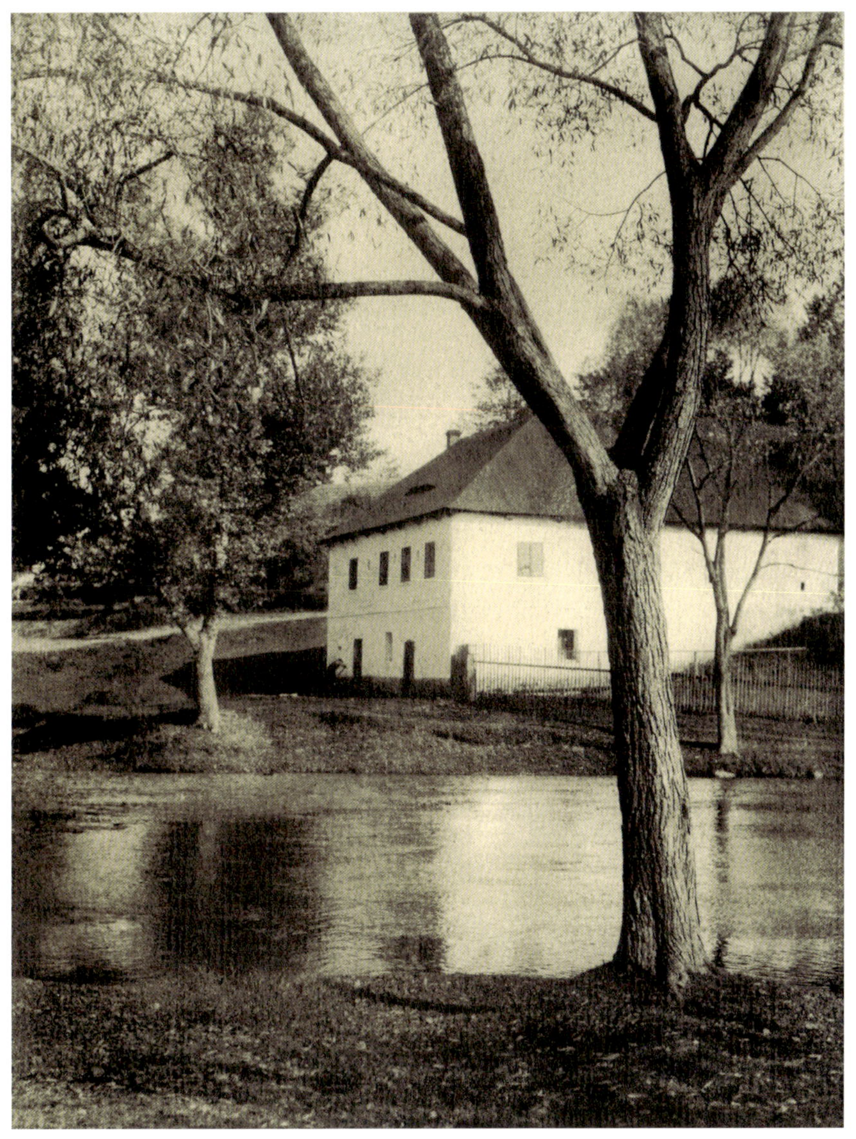

61 **Flour mill in Vítanov / Mlýn ve Vítanově** 1911–14

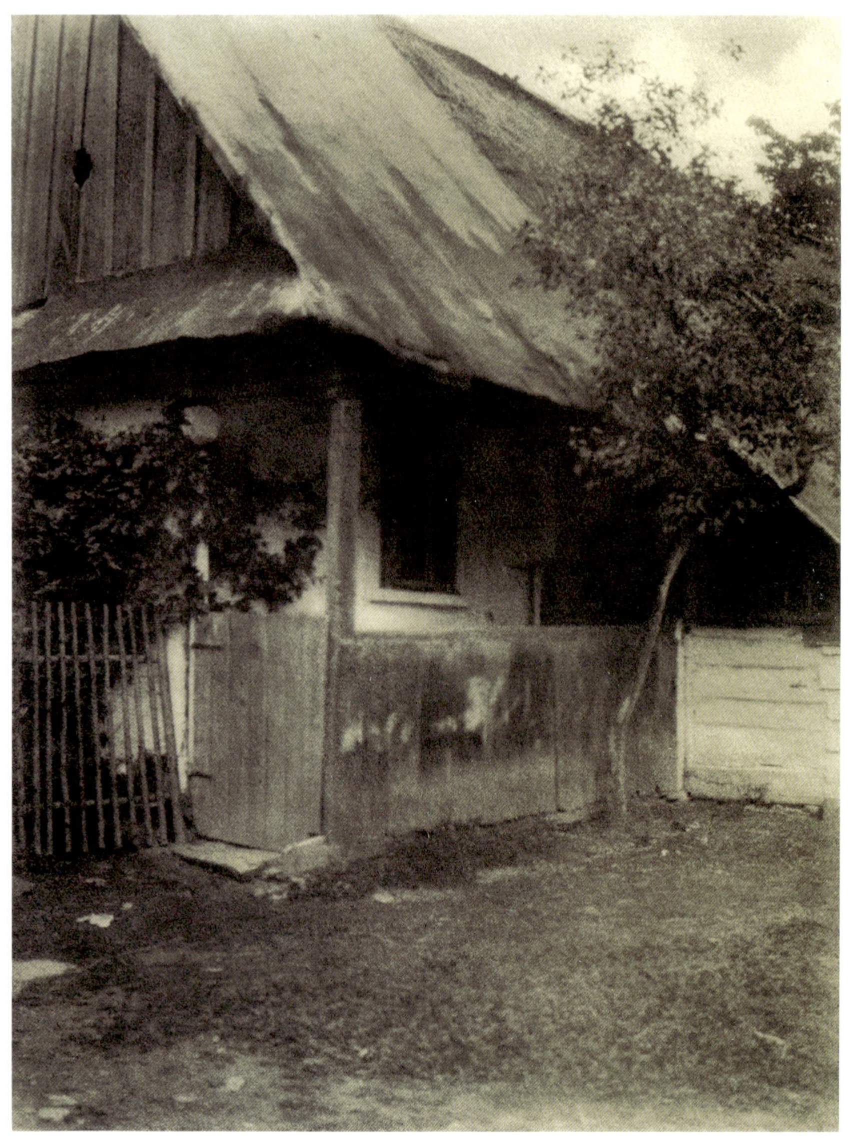

62 **Cottage near Holetín / Chalupa u Holetína** 1911–14

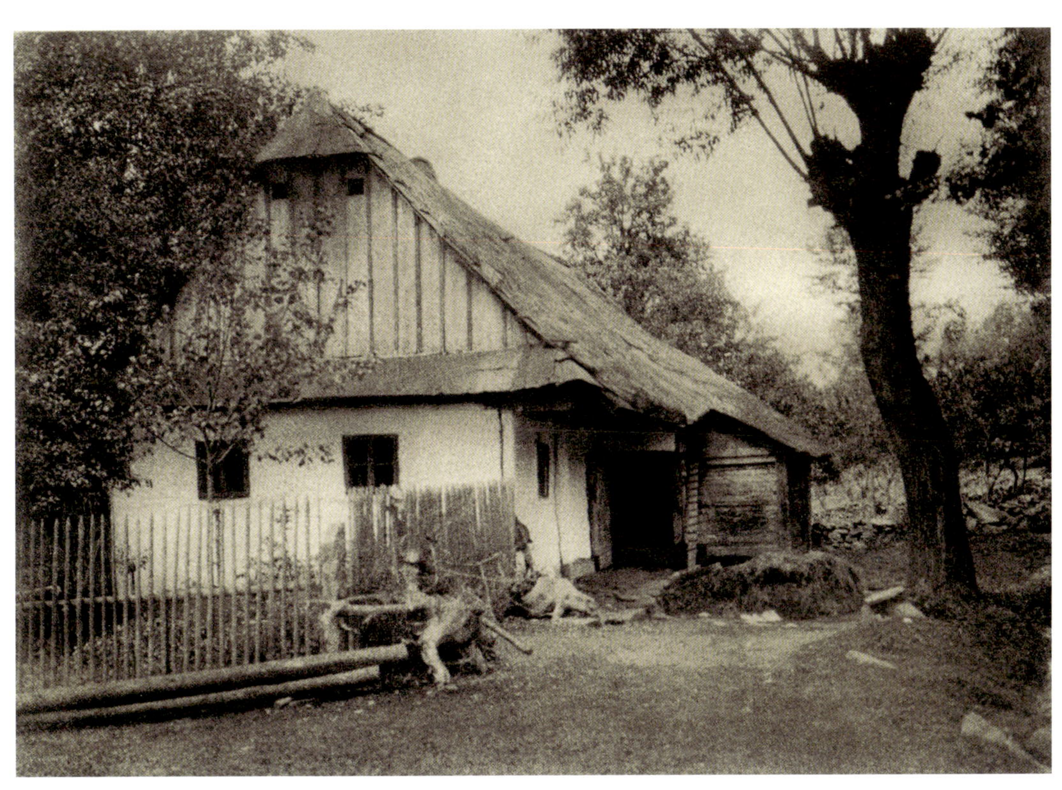

63 **Cottage in Kouty near Hlinsko / Chalupa v Koutech u Hlinska** 1911–14

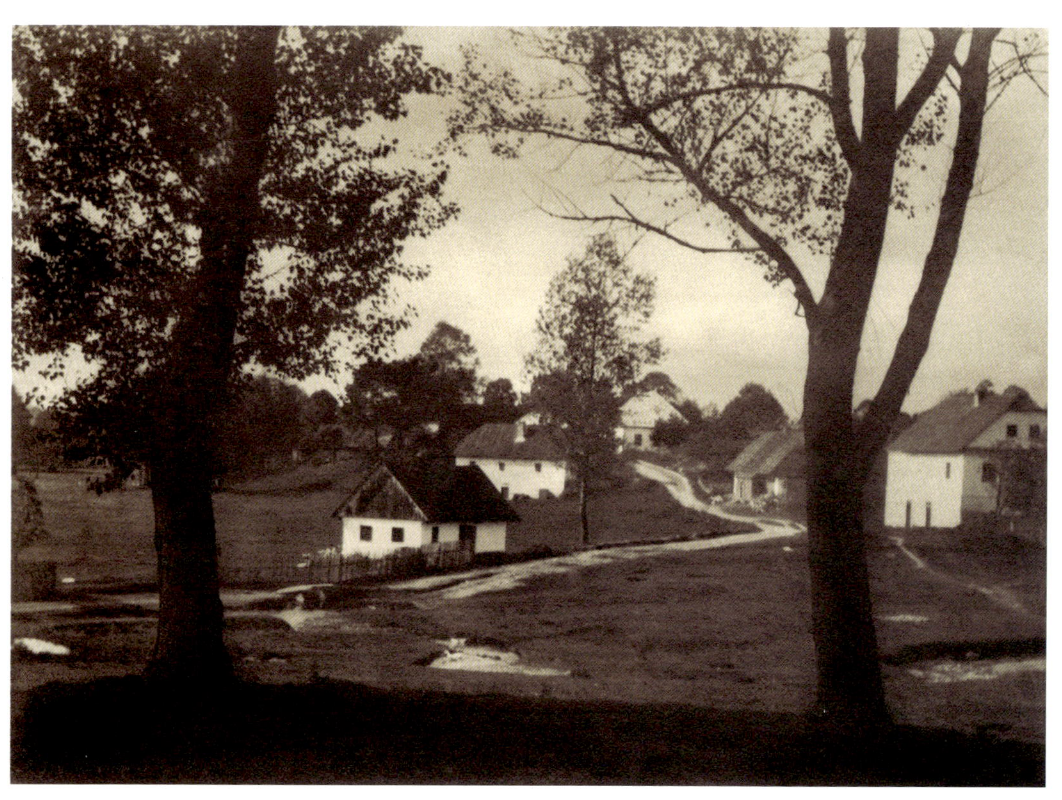

64–65 **Near Vítanov / U Vítanova** 1911–14

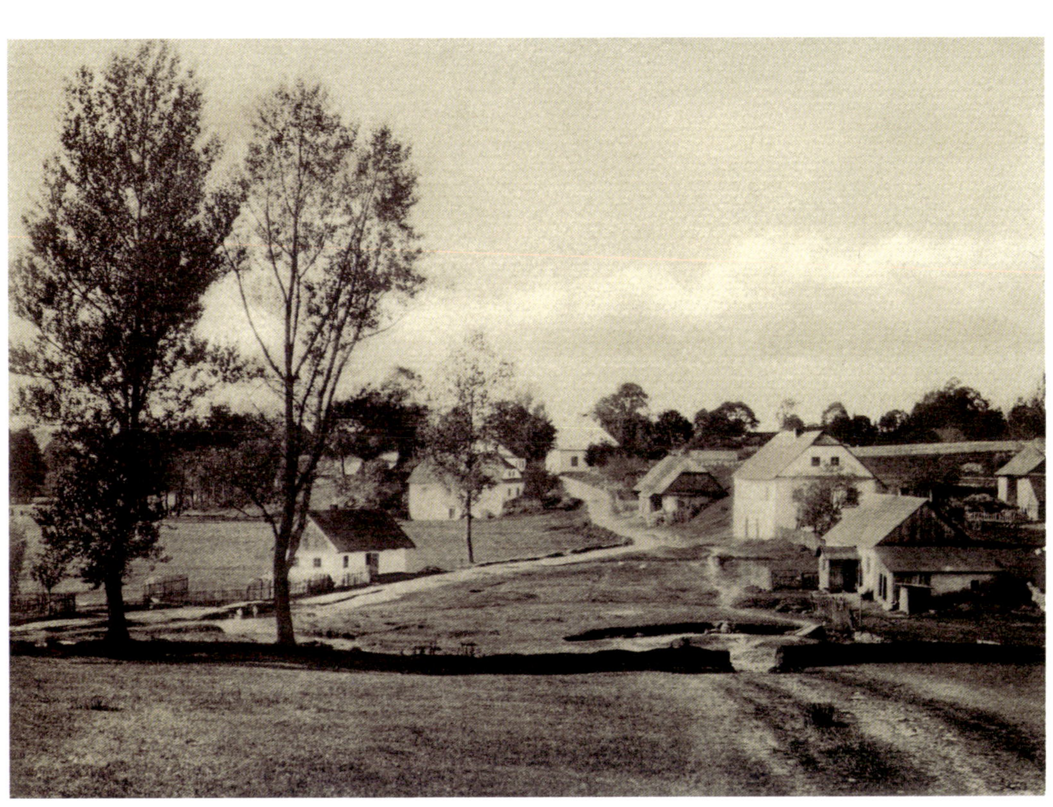

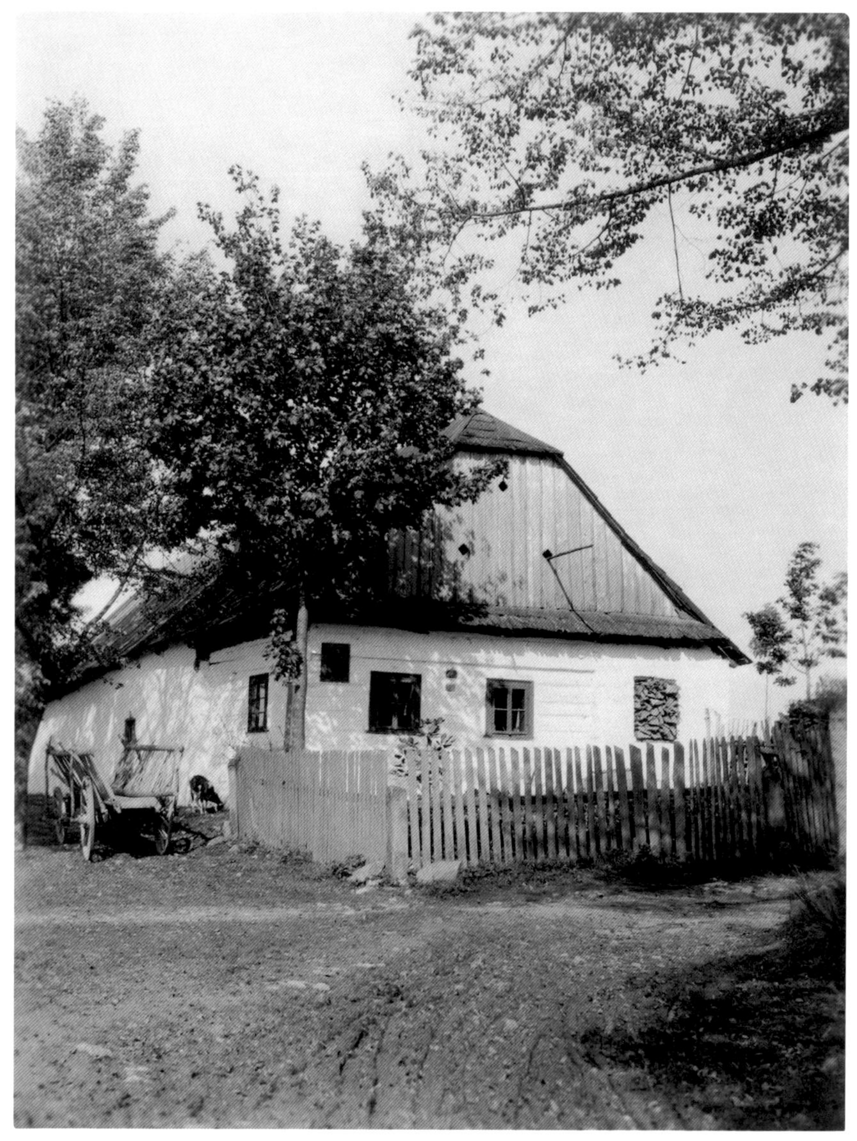

66 **Cottage in Vítanov / Chalupa ve Vítanově** 1911–14

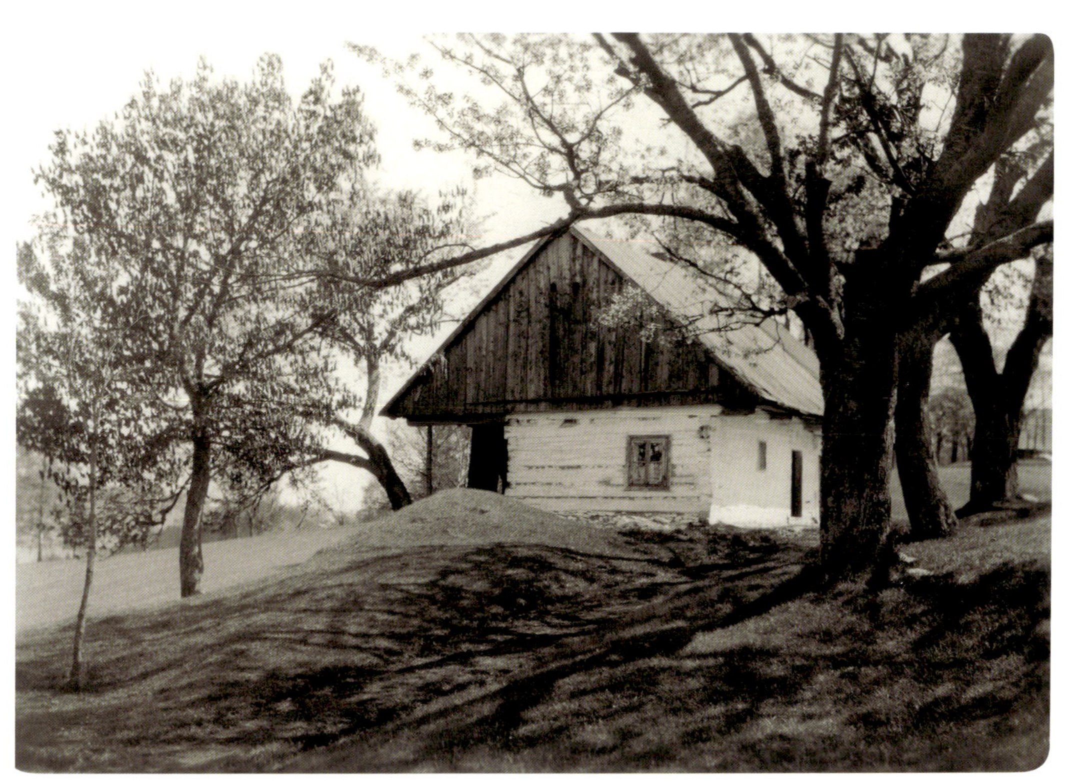

67 **Cottage / Chalupa** 1911–14

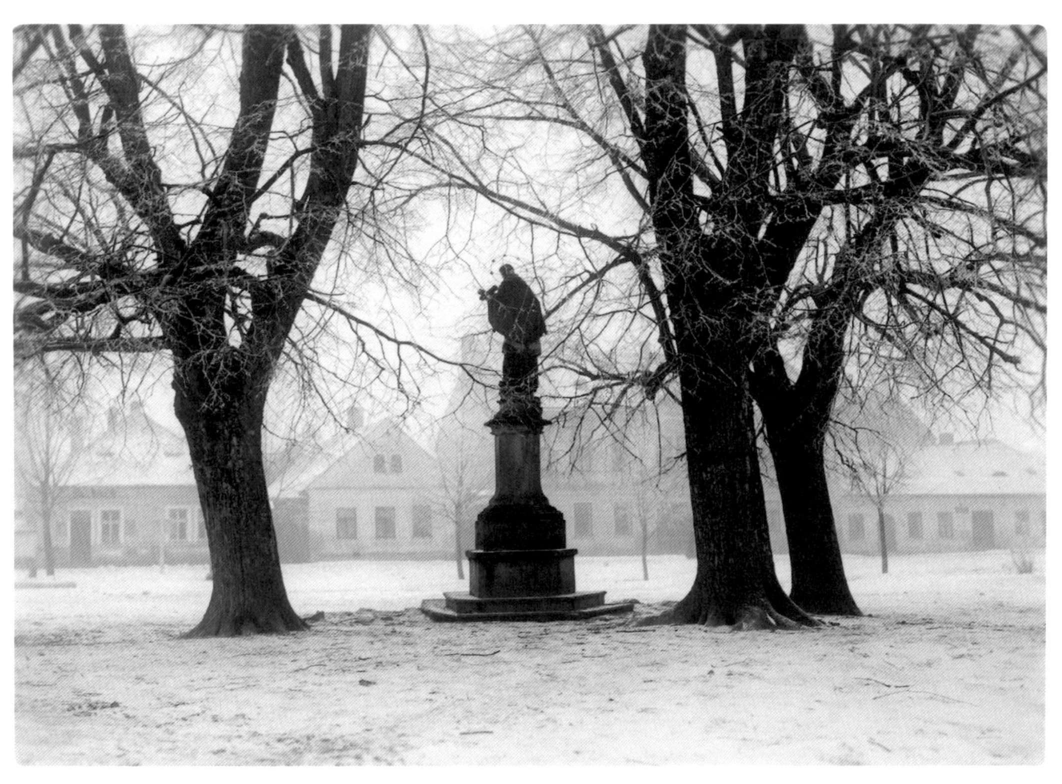

68 **Vojnův Městec** 1911–14

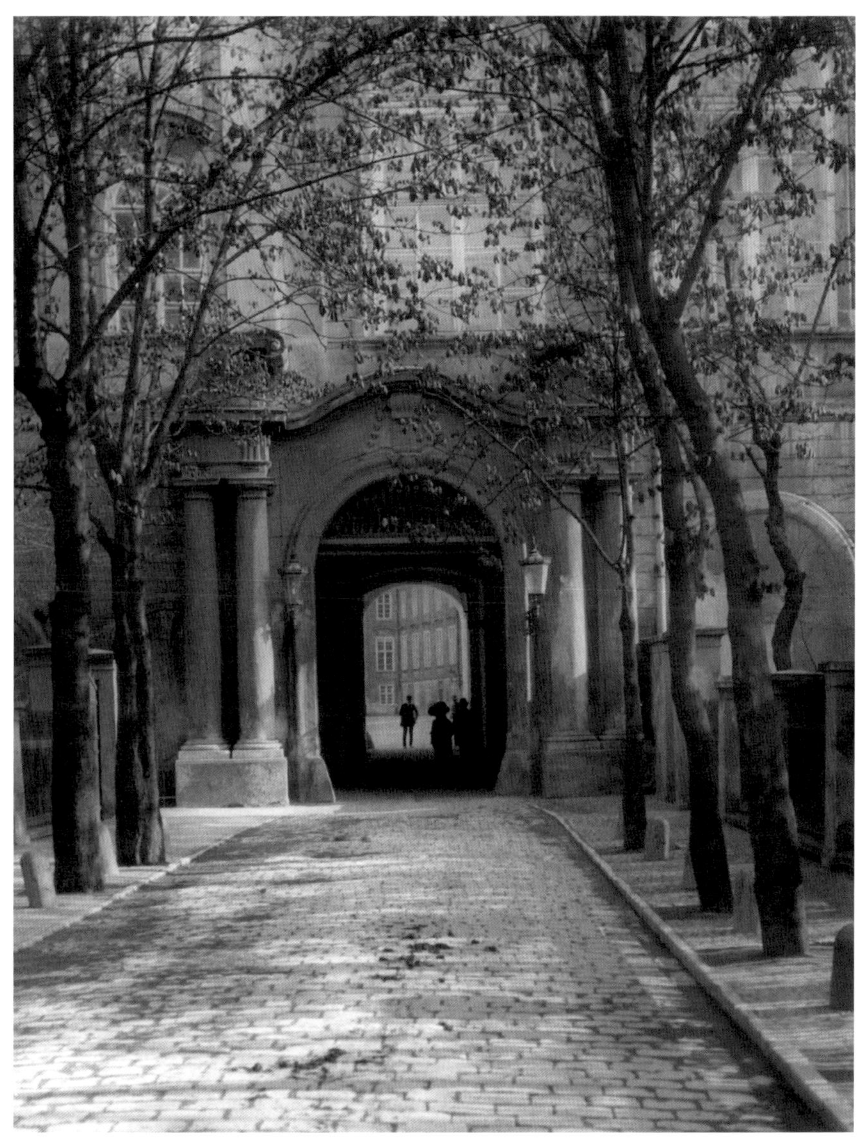

69 **Entrance to Prague Castle / Vstup do Pražského Hradu** 1912

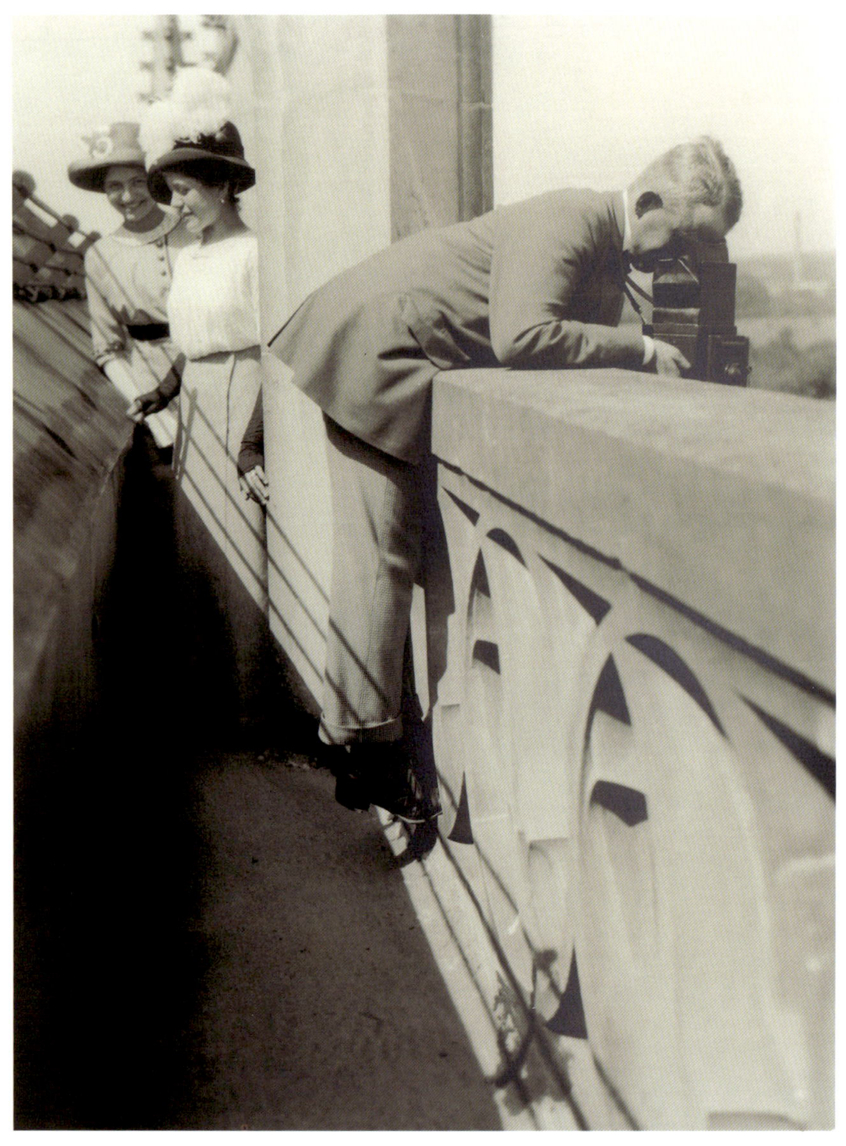

70 **Josef Binko taking photographs / Josef Binko fotografuje** 1912–13

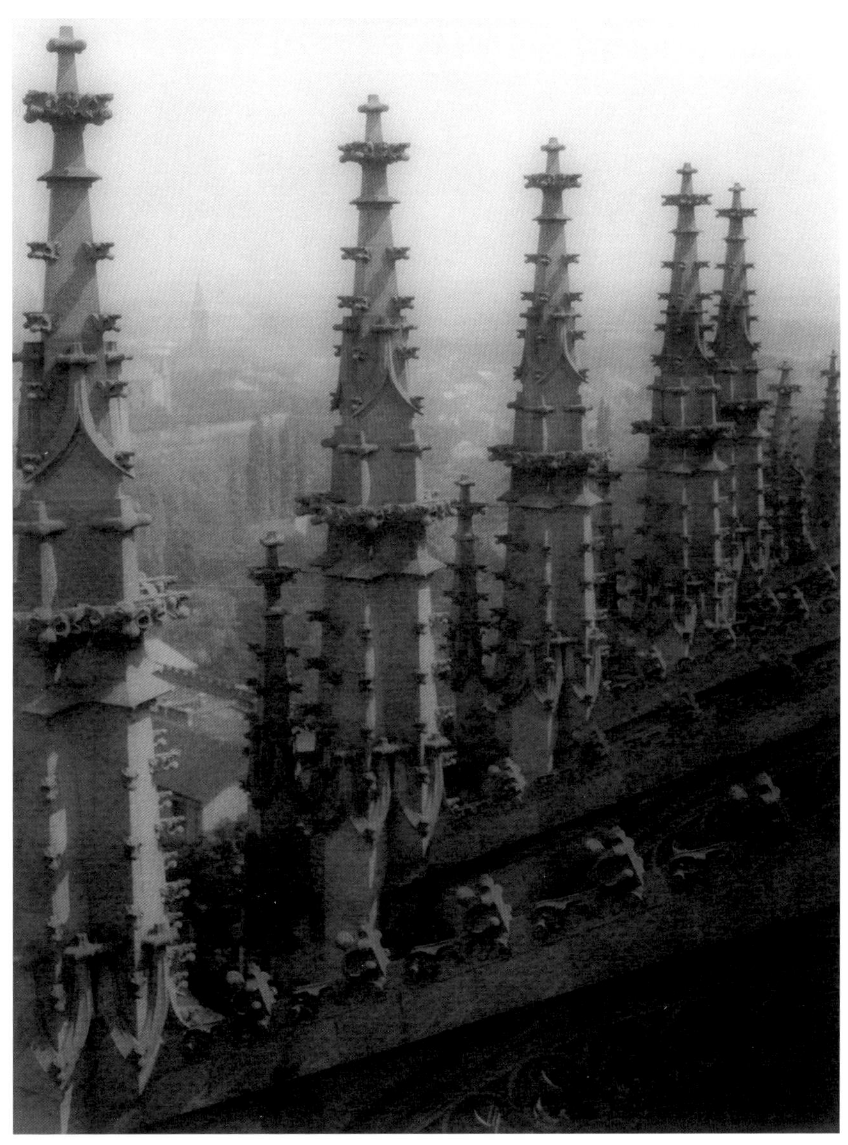

71 **Church of St. Barbara / Chrám sv. Barbory, Kutná Hora** 1912–13

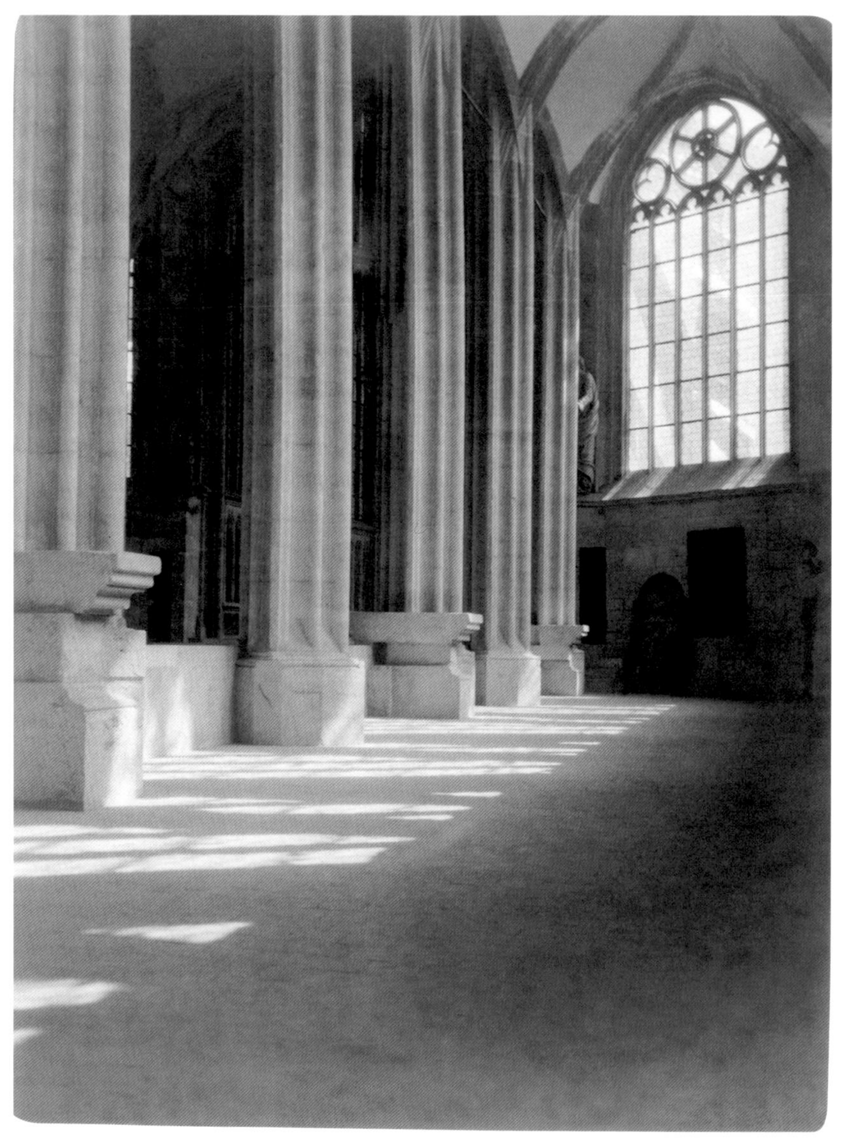

72 **Shadow and light in St. Barbara's / Světlo a stín v chrámu sv. Barbory, Kutná Hora** 1912–13

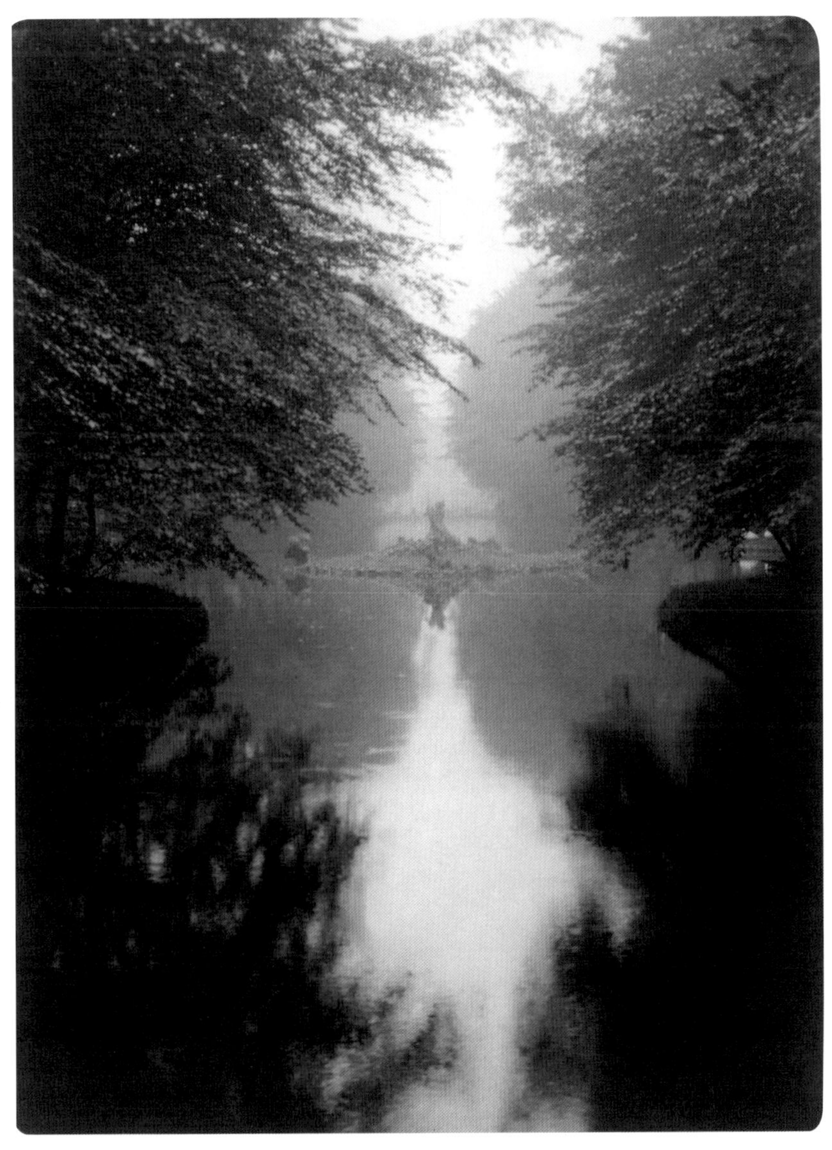

73 **Harmony in a park / Harmonie v parku** 1910–14

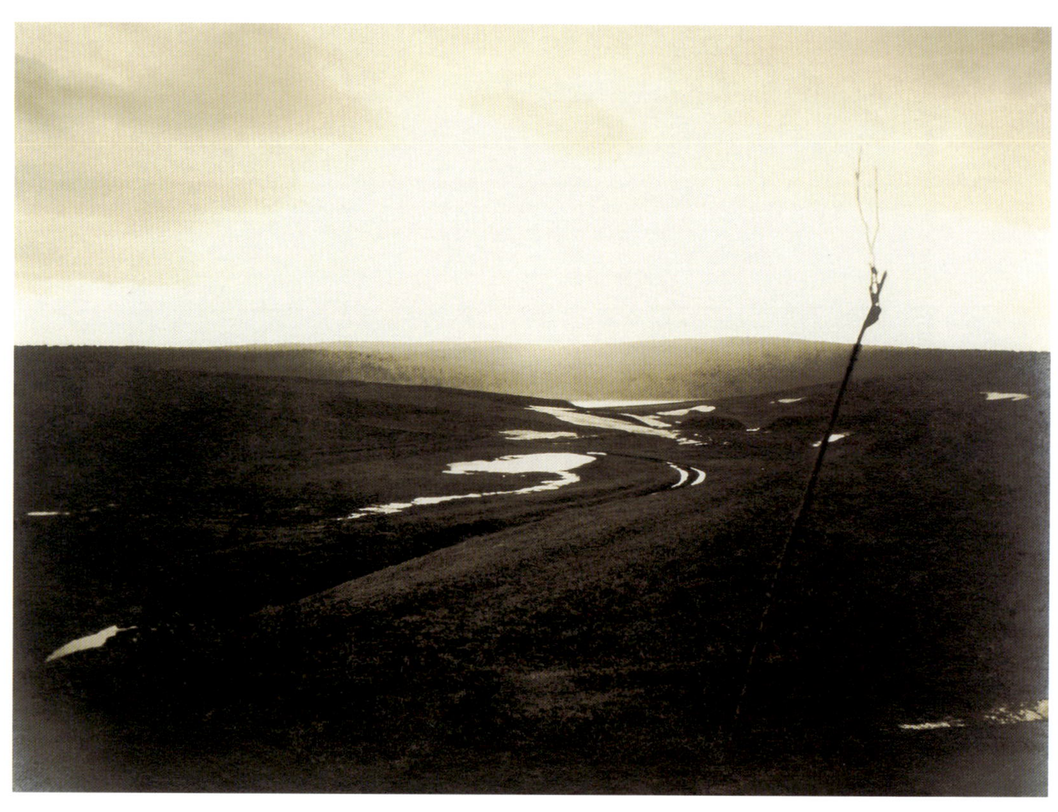

74 Early evening near Krucemburk / Podvečer u Krucemburku 1906–10

1851	On 4 August, in Krucemburk, Eduard Binko (born in Žďár nad Sázavou on 21 March 1831) married Julie Skřivanová (born in Krucemburk on 14 April 1832), daughter of the Krucemburk mayor and owner of the tannery.
	On 31 October, a son, Ladislav, was born to Eduard and Julie Binko in Krucemburk.
1869	On 21 March, Augustin Skřivan, founder of the tannery and mayor of Krucemburk from 1850–67, died in Krucemburk. The eighteen-year-old Ladislav Binko gradually took charge of the business. The modern and, at the time, unusual system of double-entry book-keeping was introduced here in this year by Antonín Skřivan, brother of Augustin.
1872	Ladislav Binko built the first steam boiler and steam engine in the tannery.
1876	On 8 August, in Kostelec nad Orlicí, Ladislav Binko married Emerenciana (also written Ema) Seykorová (born in Kostelec nad Orlicí on 20 December 1849), daughter of the co-owner of probably the largest leather factory in the Bohemian Lands.
1877	A new tannery was built in the Krucemburk leather factory; on 27 May, a son, Ladislav, was born to Ladislav and Emerenciana Binko in Krucemburk.
1879	On 7 March, a second son, Josef, was born to Ladislav and Emerenciana Binko, in Krucemburk.
1884	On 15 April, a third son, Dušan, was born to Ladislav and Emerenciana Binko, in Krucemburk.
1888	A new single-storey building was built on to the tannery with liming facilities on the ground floor and a tacking loft (drying room) upstairs. A second boiler room was also built.
1891–94	Josef Binko attended a Czech secondary school in Ječná ulice, Prague.
1894–97	Attended the Czechoslav School of Business (Českoslovanská obchodní akademie).
1895	The year of Josef Binko's earliest documented photographs.
1898	Began to work in the family factory, which was named after his great-grandfather Augustin Skřivan.
1901	After three years of practical experience, received his certificate of apprenticeship in the leather industry.
1901–03	With Josef Binko's involvement, the tannery was thoroughly modernized, including the introduction of a three-phase current drive.
1904–05	Completed his training in various tanneries with bulk-purchasing centers in countries from Germany to Croatia.
1904	Commissioned by Ladislav Binko, the sculptor Jan Štursa began work on the family tomb in Krucemburk. The Binko brothers, who met Štursa at the home of their uncle, Alois Jelínek, remained in touch with him for many years.
1906	On 8 February, Emerenciana Binková, wife of Ladislav and mother of Josef and his brothers, died in Prague; on 27 March, Julie Binková (née Skřivanová) grandmother of Josef Binko and his brothers, died in Krucemburk; on 2 August, Eduard Binko, Josef's grandfather and frequent sitter for his early photographs, died in Krucemburk.
1907	Became part-owner of the family business in Krucemburk, and began to live in Krucemburk. A large part of the production was sold by a purchasing company based in Vienna with a branch

in Pest. The company had its own warehouses and office in Stanislavov, Galicia. Binko became friends with the architect Josef Gočár (born 13 March 1880), whom the sculptor Štursa had introduced to the Binko family.

1907–08   Ladislav Binko built the "White Villa," whose exterior and interior were designed by Gočár.

1908–09   Josef Binko built the "Red Villa," which is Gočár's first independent design to be built. A darkroom was planned for the first floor (second floor, in America).

1909   On 13 September, made the earliest dated photograph, 9 × 12 cm, today in the Museum of Decorative Arts, Prague. This is a photograph of Krucemburk. Another series dates from 19 September, comprising photographs of the Krucemburk area, and another series from 25 September comprises 26 photographs of Prague. The switch over to film negatives was connected with his purchase of a Cupido camera, which was manufactured by Hüttig AG, Dresden. (It is now in the National Technical Museum, Prague).

1910   On 10 May, Josef Binko married Terezie Chladová (b. 18 October 1886). Her father was a brewer and mayor of Pardubice; one of her sisters, Antonie, married Dušan Binko; the other, Marie, married the architect Josef Gočár.

On 13–29 May, Binko and his wife traveled to Dalmatia for their honeymoon, by way of Vienna, Trieste, Miramare, Pula, Dubrovnik, and Spalato. Some of the 207 film negatives, 9 × 12 cm, which were taken on the trip, were used for a series of 103 tinted oil prints. They are now deposited in the National Technical Museum, Prague.

1911   Spring, Josef Binko adapted his darkroom, moving it to the ground floor of his villa. With considerable help from his brother Dušan he built what was then a unique vertical enlarger. Today it and other parts of the darkroom are part of the "Interkamera" permanent exhibition at the National Technical Museum, Prague. At the same time the brothers also built a projector for 12 × 12 cm slides.

On 18 February, in Krucemburk, a son, Ivan, was born to Josef and Terezie Binko.

On 20–21 September, Binko took a trip to Dresden. 39 film negatives of the journey, in 9 × 12 cm format, are deposited in the Museum of Decorative Arts in Prague. A set of contact prints is deposited in the National Technical Museum, Prague.

Twelve photographs, the first of Binko's in a magazine, were published in *Photographische Rundschau und Mitteilungen*, no. 17.

1912   From 29 June to 1 July, Josef Binko photographed Prague and members of the Sokol, a patriotic physical-education movement, at the Sixth All-Sokol Rally (27 negatives, 9 × 12 cm).

On 3–12 (?) September, Josef Binko went on his "German journey," visiting Nuremberg, Rothenburg, Ulm, Munich, Salzburg, and Königsee. Some of the 241 (9 × 12 cm) negatives from the trip were used to make a series of 43 oil prints; the series is called "Rothenburg 5. IX. 1912," and is deposited in the National Technical Museum, Prague. Eight photos were published in *Photographische Rundschau und Mitteilungen*, vol. 50 (1913), nos. 20, 21, and 23.

For his work, Josef Binko was given honorable mention by the Gevaert company.

1913   On 15–26 (?) August, Josef Binko and his friend Ludvík Boháček went on a "Second German Journey," traveling by way of Karlsbad (Karlovy Vary), Bohemia, to Bayreuth, Cassel, Eisenach, Gotha, Erfurth, Jena, and Sachfeld. 192 (9 × 12 cm) negatives of the trip are deposited in the Museum of Decorative Arts in Prague.

1914   On 21 May, a series of photographs of the painter František Kaván and his cottage was made,
        as well as many bromoil prints of the Bohemian-Moravian Uplands. After the assassination of
        Archduke Franz Ferdinand in Sarajevo, Austro-Hungary declared war on Serbia on 28 July, thus
        starting the First World War.

1917   On 13 November, in Krucemburk, a second son, Jan, was born to Josef and Terezie Binko.

1918   The Czechoslovak Republic was proclaimed on 28 October 1918. Josef Binko was invited to sit
        on the leather-manufacture committee at the Central Association of Czechoslovak Industry.

1919   On 22 January, in Krucemburk, a daughter, Věra, was born to Josef and Terezie Binko.

1920   Josef Binko became Deputy Chairman of the Leather Industry Association (and would remain
        in the post till the beginning of the German Occupation in March 1939).

1920–21 The large-scale adaptation, modernization, and expansion of the factory took place.

1923   On 31 May, in Krucemburk, Ladislav Binko, father of Josef and his brothers, died.

1923–24 Additional modernization and expansion of the leather factory took place, including the
        building of warehouses. The aim was to achieve a division in the production of vegetable
        tanning and chrome tanning, in other words to rationalize production and increase efficiency.
        A new sewage treatment plant was also built.

1925   Josef Binko apparently bought a Leica I, model A, for 35mm film, which has unfortunately gone
        missing.

1928   Growing exports led to the establishing of storehouses for the wares of Binko's factory in ten
        countries. The largest markets were in Northern Italy, Erfurth and Frankfurt for Germany, and in
        Sofia for Bulgaria and Turkey.

1932   The company, called "Koželužna Augustin Skřivan dědicové," employed 120 workers.

1935   Josef Binko bought a Leica IIIa for 35mm film, which is now the property of Jan Binko.

1938   Ivan Binko, Josef's son, began working at the Baťa Research Institute, Zlín, which he would
        eventually run.

1939   On 15 March, the German occupation of Bohemia and Moravia began.

1941   On 31 December, Ladislav Binko (the elder brother) left the company and Josef's son Jan,
        became a partner, and was trained in leather chemistry in Lyon (he was awarded the Gold Medal
        of the Syndicate of French Industry [*sic*] for his dissertation).

1942   In December, Josef Binko put together photo albums as Christmas presents for his family.

1945   On 2 December, a son, Jan, was born to Jan Binko, the son of Josef and Terezie Binko.
        On 9 May, the last day of the war in Europe, the towns of Krucemburk and Ždírec were bombed.
        "Troops of [Soviet] General Malinovsky on the first night took all the leather being made in one
        part of the factory and also the belts from the machines. Only after it was possible to establish
        normal contact with the Russian Army, could we provide all the ready leather [...] at the local
        official price, even though according to statements by Russian officers prices of leather in Russia
        were eight times higher." See Binko, "Paměti," p. 15.
        On 8 November, in a letter to the Chamber of Commerce, Prague, Josef Binko, regarding his
        acceptance of the job of Deputy Director of the leather department, lists his new (or restored)
        jobs: Deputy Chairman of the Society for the Stimulation of the Leather Industry; member of
        the Board of the State Tanning School, Hradec Králové; member of the Board of the Research

	Institute of the Tanning Industry at the Brno Polytechnic; member of the Board of the Society of Leather Chemists; and member of the Leather Experts Board at the Ministry of Industry.
1948	On 25 February, the Communist Party of Czechoslovakia seized power.
	On 28 April, the tannery was nationalized. Binko recalled in his memoirs: "In 1948, when it was nationalized, the factory was in full operation. There were supplies of raw materials to last more than six months, semi-finished goods in all stages of production, and even more than ten wagons of raw calf hide on the way from India, already paid for – and no debts with the banks or suppliers." Binko was permitted to remain in the company as a "factory expert." See Binko, "Paměti."
1949	In January, Josef Binko retired.
1953	In January, the brothers and their families were forced to move out of the White Villa and the Old House (sic).
1954	On 9 November, Dušan Binko, Josef's younger brother, died.
1960	On 11 February, Josef Binko died in the town of Vysoké Mýto.
	On 21 September, the wife of Ivan Binko sent Josef Binko's darkroom equipment and part of his archive (not including the negatives) from Krucemburk to the National Technical Museum in Prague.
1961	Binko's photographs were included in the "History of Photography I" exhibition mounted by Rudolf Skopec in Brno, which was the first time his work was exhibited in this country.
1963	On 24 December, Ladislav Binko, the eldest of the three brothers, died.
1975	Rudolf Skopec donated a set of about 2,000 of Binko's film negatives to the Museum of Decorative Arts in Prague.

Životopisná data

1851	4. 8. se v Krucemburku oženil Eduard Binko, narozený 21. 3. 1831 ve Žďáru nad Sázavou, s Julií Skřivanovou, dcerou krucemburského purkmistra a majitele koželužské manufaktury, narozenou 14. 4. 1832 v Krucemburku.
1851	31. 10. se v Krucemburku Eduardu a Julii Binkovým narodil syn Ladislav.
1869	21. 3. v Krucemburku zemřel Augustin Skřivan, zakladatel koželužské manufaktury, v letech 1850–1867 krucemburský primátor. Osmnáctiletý Ladislav Binko se postupně ujal vedení podniku; moderní a tehdy neobvyklé podvojné účetnictví zde v témže roce zavedl Antonín Skřivan, bratr Augustina Skřivana.
1872	Ladislav Binko postavil v koželužně první parní stroj a parní kotel.
1876	8. 8. se v Kostelci nad Orlicí oženil Ladislav Binko s Emerencianou (řečenou Emou) Seykorovou, narozenou 20. 12. 1849 v Kostelci nad Orlicí, dcerou spolumajitele tehdy patrně největší továrny na kůže v českých zemích.
1877	V krucemburské koželužně byla postavena nová tříslovna.
1877	27. 5. se v Krucemburku Ladislavu a Emercianě Binkovým narodil první syn – Ladislav.
1879	7. 3. se v Krucemburku Ladislavu a Emercianě Binkovým narodil druhý syn – Josef.
1884	15. 4. se v Krucemburku Ladislavu a Emercianě Binkovým narodil třetí syn – Dušan.
1888	Ke koželužně byla přistavena nová jednopatrová budova v přízemí s luhárnou a v patře se sušárnou. Byla postavena též druhá kotelna.
1891–94	Josef Binko studoval na c. k. České reálce v Ječné ulici v Praze.
1895	Z tohoto roku jsou doloženy nejstarší fotografické snímky Josefa Binka.
1894–97	Josef Binko studoval na Českoslovanské obchodní akademii (absolutorium získal 15. 7. 1897).
1898	Josef Binko zahájil praxi v rodinné továrně „Aug. Skřivana dědic Továrna na kůže" v Krucemburku.
1901	Josef Binko získal po tříleté praxi koželužský Výuční list.
1901–03	Byla provedena velká modernizace koželužny, již za účasti Josefa Binka. V závodě byl mj. zaveden pohon střídavým třífázovým proudem.
1904 –05	Josef Binko absolvoval praxi v cizích koželužnách se sběrnami od Německa po Chorvatsko.
1904	Sochař Jan Štursa zahájil na objednávku Ladislava Binka práci na rodinné hrobce v Krucemburku. Bratři Binkové, kteří Štursu poznali u svého strýce Aloise Jelínka, udržovali se Štursou mnohaleté styky.
1906	8. 2. zemřela v Praze Emerenciana Binková, manželka Ladislava Binka, matka Josefa Binka.
1906	27. 3. v Krucemburku zemřela Julie Binková, rozená Skřivanová, babička Josefa Binka.
1906	2. 8. v Krucemburku zemřel Eduard Binko, dědeček Josefa Binka, častý model jeho raných snímků.
1907	Josef Binko získal v rodinné továrně v Krucemburku vlastnický podíl a začal trvale žít v Krucemburku. Velká část výroby továrny na usně se prodávala prostřednictvím vídeňské odběratelské firmy s filiálkou v Pešti. Vlastní sklady a zastoupení měla firma v Haliči ve Stanislavově.
1907	Počátek přátelství mezi Josefem Binkem a Josefem Gočárem (* 13. 3. 1880), kterého rodina Binků poznala prostřednictvím Jana Štursy.

1907–08   Ladislav Binko stavěl tzv. Bílou vilu, kde úpravu fasád, průčelí a interiérů navrhl Josef Gočár.

1908–09   Josef Binko stavěl tzv. Červenou vilu, která je prvním samostatným dílem Josefa Gočára.
           Do prvního patra byla projektována fotokomora.

1909   13. 9. jsou datovány nejstarší filmové negativy formátu 9 × 12 cm, uložené dnes v UPM. Jedná
           se o záběry Krucemburku. Z 19. 9. pochází další série z okolí Krucemburku, z 25. 9. pak zábry z Prahy (26 kusů). Přechod na filmové negativy souvisel s koupí nového fotopřístroje značky
           Cupido firmy Hüttig AG Dresden (dnes uloženém v NTM).

1910   10. 5. se Josef Binko oženil s Terezií Chladovou, dcerou sládka a primátora Pardubic, narozenou
           18. 10. 1886. Její sestra Antonie si vzala Dušana Binka, sestra Marie architekta Josefa Gočára.

1910   13.–29. 5. podnikli Josef Binko s chotí svatební cestu do Dalmácie na trase Vídeň, Terst,
           Miramare, Pula, Dubrovník, Spalato. Z cesty se v UPM dochovalo 207 filmových negativů
           9 × 12 cm, z nichž vznikl cyklus 103 tónovaných olejotisků, uložených dnes v NTM.

1911   Na jaře Josef Binko adaptoval fotokomoru a situoval ji do přízemí své vily. S podstatnou pomocí bratra Dušana postavil na svou dobu unikátní vertikální zvětšovací přístroj, který je dnes spolu s částí komory součástí stále expozice Interkamera v NTM. Současně postavili také projekční
           přístroj pro diapozitivy formátu 12 × 12 cm.

1911   18. 2. se v Krucemburku Josefu a Terezii Binkovým narodil syn Ivan.

1911   20.–21. 9. podnikl Josef Binko výlet do Drážďan, z něhož se v UPM zachovalo 39 filmových negativů formátu 9 × 12 cm. Soubor kontaktních kopií je uložen v NTM.

1911   První časopisecká publikace snímků Josefa Binka (v Photographische Rundschau und
           Mitteilungen, č. 17). Publikováno bylo dvanáct snímků.

1912   29. 6. – 1. 7. fotografoval Josef Binko atmosféru Prahy a průvod Sokolů při VI. všesokolském sletu (27 negativů formátu 9 × 12 cm).

1912   3.–12.(?) 9. podnikl Josef Binko „Německou cestu" na trase Norimberk, Rothenburg, Ulm,
           Mnichov, Salzburg, Königsee. Z cesty se v UPM dochovalo 241 negativů formátu 9 × 12 cm,
           z nichž vznikl cyklus 43 olejotisků s názvem „Rothenburg 5. 9. 1912", uložený v NTM. Osm
           snímků bylo postupně publikováno v časopisu Photographische Rundschau und Mitteilungen
           (1913, č. 20, 21, 23).

1912   Josef Binko získal čestné uznání od firmy Gevaert za své práce.

1913   15.–26.(?) 8. Josef Binko podnikl s přítelem Ludvíkem Boháčkem „Druhou německou cestu" na
           trase Karlovy Vary, Bayreuth, Cassel, Eisenach, Gotha, Erfurt, Jena, Sachfeld. Z cesty se v UPM
           dochovalo 192 negativů formátu 9 × 12 cm.

1914   21. 5. vznikl fotografický cyklus s malířem Františkem Kavánem a jeho chalupou. V této době
           vznikají též četné bromolejotisky s náměty z Českomoravské vysočiny.

1917   13. 11. se v Krucemburku Josefu a Terezii Binkovým narodil druhý syn Jan.

1918   22. 1. se v Krucemburku Josefu a Terezii Binkovým narodila dcera Věra (později provdaná
           Nebesářová).

1918   Josef Binko se stal členem výboru Sekce průmyslu koželužského při Ústředním svazu československého průmyslu.

1920   Josef Binko se stal místopředsedou Svazu průmyslu koželužského. Ve funkci setrval až do roku
           1939.

1920–21   Velké stavební adaptace, modernizace a rozšíření továrny.

1923 31. 5. v Krucemburku zemřel Ladislav Binko, otec Josefa Binka.

1923–24 Další modernizace a rozšiřování továrny, včetně postavení skladišť. Cílem bylo dosáhnout rozdělení výroby tříslových a chromových kůží, tedy i zefektivnění a racionalizace výroby. Byla postavena i nová čisticí stanice odpadních vod.

1925 Josef Binko údajně zakoupil fotopřístroj na kinofilm Leica I, model A. Přístroj se nedochoval.

1928 Rostoucí export vedl ke zřízení skladů vlastního zboží v deseti zemích. Největší odbyt byl v severní Itálii, v Erfurtu a Frankfurtu pro Německo a v Sofii pro Bulharsko a Turecko.

1935 Josef Binko zakoupil fotopřístroj na kinofilm Leica IIIa, dodnes dochovaný.

1932 Koželužna „Augustin Skřivan dědicové“ zaměstnávala 120 dělníků.

1938 Syn Ivan nastoupil do Baťova výzkumného ústavu ve Zlíně, kde se posléze stal jeho vedoucím.

1941 31. 12. z firmy vystoupil starší bratr Ladislav Binko a společníkem se stal syn ing. Jan Binko, který vystudoval koželužskou chemii v Lyonu (za disertaci získal zlatou medaili Syndikátu francouzského průmyslu).

1942 V prosinci připravil Josef Binko rodině jako dárky k Vánocům alba fotografií.

1945 2. 12. se ing. Janu Binkovi, synu Josefa Binka, narodil syn Jan.

1945 9. 5. byly Krucemburk a Ždírec v závěru druhé světové války bombardovány. „Vojska generála Malinovského vybrala hned první noc z jednoho oddělení všechny kůže ve výrobě, a i řemeny se strojů, a teprve když bylo možno navázat normální styky s ruskou armádou, dodali jsme všechny hotové kůže... za zdejší úřední ceny, ačkoliv dle výpovědí ruských důstojníků byly ceny kůží v Rusku osmkrát vyšší .“ (viz Paměti..., s. 15)

1945 Josef Binko 8. 11. v dopisu Obchodní a živnostenské komoře v Praze o přijetí funkce náměstka generálního ředitele pro obor koženělný vypočítává své nové (nebo obnovené) funkce: místopředseda Spolku pro povzbuzení koželužského průmyslu, člen Kuratoria Státní školy koželužské v Hradci Králové, člen Kuratoria Výzkumného ústavu pro koželužský průmysl při vysoké škole technické v Brně, člen předsednictva Spolku koželužských chemiků, člen Znalců koželužských při Ministerstvu průmyslu.

1948 28. 4. byla koželužna znárodněna. Josef Binko napsal v Pamětech...: „V roce 1948 při znárodnění byla továrna v plném chodu. Surovin byly zásoby na více než šest měsíců, polotovaru v práci ve všech stadiích výroby, a dokonce přes 10 vagonů surových kipsů na cestě z Indie, předem zaplacených – a žádné dluhy bankám ani dodavatelům.“ Josef Binko dostal v továrně funkci „podnikového experta“.

1949 V lednu odešel Josef Binko do důchodu.

1953 V lednu došlo k nucenému vystěhování rodin bratrů Binkových z Bílé vily a Starého domu.

1954 9. 11. zemřel Dušan Binko.

1960 11. 2. zemřel ve Vysokém Mýtě Josef Binko.

1960 21. 9. bylo manželkou Ivana Binka převezeno z Krucemburku do NTM zařízení temné komory Josefa Binka a část archivu (bez negativů).

1961 V Brně na výstavě Dějiny fotografie I, kterou připravil Rudolf Skopec, byly vystaveny snímky Josefa Binka. Šlo o vůbec první výstavní prezentaci Binkových fotografií v českých zemích.

1963 24. 12. zemřel Ladislav Binko.

1975 Rudolf Skopec věnoval UPM soubor kolem dvou tisíc Binkových filmových negativů.

Primary Sources / Prameny

Josef Binko: *Paměti koželužny v Krucemburku*, Krucemburk 1956, MS, 15 pp. / rukopis o patnácti stranách.
Correspondence and documents in the family archives of Jan Binko, Eva Kolářová, Simona Binková, Věra (née Binková) Nebesářová. / Korespondence a archiválie v rodinách ing. Jana Binka, Evy Kolářové, dr. Simony Binkové a Věry Nebesářové.

Published photographs by Josef Binko / Přehled publikovaných snímků Josefa Binka

(The number of photographs is given in brackets. / V závorce počet publikovaných snímků.)

Photographische Rundschau und Mitteilungen 48, 1911, č. 17 (12).
Die Photographische Kunst im Jahre, 1911, s. 81, 86, 88, 93, 94 (5).
Photographische Rundschau und Mitteilungen 50, 1913, č. 20 (3).
Photographische Rundschau und Mitteilungen 50, 1913, č. 21 (1).
Photographische Rundschau und Mitteilungen 50, 1913, č. 23 (4).
Die Photographische Kunst im Jahre, 1913, s. 114, 115, 116 (3).
Photographische Rundschau und Mitteilungen 51, 1914, č. 22 (1).
Photographische Rundschau und Mitteilungen 51, 1914, č. 23 (1).

Literature / Literatura

(The number of photographs is given in brackets. / V závorce počet publikovaných snímků.)

Scheufler, Pavel: *Fotografické album Čech 1839–1914*, Praha, Odeon 1989 (1).
Encyklopedie českých a slovenských fotografů, Praha, ASCO 1993 (1).
Birgus, Vladimír & Scheufler, Pavel: *Fotografie v českých zemích 1839–1999*, Praha, Grada Publishing 1999 (1).
Scheufler, Pavel: Josef Binko – osobní data známa, *Advanced* 4, 1999, č. 6, s. 22–23 (4).
Tvář naší země – krajina domova, Lomnice nad Popelkou, Jaroslav Bárta – Studio JB 2001 (1).
Scheufler, Pavel: *Galerie c. k. fotografů*, Praha, Grada Publishing 2001 (4).
Scheufler, Pavel: Pražský hrad kamerou Josefa Binka, *Pražský hrad / Prague Castle* 8, 2002, č. 2, s. 14–17 (5).

Exhibitions / Fotografie Josefa Binka na výstavách

Dějiny fotografie II, Dům umění města Brna, listopad 1961, conceived and curated by / autor
Rudolf Skopec (catalog / katalog).
Fotografie v Čechách 1839–1914, Galerie hl. m. Prahy, zámek Trója – konírna, 1. 6. – 1. 7. 1990,
conceived and curated by / autor Pavel Scheufler (catalog / katalog).
Prague Art Nouveau. Métamorphoses d'un style, Palais des Beaux-Arts Bruxeles, říjen 1998 –
leden 1999, The "Photography" section prepared by / autor části „Fotografie" Jan Mlčoch.
Český piktorialismus 1895–1928, České centrum fotografie, Praha, 7. 12. 1999 – 14. 1. 2000,
conceived and curated by / autoři Jan Mlčoch & Pavel Scheufler (catalog / katalog).
Tvář naší země – krajina domova, Pražský hrad, Tereziánské křídlo, 26. 1. – 11. 3. 2001.
Česká fotografie 1840–1950. Příběh moderního média, Galerie Rudolfinum, Praha,
15. 1. – 28. 3. 2004, conceived and curated by / autor Jaroslav Anděl, odborná spolupráce
Pavel Scheufler.
Česká fotografie dvacátého století, Uměleckoprůmyslové museum, Praha, 23. 6. – 25. 9. 2005,
conceived and curated by / autoři Vladimír Birgus & Jan Mlčoch.

Abreviations / Použité zkratky

NTM – Národní technické muzeum v Praze
UPM – Uměleckoprůmyslové museum v Praze

List of Published Photographs

Wherever the titles are Binko's own, they are given in quotation marks. The titles of the other photos are only for orientation. Similarly, the dating is based on educated guesses (with the exception of the precisely dated travel photos from 1910–13). Photographs marked NTM are deposited in the collections of the National Technical Museum in Prague. All others come from a private collection.

15   "The Sea at Pula," 1910, from the *Dalmatian Honeymoon* series, NTM, bromoil print

16   "Between Ships," Trieste, 1910, from the *Dalmatian Honeymoon* series, NTM, bromoil print

17   "Canal Grande II," Trieste, 1910, from the *Dalmatian Honeymoon* series, NTM, bromoil print

18   "The Quay San Carlo," Trieste, 1910, from the *Dalmatian Honeymoon* series, NTM, bromoil print

19   "The Quay," Trieste, 1910, from the *Dalmatian Honeymoon* series, NTM, bromoil print

20   Binko's wife aboard the *Baron Gautsch*, 1910, from the *Dalmatian Honeymoon* series, NTM, bromoil print

21   "The *Baron Gautsch*," Trieste, 1910, from the *Dalmatian Honeymoon* series, NTM, bromoil print

22   "Kunsthistorisches Museum," Vienna, 1910, from the *Dalmatian Honeymoon* series, NTM, bromoil print

23   "San Giacomo, Ruins," 1910, from the *Dalmatian Honeymoon* series, bromoil print

24   "Diocletian's Palace, Spalato," Split, 1910, from the *Dalmatian Honeymoon* series, NTM, bromoil print

25   "Excursion to Lopud Island, the road to Aquae II," 1910, from the *Dalmatian Honeymoon* series, NTM, bromoil print

26   Binko's wife by some rosebushes, Lokrum, 1910, from the *Dalmatian Honeymoon* series, bromoil print

27   Chapel of St. Saviour, Dubrovnik, 1910, from the *Dalmatian Honeymoon* series, NTM, bromoil print

28   "A View from a Window I," Dubrovnik, 1910, from the *Dalmatian Honeymoon* series, NTM, bromoil print

29   "Roofs III," Dubrovnik, 1910, from the *Dalmatian Honeymoon* series, NTM, bromoil print

30   "Rothenburg with the Burgtor II," 5 September 1912, NTM, bromoil print

31   Dresden, 1912, NTM, bromoil print

32   "Herterichsbrunnen," Rothenburg, 5 September 1912, NTM, bromoil print

33   "Plönlein," Rothenburg, 5 September 1912, NTM, bromoil print

34   Platnéřská ulice (Platnergasse), Prague, 1910–14, oil-pigment print

35   "Red Sky in the Morning; the bastion below Prague Castle," 1906–14, NTM, gum bichromate print

36   Queen Anne's Summerhouse (Belvedere), Prague, 1906–20, NTM, gelatin silver print

37   Czernin Palais, Prague, 1906–20, NTM, gelatin silver print

38   Charles Bridge from Kampa, Prague, 1906–14, oil-pigment print

39   Francis I Bridge at the National Theatre, Prague, 1906–14, oil-pigment print

40   The former Mill pond, Krucemburk, undated, gelatin silver print, toned

41   The road from Krucemburk to Hluboká, 1910–14, bromoil print

42   The way to Škrdlovice (?) , 1910–14, bromoil print

43   "Road in Winter," 1909–11, gum bichromate print (published in a different cropped version in 1911)

44   Krucemburk in winter from the road to Hluboká, 1910–14, bromoil print

45   In the garden of the villa, 1911–12, gelatin silver print

46   In the garden of the villa, 1911–12, gelatin silver print

47   "In the Woods," 1909–11, bromoil print (published as a gum bichromate print in 1911)

48   "Dusk on the Pond," 1909–11, NTM, gum bichromate print (published in 1911)

49   Birch trees in the woods, 1909–12, NTM, bromoil print

50   In the pasture, 1906–11, NTM, gum bichromate print

51   "Goats (Dusk), near Nové Město, Moravia," 1906–11, NTM, gum bichromate print

52   The Řeka pond, 1906–11, NTM, gum bichromate print (shot with a telephoto lens)

53   Clouds in the Highlands, 1906–12, gum bichromate print

54   "Morning Mood," 1909–11, NTM, gum bichromate print (published in 1911)

55   In the Highlands, 1909–12, gum bichromate print

56–57 Cloud study, 1910–14, bromoil print

58   "Birch Trees in Jasná Pole," 1910–14, bromoil print

59   Vítanov, 1911–14, bromoil print

60   "Vítanov, the building opposite Kaván's house," 1911–14, bromoil print

61   Flour mill in Vítanov, 1911–14, bromoil print

62   Cottage near Holetín, 1911–14, bromoil print

63   Cottage in Kouty near Hlinsko, 1911–14, bromoil print

64–65 "Near Vítanov," 1911–14, bromoil print

66   Cottage in Vítanov (?), 1911–14, gelatin silver print

67   Cottage, unidentified location, 1911–14, gelatin silver print

68   "Vojnův Městec, town square with statue and linden trees," 1911–14, gelatin silver print

69   Entrance to Prague Castle from Prašný most, 1912, bromoil print

70   Josef Binko taking photographs on the roof of St. Barbara's, Kutná Hora (probably photographed
      by Dušan Binko, whose wife and her sister, the wife of Josef Binko, are also in the photograph),
      1912–13, gelatin silver print

71   Church of St. Barbara, Kutná Hora, 1912–13, bromoil print

72   Shadow and light in St. Barbara's, Kutná Hora, 1912–13, bromoil print

73   Harmony of form and light in a park, 1910–14

74   Early evening near Krucemburk, looking towards the Řeka pond, and Bílé potoky, 1906–10

Soupis publikovaných fotografií

Názvy snímků jsou orientační. V případě zjištěných autorských názvů jsou názvy uvedeny
v uvozovkách. Také datování je orientační (s výjimkou přesně datovatelných snímků z cest z let
1910–1913). Snímky označené NTM jsou uloženy ve sbírkách Národního technického muzea v Praze, ostatní pocházejí ze soukromé sbírky.

s. 2   Portrét Josefa Binka
s. 7   Josef Binko se svou chotí v roce 1910 (foto: Dušan Binko/?/)
s. 7   Kresba z náčrtníku z doby studií
s. 8   Pohled na Krucemburk s koželužnou v popředí, kolem 1895
s. 8   Pohled na Krucemburk s Červenou a Bílou vilou v popředí, asi 1910
s. 12   Červená vila, dům Josefa Binka, stavba Josefa Gočára, 1. 1. 1910
s. 12   Zadní strana pohlednice Josefa Binka Josefu Gočárovi; záběr byl nazván „domeček na prkénku".
s. 13   Jedna z mnoha variant portrétu architekta Josefa Gočára před kachlovými kamny v Červené vile
s. 17   Nákres půdorysu a zařízení hlavní stěny temné komory Josefa Binka (zpracoval ing. Jan Binko)
s. 20   Kontaktní kopie snímku manželky na palubě parníku Baron Gautsch, z něhož byl vytvořen
bromolejotisk otištěný zde v obrazové části

1   Autoportrét s rodinou, 1891–92 (v horní řadě zleva: Josef Binko – fotograf, Ladislav Binko –
bratr, „pan Losenický", uprostřed zleva: Emerenciana (Ema) Binková – matka, Juliana (Julie)
Binková – babička, v dolní řadě: Ladislav Binko – otec, Dušan Binko – bratr, Eduard Binko –
dědeček)
2   Portrét neznámé (romské/?/) dívky, kolem 1898
3   Žena s hráběmi, s úpravou pozitivu „do ztracena", kolem 1891, celloidinový papír
4   Ludvík Boháček, kolem 1907, brom
5   Josef Chlad, tchán a primátor Pardubic, 1909–1910, tónovaný slaný papír (jako pigment
publikováno 1911)
6   Eduard Binko, kolem 1900, brom
7   Ladislav Binko, kolem 1900, gumotisk
8   Ludvík Boháček, kolem 1911, pigment
9   Josef Gočár, 1909–10, gumotisk
10   Přístav na nezjištěném místě, kolem 1898, bílkový papír
11   Industrializace u řeky, nezjištěné místo, kolem 1900, gumotisk
12   U moře, kolem 1900, gumotisk
13   Nálada u moře, kolem 1904, brom
14   Moře poblíž Miramare, 1910, z cyklu Svatební cesta do Dalmácie, NTM, bromolejotisk
15   „Moře u Puly", 1910, z cyklu Svatební cesta do Dalmácie, NTM, bromolejotisk
16   „Mezi loděmi", Terst, 1910, z cyklu Svatební cesta do Dalmácie, NTM, bromolejotisk
17   „Kanál Grande II", Terst, 1910, z cyklu Svatební cesta do Dalmácie, NTM, bromolejotisk
18   „Molo St. Carlo", Terst, 1910, z cyklu Svatební cesta do Dalmácie, NTM, bromolejotisk

19   „Molo", Terst, 1910, z cyklu Svatební cesta do Dalmácie, NTM, bromolejotisk
20   Manželka na palubě parníku Baron Gautsch, 1910, z cyklu Svatební cesta do Dalmácie, NTM, bromolejotisk
21   „Parník Baron Gautsch", Terst, 1910, z cyklu Svatební cesta do Dalmácie, NTM, bromolejotisk
22   „Kunsthistorisches Museum", Vídeň, 1910, z cyklu Svatební cesta do Dalmácie, NTM, bromolejotisk
23   „St. Giacomo, zbořeniště", 1910, z cyklu Svatební cesta do Dalmácie, NTM, bromolejotisk
24   „Spalato, Dioklecián ův palác", 1910, z cyklu Svatební cesta do Dalmácie, NTM, bromolejotisk
25   „Výlet na Lopud, Cesta k Aquae II", 1910, z cyklu Svatební cesta do Dalmácie, NTM, bromolejotisk
26   Manželka u růží, Lokrum, 1910, z cyklu Svatební cesta do Dalmácie, bromolejotisk
27   Dubrovník, kaple sv. Salvátora, 1910, z cyklu Svatební cesta do Dalmácie, NTM, bromolejotisk
28   „Pohled z okna I", Dubrovník, 1910, z cyklu Svatební cesta do Dalmácie, NTM, bromolejotisk
29   „Střechy III", Dubrovník, 1910, z cyklu Svatební cesta do Dalmácie, NTM, bromolejotisk
30   „Pohled na Rothenburg z věže Burgtoru II", 5. 9. 1912, NTM, bromolejotisk
31   Drážďany, 1912, NTM, bromolejotisk
32   „Herterichsbrunnen", Rothenburg, 5. 9. 1912, NTM, bromolejotisk
33   „Plönlein", Rothenburg, 5. 9. 1912, NTM, bromolejotisk
34   Platnéřská ulice, Praha, 1910–14, olejotisk
35   „Ranní červánky, Bašta pod Hradčanami v Praze", 1906–1914, NTM, gumotisk
36   Letohrádek Královny Anny v Praze, 1906–20, NTM, brom
37   Černínský palác v Praze, 1906–20, NTM, brom
38   Karlův most z Kampy, 1906–14, olejotisk
39   Most Františka I u Národního divadla v Praze, 1906–14, olejotisk
40   Někdejší Mlýnský rybník v Krucemburku, nedatováno, brom, tónováno
41   Silnice z Krucemburku do Hluboké, 1910–14, bromolejotisk
42   Cesta do Škrdlovic (?) , 1910–14, bromolejotisk
43   „Silnice v zimě", 1909–11, gumotisk (s pozměněným výřezem publikováno 1911)
44   Krucemburk v zimě ze silnice do Hluboké, 1910–14, bromolejotisk
45   Na zahradě vily, 1911–12, brom
46   Na zahradě vily, 1911–12, brom
47   „V lese", 1909–11, bromolejotisk (publikováno jako gumotisk 1911)
48   „Soumrak na rybníku", 1909–11, NTM, gumotisk (publikováno 1911)
49   Les s břízami, 1909–12, NTM, bromolejotisk
50   Na pastvě, 1906–11, NTM, gumotisk
51   „Kozy (soumrak), u Nového Města na Moravě", 1906–11, NTM, gumotisk
52   Rybník Řeka, 1906–11, NTM, gumotisk (snímáno teleobjektivem)
53   Mraky na Vysočině, 1906–12, gumotisk
54   „Ranní nálada", 1909–11, NTM, gumotisk (publikováno 1911)
55   Na Vysočině, 1909–12, gumotisk
56–57   Studie mraků,1910–14, bromolejotisk
58   „Břízy v Jasných Polích", 1910–14, bromolejotisk

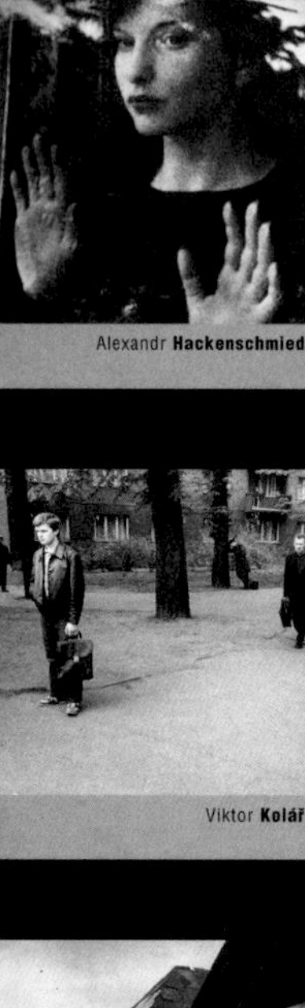

Alexandr **Hackenschmied**

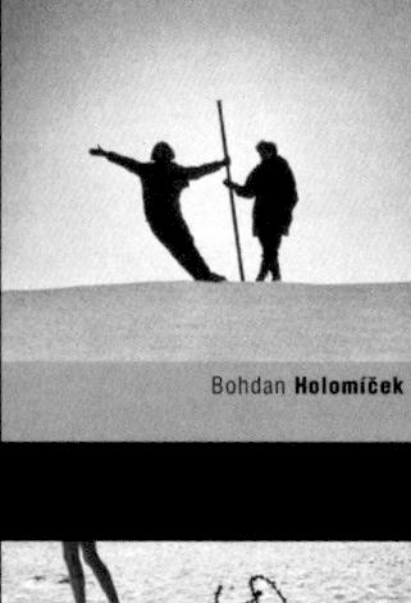

Bohdan **Holomíček**

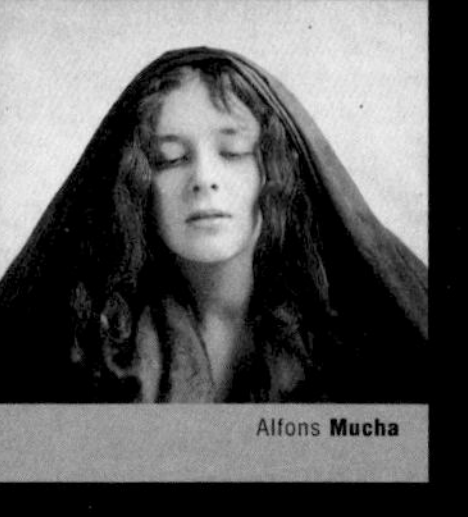

Alfons **Mucha**

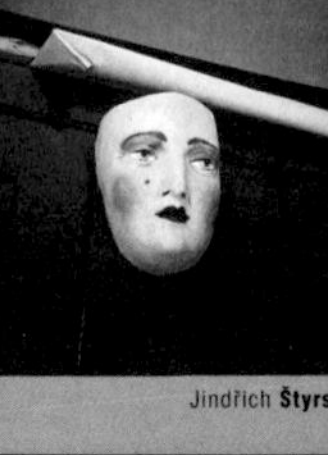

Jindřich **Štyrský**

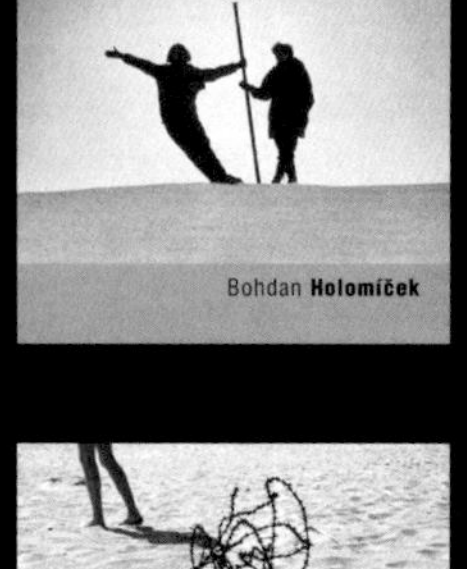

Viktor **Kolář**

Josef **Koudelka**

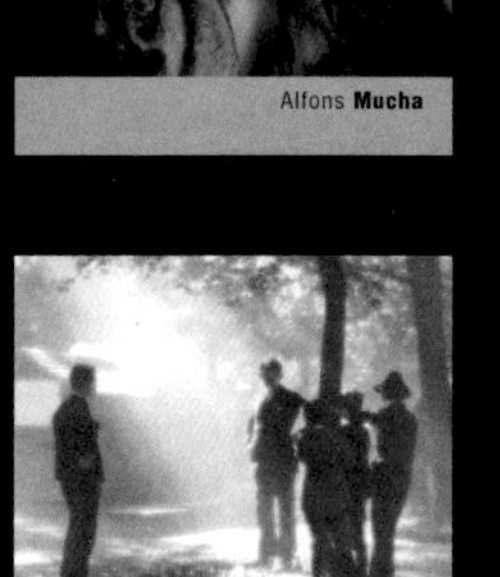

Josef **Sudek**

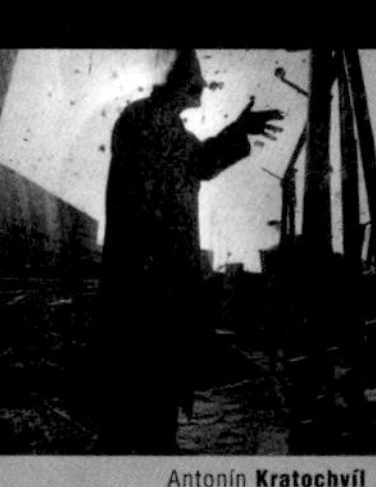

Antonín **Kratochvíl**

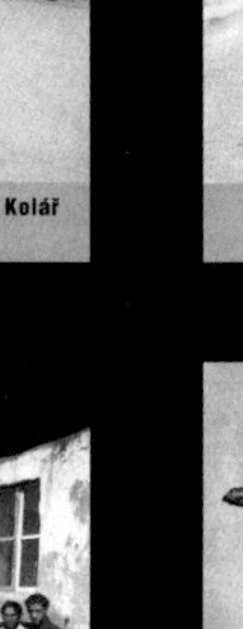

Eva **Davidová**

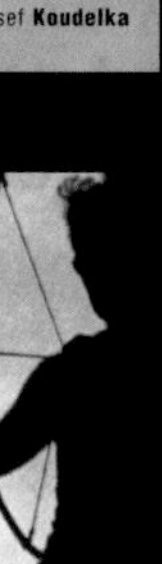

Emila **Medková**

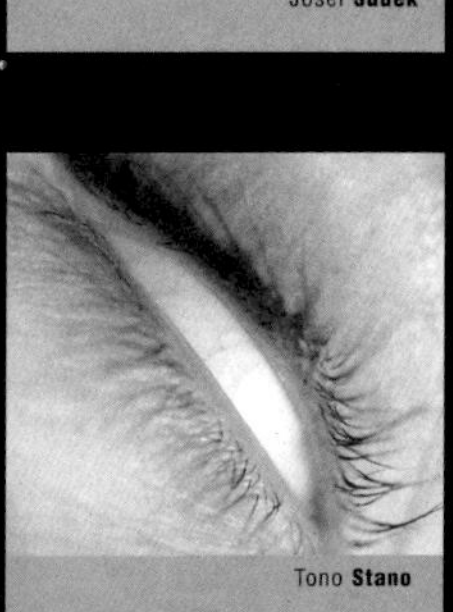

Tono **Stano**

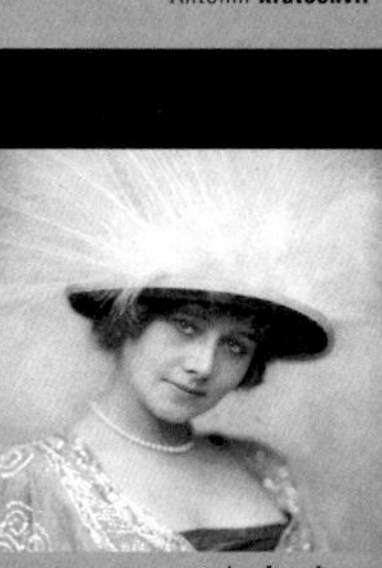

Jan **Langhans**

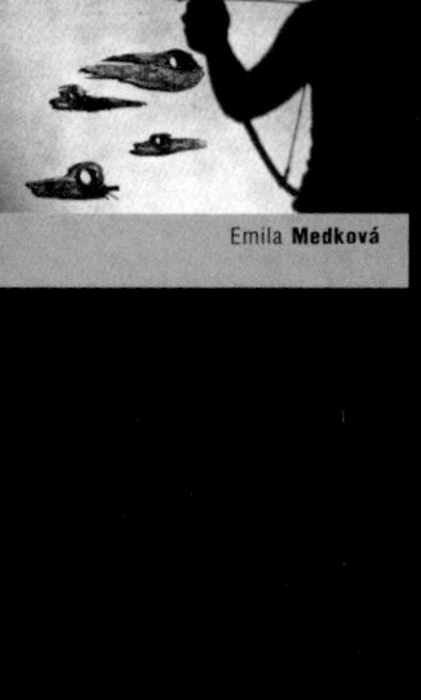

Iren **Stehli**

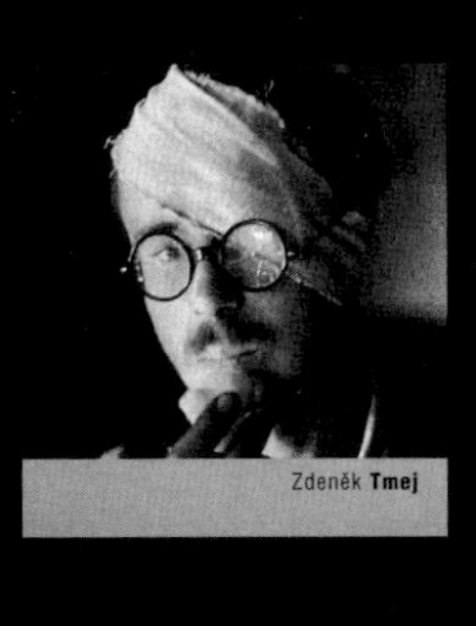

Zdeněk **Tmej**

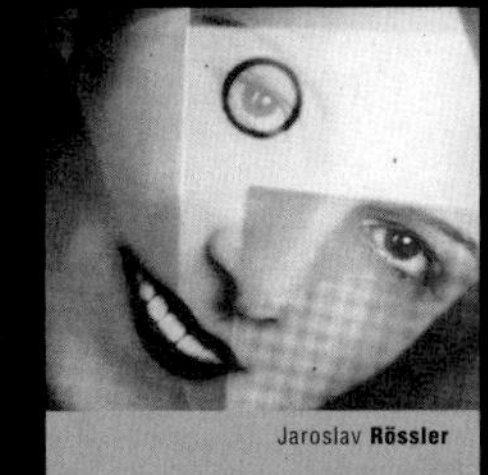

Jaroslav **Rössler**

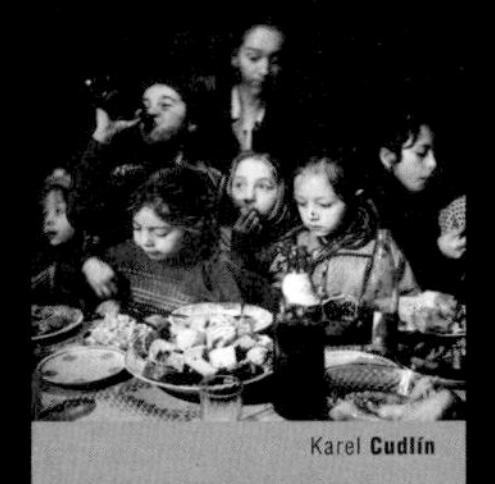

Karel **Cudlín**

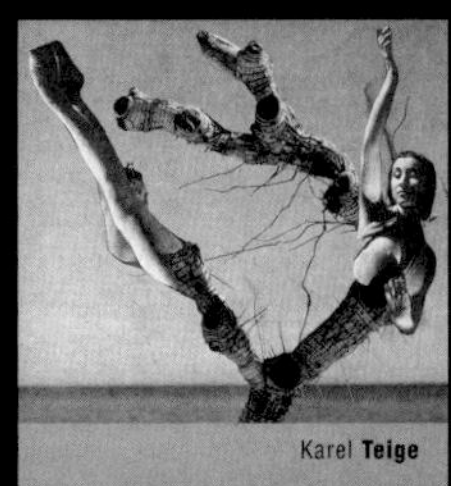

Karel **Teige**

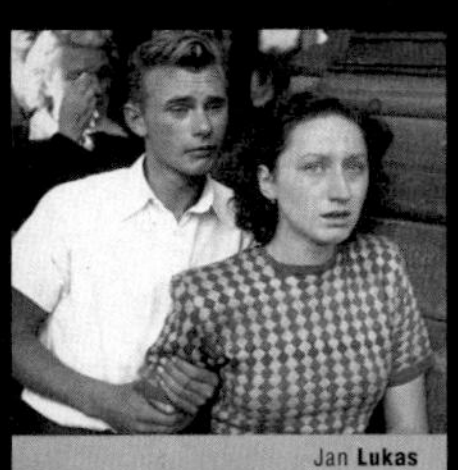

Jan **Lukas**

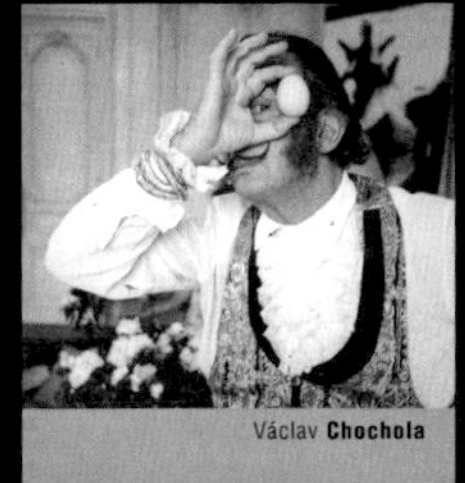

Václav **Chochola**

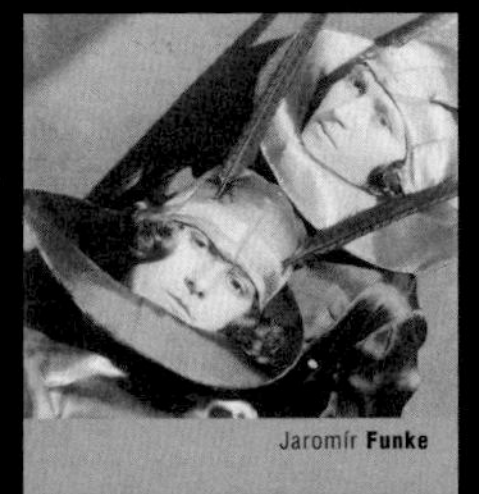

Jaromír **Funke**

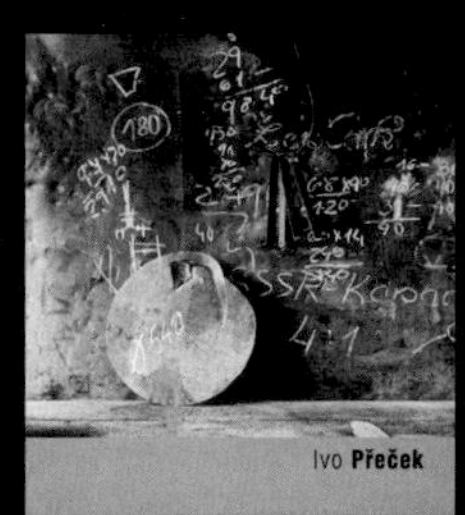

Ivo **Přeček**

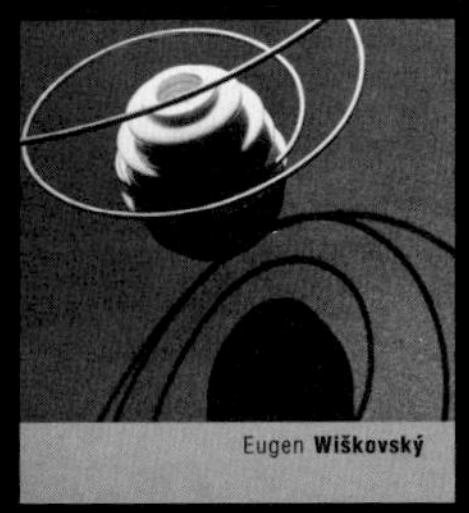

Eugen **Wiškovský**

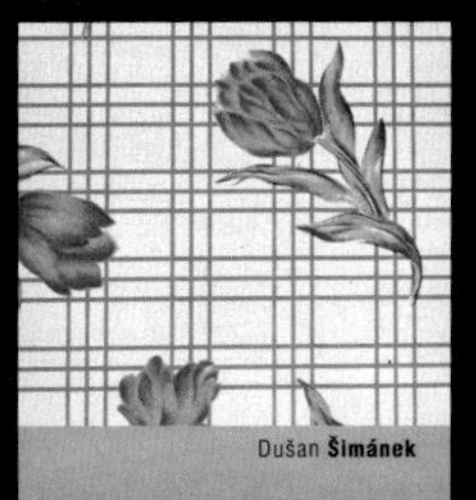

Dušan **Šimánek**

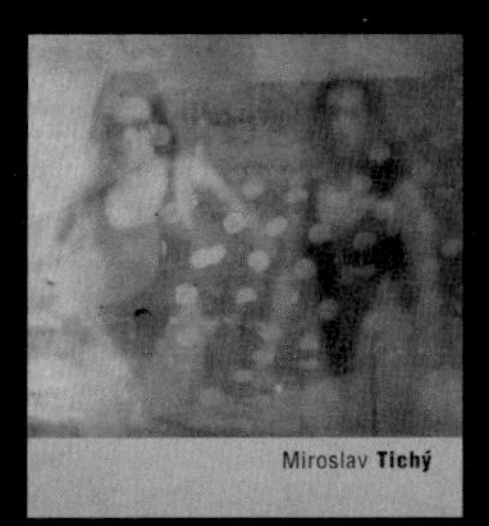

Miroslav **Tichý**

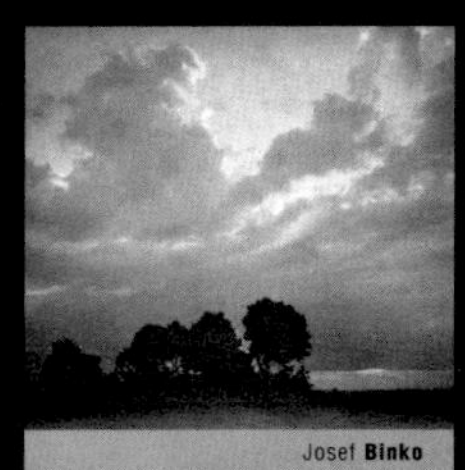

Josef **Binko**

FOTO**TORST**

Published to date / Dosud vyšlé svazky:

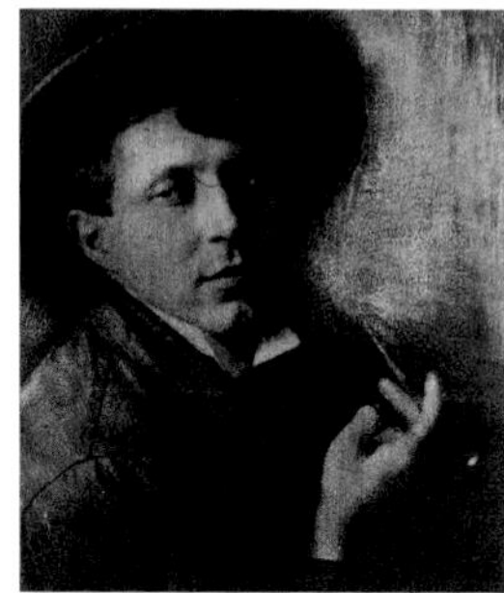

František Drtikol

1   **Alexandr Hackenschmied**
2   **Bohdan Holomíček**
3   **Alfons Mucha**
4   **Jindřich Štyrský**
5   **Zdeněk Tmej**
6   **Jaroslav Rössler**
7   **Karel Cudlín** (Out of print / Vyprodáno)
8   **Karel Teige**
9   **Viktor Kolář**
10   **Josef Koudelka**
11   **Josef Sudek**
12   **Antonín Kratochvíl**
13   **Jan Lukas**
14   **Václav Chochola**
15   **Jaromír Funke**
16   **Ivo Přeček**
17   **Eva Davidová**
18   **Emila Medková**
19   **Tono Stano**
20   **Jan Langhans**
21   **Eugen Wiškovský**
22   **Dušan Šimánek**
23   **Miroslav Tichý**
24   **Josef Binko**
25   **Iren Stehli**

Soon to be published / Připravujeme:

František Drtikol

Also available through D. A. P. / Distributed Art Publishers
155 Sixth Avenue, 2nd Floor, New York, N. Y. 10013, USA
Tel: ++1 (212) 627-1999 Fax: ++1 (212) 627-9484

Josef Binko

by Pavel Scheufler
Photo selection: Pavel Scheufler
Translation: Derek Paton
Graphic concept: Studio Najbrt, Prague
Graphic design: Pavel Lev, Studio Najbrt
Lithography: Art D, Prague
Printed by Trico, Prague
Copy editors: Jan Šulc, Lenka Urbanová, and Derek Paton
Published by TORST
Address: Opatovická 24, Prague 1
CZ-110 00, Czech Republic
foto@torst.cz
First edition, 2006

Also available through D. A. P./Distributed Art Publishers
155 Sixth Avenue, 2nd Floor, New York, N.Y. 10013, USA
Tel: ++1 (212) 627-1999 Fax: ++1 (212) 627-9484